D0283680

The Historian at Work

The Historian . . . loaden with old Mouse-eaten Records, authorising himselfe for the most part upon other Histories . . . better acquainted with a thousand yeres ago, than with the present age . . . curious for Antiquities, and inquisitive of Novelties, a wonder to yoong folkes, and a Tyrant in table talke . . .

Sir Philip Sidney, *The defence of Poesie* (1595)

The Historian at Work

edited by

JOHN CANNON

Professor of Modern History, University of Newcastle upon Tyne

London
GEORGE ALLEN & UNWIN
Boston   Sydney

First published in 1980

GEORGE ALLEN & UNWIN LTD
40 Museum Street, London WC1A 1LU

© George Allen & Unwin (Publishers) Ltd, 1980

British Library Cataloguing in Publication Data

The historian at work.
 1. Historiography – Europe
 I. Cannon, John
 907'.2'04   D13.5.E9

 ISBN 0-04-901025-5
 ISBN 0-04-901026-3 Pbk

Typeset in 10 on 11 point Times by Watford Typesetters Ltd
and printed and bound in Great Britain by
William Clowes (Beccles) Limited, Beccles and London

Contents

Preface

The suggestion for a volume of essays of this nature arose out of our experience in running a first-year class on The Study of History at the University of Newcastle upon Tyne. It soon became clear that one of the difficulties was to provide enough suitable reading matter. E. H. Carr, *What Is History?*, was a trusted friend but, first published in 1961, has begun to lose impetus. G. R. Elton's *The Practice of History* (1967) and *Political History – Principles and Practice* (1970) and G. Kitson Clark, *The Critical Historian* (1967) have much of value on certain aspects of the historian's task but did not attempt the historiographical side. Arthur Marwick's *The Nature of History* (1970) is in many respects a remarkable *tour de force*, but the very attempt to cover so much ground meant that many historians could be given only one paragraph and the result, for some students at least, was a blur of great names. Other volumes, particularly on the philosophy of history, are positive deterrents to further study.

We were tempted to try a thematic treatment for the volume and some readers may feel that we should have done so. It would have been interesting to have chapters devoted to specific kinds of history and to have offered examples of legal historians, diplomatic historians, military historians, and the like. But what would one do about political historians? How could we agree upon one to represent the whole *genre*? And if military historians, why not naval historians, transport historians, medical historians, historians of science and architecture, of thought and music?

In the end, we drew up a list of historians who had made outstanding contributions to the development of the subject. We then modified our original selection in the light of the interests of our contributors. Compiling lists of the eleven historians to be included called to mind happy hours at school devising the best-ever English cricket team, from Grace, through Woolley and Walter Hammond, to M. C. Cowdrey and Geoffrey Boycott. Who would be wicket-keeper? Strudwick, Duckworth, Ames, Evans, Knott? Was Stubbs worth a place in the first team? If Acton came in, who should be left out? In the end, the final selection will no more please all historians than the best-ever cricket team commands total approval from all cricket-lovers.

We start with Gibbon, at the point when history was beginning to emerge as a separate discipline and when some of the modern techniques of research were being developed. It may appease readers who are at a loss to understand why we have excluded Raleigh and

Clarendon, Vico and Voltaire, Michelet and Carlyle, Stenton, Pirenne and Froude, to know that they were at least discussed. Our list does not claim to be either authoritative or exhaustive. We merely hope that readers of this volume will have started to acquire some understanding of the way in which certain fine historians saw their subject, and what made them fine historians. In particular, we have tried to place each historian firmly in the political and intellectual context of his own day.

I should perhaps add that the first chapter, which attempts to provide some talking-points on certain problems in the writing of history, is a purely personal statement. I should be greatly surprised if any of the other contributors agreed with all of it, and it is possible that none of them agree with any of it.

Acknowledgements

It is a great pleasure for me to have the chance to thank the many people who have helped in preparing this volume. Several of my colleagues in the University of Newcastle upon Tyne have given me assistance on various points and I must particularly thank Dr Anthony Stanforth and Miss Elizabeth Skinner of the Department of German, Mrs Jane Heal of the Department of Philosophy and Miss Elizabeth Redgate of the Department of History. Miss Pat Murrell, a research associate in the Department of History, read the typescript and saved me from many errors.

In bibliographical and typographical matters, I have been very greatly helped by Miss S. F. Hearder of the University Library, Reading. Dr Hamish Scott of the University of St Andrews read my own chapter on Namier and offered me much helpful advice.

Finally, I must acknowledge the comments made by the '78 intake of History students at Newcastle, who were shown an early draft of my first chapter. In fairness to them, I should place on record that they did their best to persuade me to abandon the joke about the red-haired girl from Beccles.

Newcastle upon Tyne
Boxing Day 1979   JAC

Note on Contributors

BURKE, Ulick Peter, MA (Oxon.), is a Fellow of Emmanuel College, Cambridge and a University Lecturer; educated at St John's and St Antony's, Oxford; taught in the University of Sussex 1962–78; publications include *Culture and Society in Renaissance Italy, Venice and Amsterdam* and *Popular Culture in Early Modern Europe.*

CANNON, John Ashton, MA (Cantab.), PhD (Bristol), is Professor of Modern History in the University of Newcastle upon Tyne; educated at Peterhouse, Cambridge; his publications include *The Fox–North Coalition, Parliamentary Reform, 1640–1832* and an edition of the *Letters of Junius.*

DERRY, John Wesley, MA, PhD (Cantab.), is Reader in History in the University of Newcastle upon Tyne; educated at Emmanuel College, Cambridge, and subsequently Fellow of Downing College; among his books are *The Regency Crisis, Charles James Fox, Castlereagh* and *English Politics and the American Revolution.*

LOYN, Henry R., MA, D.Litt. (Wales), is Professor of History at Westfield College, London; he is President of the Historical Association; his books include *Anglo-Saxon England and the Norman Conquest, Norman Britain* and *Medieval Britain* (with Alan Sorrell), *The Reign of Charlemagne* and *The Vikings in Britain.*

McCORD, Norman, BA (Dunelm.) PhD (Cantab.), holds a personal chair in social history at the University of Newcastle upon Tyne; he took his first degree at Newcastle and did postgraduate research at Trinity College, Cambridge; among his interests are archaeology, aerial photography and local history; his books include *The Anti-Corn Law League.*

RAMM, Agatha, MA, D.Litt. (Oxon.), is a fellow of Somerville College, Oxford, and a university lecturer; educated at Bedford College, University of London; among her publications are *The Political Correspondence of Mr Gladstone and Lord Granville, 1868–1886,* 4 volumes, *Germany, 1789–1919* and *Sir Robert Morier, Envoy and Ambassador in the Age of Palmerston.*

SPECK, William Arthur, MA, D.Phil. (Oxon.), is Reader in History in the University of Newcastle upon Tyne; he took his degrees at the Queen's College, Oxford; he is author of *Tory and Whig, Jonathan Swift* and *Stability and Strife, 1714–60.*

TAYLOR, Joan, BA (London), is Senior Lecturer in History in the University of Newcastle upon Tyne, where she has also been Dean of the Faculty of Arts; she took her first degree at Westfield College, London, and held a travelling studentship in Vienna; her interests include modern international relations and the impact of Europe on the non-European world.

WARMINGTON, Brian Herbert, MA (Cantab.), is Reader in Ancient History in the University of Bristol; educated at Peterhouse, Cambridge,

THE HISTORIAN AT WORK

his publications include *The North African Provinces from Diocletian to the Vandal Conquest, Carthage* and *Nero – Reality and Legend.*

WATT, John Anthony, BA (Leeds), PhD (Cantab.), is Professor of Medieval History in the University of Newcastle upon Tyne; his post-graduate study was undertaken at Peterhouse, Cambridge; he is the author of *The Theory of Papal Monarchy in the Thirteenth Century* and *The Church in Medieval Ireland.*

WHITTAM, John Richard, MA, B.Phil. (Oxon.), PhD (London), is Senior Lecturer in History at the University of Bristol; educated at Worcester College and St Antony's College, Oxford; has written several articles on modern Italian history and his book *The Politics of the Italian Army* was published in 1977.

1 *The Historian at Work*

'Great abilities', declared Dr Johnson in his confident way, 'are not requisite for an historian; for in historical composition, all the greatest powers of the human mind are quiescent.' Fifty years later, Thomas Babington Macaulay, in an essay for the *Edinburgh Review*, was of the opposite opinion. 'To write History respectably', he observed, 'is easy enough; but to be a really great historian is perhaps the rarest of intellectual distinctions.'[1]

Such a pronounced disagreement is not wholly to be explained by the fact that Johnson was not an historian while Macaulay, in 1828, aspired to be one.[2] There is not, perhaps, much point in debating how intelligent an historian has to be: intelligence does not come amiss in any human activity. More useful is whether a particular kind of intelligence is needed and what are the problems in historical study that demand intelligent consideration. This is all the more necessary because there exists among the general public a suspicion that historical writing is really a brisk and straightforward business of finding out what happened and putting it down, but that historians pretend that it is full of difficulties in order to protect their own mystique.

The temptation may be to agree with Johnson. Historical study does not demand the kind of mind that one expects, say, in philosophers and mathematicians. Historians are said to mature slowly: G. G. Coulton, the mediaevalist, did not obtain his first university appointment until he was 61, but was still lecturing at the age of 88. What historians do need is a combination of talents that is a little rare. They must be capable of tasks of often minute and repetitive drudgery – working out accounts, searching for genealogical evidence, adding up votes, recording place-names, computing crimes, comparing baptisms and burials – without allowing it to blunt their intellect. They must retain, amid these inescapable chores, the capacity to see the wood for the trees: to stand back from the evidence they have so painstakingly amassed and ask interesting, important and perhaps irreverent questions. One of the most celebrated of twentieth-century historians, Sir Lewis Namier, had just this combination of talents: he was as much at home discussing the distribution of property in Huntingdon in 1754 as the great clash of Teutons and Slavs that has convulsed modern Europe.

But the prime reason why the study of history is a demanding one is that so much is necessarily left to the discretion of the historian. His first task is to decide what problem or period he is to examine. Gibbon pondered several subjects, including a History of Switzerland, before he hit upon the one which brought him fame. Although the historian can seek advice from his friends, the choice is ultimately his alone: if he chooses a dull or overworked subject, he is likely to fail. Often the single most important decision the historian takes is to decide his field of postgraduate study, since this may well lead to a lifetime of work on related problems. It is difficult to believe that a history of Switzerland, however distinguished, could have brought Gibbon such lasting acclaim.

Having embarked on his chosen theme, the next problem the historian faces is the accumulation and selection of evidence. The process of selection is of particular importance. The historian is essentially a bringer of order to the past, a perceiver of patterns. The events of the past are myriad in number, most of them neither recoverable nor of interest. Even the tiny fragment which survives in the shape of historical evidence presents the most bewildering variety of sequences, connections, relationships, parallels, contrasts and irrelevancies. In order to function at all, the historian must simplify.[3] At every turn, he is forced to resort to historical shorthand. Imagine what an infinite confusion of persons and events is brutally summarised in the phrase 'the fifteenth century'. Historians who would be embarrassed to think in terms of centuries take refuge in 'crucial decades'. It is not that they really believe that history moves in such obligingly manageable chunks of time but that they need desperately to impose some order on their sprawling materials. So we talk of 'Christendom', 'the absolute monarchies', 'the ruling classes', 'the great powers' and on to such weather-beaten conglomerates as 'the Renaissance', 'the Enlightenment' and 'the industrial revolution'. With each phrase we trample upon the subtleties and complexities of the past. But, dislike these categories as many of us do, deride them for their crudity as most of us can, it is hardly possible for history to be written without them. Time after time, iconoclasts have set out to destroy them, only to find that they rise again to discomfit their assailants.

If to simplify is the first task of the historian, the second is to resist oversimplification – to qualify, reserve, distinguish and discriminate. We debate, apparently everlastingly, whether 'bastard feudalism' is an apposite term, whether 'a revolution in government' is too bold a claim for Thomas Cromwell's work, whether Romanticism is a concept of any value to the historian. We argue whether Dr A has pushed his thesis too far and whether Professor B has done justice to the counter-arguments. Like a sculptor, we chisel away at a granite block until it takes a shape we can recognise in the historical past.

It has been suggested that there are two kinds of historians: those who construct patterns and theories and those who destroy them, the synthesisers and the demolition men. J. H. Hexter, in a characteristically ebullient phrase, has called them the splitters and the lumpers:

> Historians who are splitters like to point out divergencies, to perceive differences, to draw distinctions . . . they carry around in their heads lists of exceptions to almost every rule they are likely to encounter. They do not mind untidiness and accident in the past; they rather like them. Lumpers do not like accidents . . . instead of noting differences, lumpers note likeness; instead of separateness, connection. The lumping historian wants to put the past into boxes.[4]

In fact, every historian needs to be both lumper and splitter, formulating his hypothesis and then doing his best to punch holes in it, preferably before the reviewers do. In the last analysis, it must be for the historian himself to decide whether he has struck a fair balance between simplifying and oversimplifying. If he does not simplify enough, he runs the risk of being chaotic, unintelligible, unreadable, even unpublishable: if he simplifies too much, he will bore and distort. There is neither litmus paper nor light meter to guide him: it is a matter for his judgement.

The question of how much to leave out is particularly acute when we are dealing with the larger problems of historical interpretation. It arises from the seamless web of history, that intricate network of relationships which has led some philosophers to deny that historical explanation can have any validity. 'The strict conception of cause and effect appears to be without relevance in historical explanation,' wrote Michael Oakeshott: since no historian can offer a complete account of change, he cannot offer any account.[5] The first time I read this I was greatly alarmed, not least because it seemed to threaten the livelihood of myself and my colleagues; but, upon reflection, it appears to me to be based upon a fairly simple misunderstanding – that the only true account of an event must be a *total* account. In everyday life, we have accounts which, though not total, are perfectly adequate to the question asked. It is not a false answer to the question 'How was she knocked down?' to reply that she was knocked down by a drunken taxi-driver. We all understand that, given unlimited time, we could improve upon the explanation by adding that the taxi-driver had been driven to drink by the demands of the Electricity Board, or even that he would not have been there at all had not his father met his mother thirty years before in Beccles and been attracted by her red hair.

Even if we are satisfied that historical explanation is possible, it remains rather difficult. We have to break the links of causation somewhere and we have to content ourselves with distressingly approximate explanations. Suppose we are asked why the Austrians attacked the Serbians in 1914.[6] Though we understand that there must have been thousands of motives involving millions of people, a lecturer who began by remarking that he would deal only with the first seven hundred factors would not greatly endear himself to his audience, however much they ought, in theory, to admire the rigour of his approach. We therefore disregard the motives of thousands of soldiers who were 'doing their duty' or 'obeying orders', and concentrate on the views of Count Berchtold, who was Austrian foreign minister. We restrict ourselves to four or five fundamental causes, leaving the audience to understand that the last word has not been said upon the subject. But the selection of what are the four or five fundamental causes is for the historian to make: it does not make itself. Nor is there any way of demonstrating, beyond doubt, that we have chosen the right causes or put them into the right order. In fact, a number of academic controversies have arisen from taking causes which had previously been regarded as of only marginal importance and promoting them to a higher order in the explanation.

This element of judgement, which I am emphasising, is peculiarly necessary in the task of evaluating evidence. Sir Herbert Butterfield once remarked that it was a mistake for the historian to regard himself as a judge when his proper role was that of a detective.[7] But though it is not the historian's duty to pass sentence, he is certainly under an obligation to review the evidence. The compilation of evidence, difficult though it may be, is usually much easier than the evaluation and assessment of it.

There are countless hazards in deciding how much weight can be placed upon particular evidence. Though the evidence itself may be true, it may be unrepresentative; it may be at variance with other evidence; it may answer only an aspect of the question posed, and that not necessarily the most important. At a second stage comes evidence which has been warped by political, religious or other prejudice. A famous example of touching up events out of all recognition is the sinking of the French warship *Vengeur* in the action of the Glorious First of June in 1794. According to the account given by Bertrand Barère to the Convention, the *Vengeur* went down with all hands, the tricolour flying and the guns blazing revolutionary defiance. More than forty years later, proof was forthcoming that in fact the *Vengeur* had struck her colours, two hundred of the crew were saved, and the captain was on an English vessel eating cold mutton pies when his ship went down. Thomas Carlyle, who had been taken in by Barère's version, added a hasty revision to his *French Revolution*, 'with resentful brush'.[8] Truth is always a casualty in wartime, and a more modern legend credited the Royal Air Force with shooting down 185 German planes on 15 September 1940 at the height of the Battle of Britain. Though political and national bias is fairly easily detected, there are other forms which are more insidious. The reports of the Royal Commissions on the Poor Law in 1834 and the employment of children in mines in 1842 have been shown to be tendentious, the motive in these cases being largely humanitarian. In a third category, one which the historian comes across surprisingly often, is evidence which has been deliberately planted to deceive: it may come from a compulsive liar or an occasional liar;[9] from a forger, or the victim of a forger.[10]

Even when we are dealing with what we might call uncontaminated evidence, the interpretation may be very uncertain. Let us take an example. In *England in the Seventeenth Century*, Maurice Ashley quoted the story of a farm labourer, who was turned away from the field of Marston Moor muttering, of king and Parliament, 'What, has them two fallen out then?' What are we to make of that? Can the historian legitimately infer that the lower orders of Stuart England knew little of and cared nothing for the concerns of the governing class? Or is it that, by some quirk, the views of the local village idiot have been preserved to confuse posterity?[11]

The difficulty is that in evaluating his evidence, the historian can appeal, for the most part, only to probability and common sense, neither of which is a very precise yardstick. Even the revised version of the *Vengeur* episode might be queried by the argument that all English eye-witnesses had conspired to discredit French valour. Rarely can historical probability be expressed in mathematical terms, and the definition of common sense as the opinion of the average intelligent man does not get us very far, since average intelligent men display a great gift for disagreeing. Scholars from other disciplines are often shocked at the crudity of the historian's approach and complain of the low standard of historical verification. The historian must bear this reproach as best he can, because it derives from the nature of his subject: he must not be goaded into claiming an accuracy which the material he uses will not normally permit.

Some of my professional colleagues will, I am sure, feel that this exposition is quite unnecessary and far removed from anything they experience when engaged in the writing of history. Indeed, there are very distinguished historians who are impatient with any discussion of historical method, as though it served only to make the historian self-conscious. They remind one of trapeze artists who can perform only provided they never look down. Professor Richard Cobb, in *Second Identity*, has expressed this point with engaging vivacity:

I do not know what history is about, nor what social function it serves. I have never given the matter a thought. There is nothing more boring than books and articles on such themes as 'What is History?', 'The Use of History', 'History and Something Else'.[12]

This is delightful swashbuckling stuff and, of course, it would be tedious if we all gave up writing history in order to concentrate on historiography. But, coupled with the advice to get on and consult the documents, it smacks of the Rankean thesis that all historians need to do for the past is to explain 'how it really was'.[13] The writing of history is not, however, a straightforward activity like growing mushrooms or tracing gas leaks, which can be performed quite adequately in an unreflecting way.

The thesis that historical composition is comparatively simple can itself contribute to error if it discourages historians from examining the assumptions on which their work is based. Weeks of careful and painstaking research can be ruined by the unguarded acceptance of false assumptions.[14] The historian must, for example, always consider to what extent the answers to his questions are determined by the categories of evidence he is consulting: those who devote their time to the investigation of police and criminal records need to remind themselves of the many thousands of unrecorded acts of kindness and sympathy if they are not to finish up with a distorted and melancholy view of human nature.[15] In the same way, those who exploit the vast treasure trove of information contained in Royal Commissions and government inquiries must remember that these sources have an inherent bias towards gloom, since governments do not often set up commissions to inquire into harmony and contentment.[16] The *cahiers de doléances*, submitted to the Estates-General in 1789, are a magnificent source for French society on the eve of the revolution, but they cannot tell us the whole truth since they are concerned mainly with what was wrong in that society.

One objection to the amount of emphasis I have placed on the historian's discretion is that it flirts dangerously with the view that historical writing is basically subjective: that all history is, in essence, the product of the historian's mind, and therefore that all historians may be equally right or wrong. This is, if I understand it, the chief criticism levelled by Professor G. R. Elton at parts of E. H. Carr's *What Is History?*. Carr, in Elton's judgement, puts excessive emphasis on the role of the historian and underestimates the extent to which the evidence itself determines the conclusions reached. I agree with Elton in disliking the distinction Carr makes between facts and *historical facts*: indeed, I can hardly think of a form of words more likely to cause confusion. All that I take Carr to mean is that a neglected or disregarded fact may be turned into an interesting fact by being incorporated into an historical exposition.[17] But I am not sure that Professor Elton's other comments quite meet the point. He is certainly right to insist that, in his interpretation, the historian does not have a free hand: it is not an irresponsible discretion that he exercises and he is restrained at all times by the evidence before him. When dating a letter, editing a cartulary, exposing a forged document or composing a close narrative, these restraints will be very severe. But most historians are called upon, particularly as teachers and lecturers, to pronounce on broader themes – the reasons for the decline of Rome, the spread of heresy in the Middle Ages, the growth of nationalist feeling in the nineteenth century – and here the same degree of proof cannot be expected. Professor Elton's example is not really decisive. 'No matter how many observers', he tells us, 'concern themselves with such questions as the day on which Britain declared war on Germany in 1914 . . . they will all come up with the same answer.'[18] One would hope so. But the fact is that historians do *not* much concern themselves with such matters because there is no problem to discuss. They do consider whether Grey's foreign policy contributed to war, to what extent colonial rivalries were involved, and how much blame should be attached to the German High Command, and on these matters they notoriously do not come up with the same answer. The emphasis given to each factor, the order of priorities, is a matter for the historian's judgement: the facts do not provide it. But far from conceding that this opens the gate to academic anarchy, each historian as good as his neighbour and each entitled to his opinion, it is the quality of this judgement which helps to distinguish the good historian from the bad.

The argument whether history should be objective or subjective has been much debated without being, in my view, greatly advanced. The truth is that these words are two straitjackets and the historian does not feel very comfortable in either. If by 'objective' we mean totally impartial history, uncoloured by personal feelings or opinions, the kind of history that might be produced by computer, it is out of the question: there must always be a process of selection and that selection can be made only in the light of the historian's own judgement as to what is important. Even the computer must first be given its programme. But this is not an invitation to veer wildly to the other extreme. If by purely subjective history we mean history that flies in the face of the evidence, a mere matter of opinion, whimsical and idiosyncratic, it is of no great interest. There is a more subtle relationship between the historian and the facts of the past than can be expressed in these two words.

This disagreement between those who emphasise the objectivity of past happenings as against those whose emphasis is on the role of the historian arises partly from the confusion over the two meanings of the word 'history'. We use the same word to mean not only the events of the past, what actually happened, but also our analyses of and commentaries upon what happened. The distinction can be seen at its clearest in the careers of statesmen-historians like Clarendon and Churchill, both of whom 'made history' and 'wrote history'. If we use the term 'history' mainly in the first sense, we tend to finish up arguing for the objectivity of the subject: if we use it mainly in the second, we finish up as exponents of subjective history. The truth lies between.

There have been many primitive societies which have had neither oral nor written record: it is only in the first sense, therefore, that their history existed. When we turn to modern Europe and to the historians discussed in this volume, it is hard to deny that their characters, interests and circumstances were of critical importance in deciding the nature and quality of the history they produced. Do we really believe that Gibbon and Macaulay, de Tocqueville and Namier would have been better and more interesting historians had they blotted out their own personalities and confined themselves to mere paraphrases of the evidence they had discovered? The historian is not a chronicler of past events but an interpreter of the past and his success or failure depends to a considerable extent upon the balance he succeeds in striking between himself and the past. There are historians who are tediously obtrusive, though perhaps it would be prudent not to identify them, and others who are self-effacing to an unreasonable degree: to get the right balance is another of those nice decisions the historian is called upon to make and one where, he may be sure, he will not please everybody.

This discussion draws attention to one of the difficulties commonly experienced by university students, particularly in their first year of study. They not infrequently complain of a sense of helplessness in the face of a barrage of conflicting interpretations. Matters to which the protagonists may have devoted thirty years of study are laid before the student who is expected to provide an instant judgement on the basis of a few days' reading. The temptation to retire into a mindless subjectivism, where everything is a matter of opinion, may seem overwhelming. First, there are two words of solace. The extent to which all history is open to argument is exaggerated by the fact that much writing and most lecturing takes place within the disputed areas: outside those are large areas where a general interpretation is commonly accepted. All essays, if properly devised, will explore some problem, examine some controversy or demand some technique, in order to give the student an opportunity to develop and demonstrate judgement. An essay which invited the student to discuss the proposition that Drake made a substantial contribution to the defeat of the Armada would not seem very challenging. Secondly, although students frequently complain of the swing of the pendulum in historical controversies, it is very rare for those controversies to return to their original starting-point. Namier and Sedgwick, in the 1930s, helped to destroy the myth that Bute and George III wished to establish absolutism: now, although Namier's interpretation has itself been challenged and stands in need of modification, no informed historian could possibly revert to the original view.

These are but general comforts. There is more urgent advice for the fresher cast adrift on the choppy sea of historical controversy. Are the scholars in contention equally expert? It is surprising how often a well-argued work of genuine scholarship is placed on a par with the most derivative textbook. When were the competing works written? It does not follow that the most recent is the most reliable, but it is essential to know how the dispute has developed in order to avoid going round in circles. What is the precise point at issue? Is it a disagreement about brute fact, which can be settled fairly easily, or does it depend upon definitions? Would reference back to the original documents, if possible, resolve the difficulty? Is there some third party to whom appeal can be made? Are there reviews of the books in question which might suggest lines of comment? Is there any reason to suspect, on the part of the authors concerned, a particular prejudice or bias? The questions and advice can be multiplied. But, at the end of the day, the student, however fresh, must fall back upon his own common sense, advance his own definitions, provide his own criteria, list his own priorities, appeal to his own knowledge of human nature, and form his own conclusions. It is a tall order and infinitely worthwhile.

One of the most frequent warnings given to student historians is to beware of hindsight. I must confess that I am not sure what this means. Hindsight may be defined as knowledge withheld from the participants in history, or wisdom after the event. But all historical evidence is necessarily procured after the event and a strict adherence to the precept would put historians out of business. It cannot therefore mean a ban on knowledge *acquired* after the event. At most, it must mean that the historian should not take into account knowledge *relating to* events subsequent to the ones he is discussing. But there is no reason why we should lay this aside and every reason why we should employ it. It is one of the historian's trump cards. If we are to judge the work of Frederick the Great while resolutely ignoring, or pretending not to know, anything that happened after 1786, we limit ourselves quite unnecessarily. Does the catastrophe of Jena in 1806 cast no doubt on Frederick's achievements? Is it not important that we should take account of the repeated difficulties of establishing a permanent regime in France in the nineteenth century in order that we should be more understanding of the mistakes made by the revolutionaries, by Napoleon Bonaparte, by the restored Bourbons and by

Louis Philippe? Do not the repeated instances each time add something to our total appraisal of the shattered nature of French society after 1789?

The proposition that we should put aside hindsight seems to me to be based upon a fundamental misunderstanding. It presumes that the past itself was static. Let us suppose that an historian, in the mistaken belief that he is fulfilling his professional duty, gives himself a kind of scholarly amnesia and, in order to escape the danger of hindsight, tries to see the past only as contemporaries saw it. The first difficulty he will face is *which* contemporaries he is to impersonate, the intelligent and well informed, the stupid and ignorant, the old or the young? It is naive error to imagine that at some time in the past there was a common body of knowledge or opinion. His second difficulty is greater. At what point in time does he propose to station himself? The past was itself unfolding to contemporaries: they used hindsight in their own estimates of the situation and the passage of a few years, months, or even days could make the most profound difference in the way *they* looked at things. Will he pitch camp on 11 October 1066, just before the Battle of Hastings, or on the 15th, the day after: it might make some difference to his point of view. If he stops the historical clock at 1486 there is not much reason to believe that Bosworth was not just another in the long line of battles – St Albans, Wakefield, Mortimer's Cross, Towton, Barnet, Tewkesbury – which had failed to bring the Wars of the Roses to an end: by 1500 it was becoming clear that the new dynasty might well survive and the significance of Bosworth changed accordingly. If we are to pledge ourselves never to make use of *subsequent* discoveries or exposures, it is our historical duty to go on maintaining the guilt of Archbishop Plunket, since Titus Oates was not unmasked as a scoundrel until well after the archbishop's execution. Are we to ask how contemporaries saw events on 30 September 1938 when it was at least possible that Chamberlain had obtained 'peace in our time' or on 16 March 1939 with Czechoslovakia occupied by Hitler's troops and Chamberlain's policy in ruins? Since contemporaries cannot be denied the right to use hindsight – that is, to revise their opinions in the light of later evidence – I do not see why the historian should be denied it.

What is meant by the warnings to eschew hindsight is something different: that we should not condemn the ability of people in the past by an appeal to subsequent events which they could not reasonably have been expected to foresee, nor their morality by an appeal to standards to which they did not subscribe. It is certainly necessary to remind ourselves constantly that our predecessors did not know what the outcome of events would be and that, had they done so, they might have behaved very differently. Otherwise we slide easily into a patronising attitude towards the past, until it seems to be peopled with nobody but fools and incompetents, hell-bent on disaster. One of the most important obligations of the historian is to keep good faith with the dead and not to score cheap points off them. Yet it may well be that the historian, in order to be fair, needs to employ hindsight. If we close our inquiry into the problems of the Habsburg Empire with the death of Joseph II in 1790, we shall be tempted to agree with him that he had failed in all his enterprises: it is necessary to continue the survey at least until 1848 to appreciate the extent to which Joseph marked out the future pattern of Austrian development. We rescue him from his own harsh assessment.

This is part of the wider problem of the relationship between past and present. The need to study history 'for its own sake' or 'for the sake of the past' has been asserted with vigour. Sir Herbert Butterfield, in an influential passage, insisted that the ultimate in unhistorical attitude was to 'study the past with one eye, so to speak, upon the present . . . the source of all sins and sophistries in history'. Thirty-six years later, Professor Elton was in full agreement: to study the past for the light it throws upon the present was, he declared, 'the cardinal error'.[19]

Despite the eminence of its exponents, this seems an unreasonably extreme and purist point of view. Why should it be so totally reprehensible, to demand such thunderous anathemas, to turn to the past to help understand the present? Is it not a very natural and proper question, confronted, shall we say, by the violence in Northern Ireland, to ask how this came about? Does not a situation like the present division of Germany cry out for an historical explanation if we are to make sense of it? Why should the historian turn away customers when he has so few?

Of course, one understands why Sir Herbert Butterfield and Professor Elton should have perceived dangers. To ransack the past seeking ammunition for present political and religious controversies is easy enough, and those who look will assuredly find it. But it seems to me rather a doctrine of despair to presume that no historian is capable of relating past to present in a square and honest way. It is wrong to give a theme prominence in its own period merely because it was to acquire importance subsequently, but it cannot be wrong to point out that it *was* to become important. To write as though Winstanley and the Diggers in Stuart England were more than an obscure and unimportant group would be unscholarly; yet the later discussions of collectivist solutions to political and social problems mean that they have acquired a greater interest for people today. Is it so very difficult for historians to proffer these two evaluations – to wear bifocal glasses – to peer at both past *and* present? Are readers really so simple that they cannot comprehend that events and actions have a changing significance as the long perspective of human history unfolds?

The phrase 'to study the past for its own sake', far from being translucently clear, is fraught with ambiguity. Let us take an example. Suppose I play tennis regularly with an earnest friend who assures me that he plays solely to keep fit: I may be provoked to reply that I play tennis for its own sake. Strictly speaking, this is nonsense. Tennis is not concerned whether I play or not. What I really mean is that I play for my own pleasure. But whether we play for pleasure or to keep fit, it is for *our* purposes that we play. In the same way, it must be a matter of indifference to the past whether we study it or not: Lord North was certainly interested while alive to know what historians would make of him, but I doubt if he is much interested now. In other words, we study the past for *our* sake, and what the phrase hints at is the very real pleasure and satisfaction we feel from trying to understand it. Once we have established that we all study the past for our own sake, there seems little reason to be dogmatic about the precise motivation. To try to reconstruct what life was like, say, in AD 655 is an admirable objective, but it does not follow that it should be regarded as the only legitimate objective for studying the past. If one historian studies the past because that gives him intellectual pleasure *per se* and another because he hopes the better to understand the present, why should they quarrel? Each is a perfectly respectable motive and, in practice, most of us manage to combine them.

A further difficulty is that the phrase draws far too sharp a distinction between present and past. We understand that the present is disappearing into the past all the time. Indeed, the historian can hardly talk about the present because, by the time he has evidence to examine, it has become the past. So what we are being told is that we should not study the distant past in order to understand the more recent past. Put like that, it sounds a rather odd proposition. Not only is the historian justified in examining the 1620s in order better to understand the 1640s, but he would be singularly foolish not to do so. But if it is not suspect to make use of the 1620s for the light thrown on the *then* future, is there some mysterious date at which it becomes suspect? It seems to me that, far from shunning the present as though to guard against some vulgar contamination of the mind, the historian should reflect constantly on the endless, delicate and changing relationship of past and present. The reader's safeguard against distorted history is not that the historian banishes the present but that he confines his arguments scrupulously to those which his evidence will support.

The fear that our understanding of the past will be distorted by the intrusion of the present seems to be one to which British historians are peculiarly prone. Perhaps the exuberance of the liberal tradition in Victorian historiography provoked an excessive reaction, which has yet to subside. Other nationalities seem less anxious. J. H. Hexter, the American historian, has stood the argument on its head, insisting that the systematic methods of inquiry he adopts in his professional study of seventeenth-century England give some coherence to the fitful attention he pays to contemporary American affairs: 'instead of the passions, prejudices, assumptions and prepossessions . . . of the present dominating my view of the past, *it is the other way about*'.[20] The Dutch historian H. R. Hoetink has denounced as a platitude the proposition that the past can be understood from within, arguing that any attempt to do so is doomed to failure.[21] But the most determined repudiation of any divorce between past and present came from Marc Bloch, in his moving testimony *The Historian's Craft*, written in part in German captivity during the Second World War.[22] The relationship of past to present was, in his view, so close that an historian who tried deliberately to banish the present placed himself at a grave disadvantage in trying to understand the past. The lines of connection, Bloch argued, ran both ways:

> This faculty of understanding the living is, in very truth, the master quality of the historian . . . . A great mathematician would not, I suppose, be less great because blind to the world in which he lives. But the scholar who has no inclination to observe the men, the things, or the events around him will perhaps deserve the title, as Pirenne put it, of a useful antiquarian. He would be wise to renounce all claims to that of a historian.[23]

Though Bloch, in this instance, was betrayed into an excess of zeal, it is significant that a number of the historians discussed in this volume played an important part in the public life of their day – Gibbon, Macaulay and de Tocqueville as Members of Parliament, Bloch and Wheeler as soldiers, Marx as a journalist and political agitator, Namier as a propagandist for the cause of Zionism.

The advocates of studying the past for its own sake have an important point to make, even if the phrase is not felicitous and the argument is sometimes put too stridently. They are right to insist, not only that if our basic appraisal of the past is faulty it can be of no value, but that it is likely to be faulty if we approach the past impatient to wrest from it precepts and morals for present-day use. First and foremost must come the desire to know the truth of the matter, even if that truth turns out to be unpalatable, confusing and quite useless for present-day controversy. F. W. Maitland, the mediaevalist, was an historian who did believe that an understanding of the past might be a guide to action: 'we study the day before yesterday, in order that yesterday may not paralyse today, and today may not paralyse tomorrow'. He even talked of the 'liberating force' of legal history. But he was sober enough to realise the dangers in his approach to the past, and he put the point with characteristic moderation and good sense:

I get more and more wrapped up in the middle ages, but the only utilitarian justification that I ever urge in *foro conscientiae* is that, if history is to do its liberating work, it must be as true to fact as it can possibly make itself; and true to fact it will not be if it begins to think what lessons it can teach.[24]

It follows from the preceding exposition that, like Professor Cobb, I am doubtful whether there is such a thing as historical method in the strictest sense, though much has been written about it and many courses have been devoted to it.[25] That there are important historical techniques to be learned and practised I do not, of course, deny: nor is the remark intended as an encouragement to, or apology for, slipshod or inaccurate scholarship. But what passes for historical method is usually no more than the acquisition of necessary, but routine, skills. Historians must check and cite their sources meticulously, just as a surgeon must make sure that his scalpels are sharp and sterilised. But good scalpels do not make a fine surgeon, nor do good techniques, in themselves, make fine historians. 'Accuracy', A. E. Housman once remarked, 'is a duty not a virtue.'[26]
We should not make a fetish of historical technique. The command of foreign languages, knowledge of sources, familiarity with statistical method, palaeographic expertise, acquaintance with computer techniques – these are assets of great value to any historian. The careful and dexterous use of his own language is of such importance that it is hard to think of a really good historian who is defective in this respect. Nevertheless, in the last analysis, it is insight, understanding, range, application and passionate devotion to historical truth that are the supreme historical virtues. When we contemplate the great historians of the past – Clarendon, Gibbon, Macaulay, Acton, Pirenne – it is not usually their technical prowess we marvel at: nor, when their deficiencies are pointed out and their conclusions modified, do we cease to think of them as great historians.
Another difficulty is that some of the historical techniques which are much recommended, particularly to students, are almost impossible to practise. We are told, for example, how necessary it is for the historian to examine all the evidence before venturing an opinion – indeed, this is sometimes held out as one of the most salutary lessons which historical training can inculcate. In practice, there is no historian, however dedicated or long-lived, who could approach such perfection, save possibly in some very remote corner of the subject. It is for the historian to decide when he can go into print or when more needs to be done; knowing when to cut his losses, when the law of diminishing returns has set in, is another nice decision for him to make. Nor can the historian, as he is sometimes advised to, approach his sources without preconceived opinions. He must already have some idea what

questions he intends to ask and where he can hope to find the answers, even though he reserves the right to modify his thesis, or even abandon it, in the light of the evidence he obtains. He would otherwise drift from record office to record office inquiring whether the archivist had any interesting manuscripts.

This reiterated emphasis on the discretion of the historian helps to explain why the writing of history, which looks at first sight a simple business, turns out to be unexpectedly difficult. Since so much depends upon their understanding of human nature, it follows that few historians can ever feel totally equipped for their profession, quite incapable of adding any more experience to the amount they bring to bear on the problems of the past. This is, I think, what Namier meant when he wrote of the study of history that 'a great deal of previous experience and knowledge, and the scientific approach of the trained mind, are required, yet the final conclusions (to be re-examined in the light of evidence) are intuitive: an art'.[27]

NOTES: CHAPTER 1

1 *Life of Johnson*, ed. G. B. Hill, Vol. I, p. 424. In a later discussion, Johnson argued that the basic facts, the raw materials of history, were all provided: the rest, 'the colouring, all the philosophy of history is conjecture'. Boswell sensibly objected that Johnson would reduce history to no better than an almanack 'a mere chronological series of remarkable events'; ibid., Vol. II, pp. 365–6. Macaulay's observations are in the *Edinburgh Review*, vol. 47, 1828, p. 331.

2 Macaulay was sketching out the requirements for a greater historian than had then appeared: 'an historian, such as we have been attempting to describe, would indeed be an intellectual prodigy'. Macaulay was then a young man in the process of establishing his reputation: the *History* did not appear until 1848. He may therefore, at least on this occasion, be acquitted of the charge of overweening vanity.

3 I do not, of course, deny that on specific questions the difficulty may well be lack of evidence rather than too much. But, as a general proposition, it must be very rare for an historian to complete a book, or even an article, confident that he has seen all the available evidence on the subject.

4 *Times Literary Supplement*, 24 October 1975, pp. 1250–2.

5 *Experience and its Modes* (1933), p. 132. Contrast the philosopher's view with that of the practising historian, as put by Richard Pares in *The Historian's Business* (1961), pp. 6–7: 'Historians, in asking why and why not, are seeking for a coherent system of explanations, and above all of causation, for history is especially a study of causality.'

6 I have deliberately framed the questions in the kind of loose way we often adopt, though, in strict fact, very few Austrians attacked anybody in 1914. Accurate and precise framing of questions is an important part of the historian's task.

7 *The Whig Interpretation of History*, first published 1931, Pelican edition 1973: all references are to the latter; p. 79. See also Dom David Knowles, *The Historian and Character, and Other Essays* (1963), p. 13: 'the historian

is not a judge, still less a hanging judge'. Both authors were engaged in a discussion of moral judgements in the writing of history.

8   The full account is 'On the sinking of the *Vengeur*', in *Critical and Miscellaneous Essays*.

9   A recent example of a compulsive liar is Sir Edmund Backhouse, whose whole life, brilliantly reconstructed by Professor Trevor-Roper, was a fantasy. Occasional liars are too numerous to list.

10 My favourite forgers are Charles Bertram, whose bogus chronicle by Richard of Cirencester deceived historians of Roman Britain for more than a century, and Thomas J. Wise, the bibliophile. The most incompetent forger I have had to deal with was Olivia Wilmot Serres who, among other things, claimed to be the rightful Princess of Cumberland. All three are in the *Dictionary of National Biography*. For a talented French forger, Vrain-Lucas, see Marc Bloch, *The Historian's Craft*, translated P. Putnam (1954), pp. 95–7.

11 p. 79. In practice, the example makes the point that a piece of evidence, in isolation, may be of little value, and no historian would try to answer my question without further examining literacy rates, petitions, circulations of pamphlets and the like.

12 *Second Identity* (1969), p. 47.

13 ibid., p. 18. 'Why, one wonders', continues Cobb, 'when reading certain sections of *Past & Present*, why do historians spend so much time arguing, imposing definitions . . . when they could be getting on with their research?' But it is a strange historian who does not need definitions. Ranke's famous phrase 'wie es eigentlich gewesen' is commented on in Chapter 3 by Dr Agatha Ramm.

14 I am far from wishing to throw stones at other historians. When attempting to work out the total electorate in eighteenth-century England for *Parliamentary Reform, 1640–1832*, I went to considerable trouble to see as many poll books as possible in order to get precise figures. But I was obliged to assume that in hotly disputed contests, most eligible voters took part. Professor D. C. Moore in *The Politics of Deference* (1976) rightly objected that this was an unproven assumption and later research by Professor Geoffrey Holmes has cast further doubt on it. In other words, while endeavouring to establish the electorate to within a few hundreds, my margin of error may have been 20 or 30 per cent. I give this hostage to Professor Cobb as proof that not even an interest in the theory will necessarily save an historian from mistakes.

15 Part of the value of reading letters and diaries is that they record acts of kindness (as well as meanness) which rarely get into formal and official documents. They also serve as a warning against stereotyped history by reminding us of the great variety of human behaviour. The early 1870s might appear to be the highwater mark of Victorian earnestness, with Mr Gladstone at No. 10 Downing Street and the queen still in mourning for Prince Albert. But in Kilvert's diary for that period we read of an Anglican clergyman bathing nude on Weston beach. Kilvert later records a party of dissenting ministers on Llangorse Lake, tickling girls into squeals of laughter.

16 See review by Professor Norman McCord of J. T. Ward, *The Age of Change, 1770–1870* in *Times Higher Education Supplement*, 23 January 1976: 'I noted how much of our available source material is inherently biased in favour of the unusual rather than the typical and in the direction of things which have gone awry rather than anything that has gone well.'

17 G. R. Elton, *The Practice of History* (1967), particularly pp. 51–5, and E. H. Carr, *What Is History?* (1961), pp. 4–7. The same logic forces me to concede that it may also be turned into an uninteresting fact. Charles XII

of Sweden and John Wesley shared the same birthday but I am not sure
that this is a very fruitful pattern to have perceived.

18 p. 80.
19 *The Whig Interpretation of History*, p. 30; *The Practice of History*, p. 48.
20 'The historian and his day', in *Reappraisals in History* (1961), p. 9.
21 'Les notions anachroniques dans l'historiographie du droit', in *Tijdschrift voor Rechtsgeschiedenis*, vol. 23 (1955).
22 Bloch is discussed by Professor H. R. Loyn in Chapter 8.
23 *The Historian's Craft*, pp. 43–4.
24 *The Collected Papers of Frederic William Maitland* (1911), Vol. III, p. 439; C. H. S. Fifoot, *F. W. Maitland. A Life* (1971), p. 143. These references are from P. B. M. Blaas, *Continuity and Anachronism: Parliamentary and Constitutional Development in Whig Historiography and in the Anti-Whig Reaction between 1890 and 1930* (1978), pp. 246–7. Maitland is discussed by Professor J. A. Watt in Chapter 7.
25 In *A Sense of Place* (1975), p. 47, Richard Cobb gave his answer to an earnest inquirer: 'I shocked him very much by saying that no such method existed, that the methodology of history was the invention of solemn Germans.' For an excellent statement of the contrary case, see G. R. Elton's presidential address to the Royal Historical Society in November 1976, *Transactions of the Royal Historical Society*, 5th series, vol. 27, pp. 197–211.
26 Quoted E. H. Carr, *What Is History?*, p. 5.
27 'History', in *Avenues of History* (1952), p. 8. Namier is discussed in Chapter 9.

NOTE ON FURTHER READING

Many professional historians have been tempted, at some stage in their careers, to reflect upon their craft and it is not possible to do justice to all the contributions. Controversies which seemed of importance to earlier generations – for example, whether history is an art or a science, or whether historians should pass moral judgements – have ceased to be captivating. Readers who (rightly) are unwilling to take this opinion on trust should begin with J. B. Bury's inaugural lecture at Cambridge (1903) entitled 'The science of history', reprinted in *Selected Essays*, followed by G. M. Trevelyan's riposte 'The latest view of history', *The Independent Review* (1903–4), vol. I, pp. 395–414. The argument over moral judgements produced a celebrated exchange between Lord Acton and Bishop Creighton and still sends up occasional showers of sparks: for an introduction, see G. Himmelfarb, *Lord Acton: A Study in Conscience and Politics* (1952), pp. 158–62.

Perhaps the best introduction to modern historiography is Herbert Butterfield's *The Whig Interpretation of History* (1931, reprinted in 1973 as a Pelican): it is a warning against history distorted by present-day bias and an appeal for the past to be studied for its own sake. It is a pity that Sir Lewis Namier did not write more on historiography: what he had to say is mainly included in one laconic essay, 'History', in *Avenues of History* (1952). It is typical Namier, loose in construction but full of insight. Geoffrey Barraclough in *History in a Changing World* (1955) offered objections to parts of the Butterfield thesis and made interesting comments on concepts of mediaeval history (Chapters I and IV). Richard Pares, *The*

Historian's Business (1961) and Dom David Knowles, *The Historian and Character, and Other Essays* (1963) repay attention. E. H. Carr's *What Is History?* (1961) produced some lively controversy. G. R. Elton, *The Practice of History* (1967), accused Carr of a naive belief in progress and argued that his approach led to relativism: he followed this up with *Political History – its Principles and Practice* (1970). J. H. Plumb, *Men and Places* (1963), has important observations, particularly on history and biography, and in *Death of the Past* (1969) he discussed the social function of history. Arthur Marwick, *The Nature of History* (1970), attempted a very ambitious historiographical survey, but his assessments are always of value. A good straightforward guide to many historical problems and controversies is David Thomson's *The Aims of History* (1969). Richard Cobb sprinkles his books with engaging and provocative comments: see particularly *A Second Identity* (1969) and *A Sense of Place* (1975). A recent work by P. B. M. Blaas, *Continuity and Anachronism: Parliamentary and Constitutional Development in Whig Historiography and in the Anti-Whig Reaction between 1890 and 1930* (1978), is as indigestible as its title suggests, but has valuable studies of Pollard, Maitland and Tout.

2 *Edward Gibbon*

Edward Gibbon was born in May 1737 at Putney, son of Edward Gibbon, a Member of Parliament 1734–47 and Alderman of London 1743–45; attended Westminster School and Magdalen College, Oxford. In 1753 converted to Catholicism and sent by his father to Lausanne where he returned to Protestantism, read and studied privately until 1758. Commissioned service in the Hampshire militia from 1760–2; published *Essai sur l'étude de la littérature* in 1761. Conceived the idea of *Decline and Fall* on a visit to Rome in 1764 and began preliminary work in 1768. On death of father in 1770, settled in London, mixing in literary and political circles; became MP for Liskeard 1774. Published Volume I of *Decline and Fall* in 1776; appointed to Board of Trade by North in 1779. Volumes II and III published in 1781. Obtained seat at Lymington the same year through ministerial patronage but place at the Board of Trade abolished 1782. Volume IV written in 1783. Abandoned his parliamentary career and settled from 1783 onwards in Lausanne, where volumes V and VI written between 1784 and 1787. Volumes IV, V and VI published in 1788; between 1788 and 1793 wrote portions of his *Memoirs*, published posthumously by his friend Lord Sheffield; returned to England 1793 and died in London in January 1794.

The author of the *History of the Decline and Fall of the Roman Empire* was a member of no university or learned society, worked entirely alone and never showed a page of his manuscript to other scholars or corresponded with them about his *History*. Apart from some nine years as a mute Member of Parliament he lived the life of a 'gentleman and a scholar'; while he was happy enough in London, mixing in the vigorous society of the Literary Club with such figures as Reynolds, Sheridan, Fox and Johnson, he was even happier living in a provincial Swiss city, Lausanne. His early work was written in French and his *History* shows throughout the influence of the French Enlightenment as well as characteristically English attitudes, themselves so much admired by Voltaire and others.

His *Decline and Fall* is the first historical work of true greatness which could be described as modern in the sense of being a comprehensive narrative treatment of a large theme, having full mastery of all available original and secondary source material, and written from a consistently secular, non-religious viewpoint. It is also a work of the highest artistry and a masterpiece of English prose. It had an instant success in England and on the Continent and has remained one of the most widely read works of history; yet Gibbon was not an innovator and founded no historical school. The reason for some of these apparent contradictions may be found in the intellectual progress of a life largely spent in the pursuit of learning.

Gibbon's grandfather, the son of a linen draper, made a fortune as a purveyor to the British army in the wars of Queen Anne and as a director of the South Sea Company. Much of it was forfeited on the collapse of the company but he amassed another fortune, the bulk of which came to Gibbon's father. The latter sought success in society and politics but although he was a Tory MP from 1734 to 1747 and an Alderman of London he made little mark and withdrew to a small estate at Buriton in Hampshire where his extravagance and incompetence gradually diminished his inheritance.

The historian was born at his father's house at Putney in 1737. He was sickly throughout his childhood and apart from three years at Westminster School was taught by private tutors. His poor health turned him into an avid reader at an early age. In 1752 he entered Magdalen College, Oxford. Late in life, in some of the best-known pages of his *Memoirs*, Gibbon attacked his college and university with virulent sarcasm for ignorance, indolence and greed.[1] His precocious reading had perhaps given him expectations which were bound to be disappointed by the low state of learning in English (though not Scottish) universities of the time. He did, however, take full advantage of what he admitted was a 'numerous and learned' library. More important was a development in Gibbon's religious views which affected the course of his life. The family tradition was High Church and Gibbon records that in his childhood he used to discuss religion with a pious aunt. While at Oxford he read Conyers Middleton's *Free Enquiry*, published in 1749. Far from accepting Middleton's disbelief in miracles, Gibbon concluded that since he himself accepted the miracles of the early church he should also accept much else from pre-Reformation times which was rejected by Protestants. After reading Catholic writers such as Bossuet and Robert Parsons, he was received into the Catholic Church by a priest at the Sardinian Embassy. Gibbon later sought to portray his conversion as an intellectual error but could not deny that there was a strong element of religious enthusiasm involved. The devastating effect it had on the course of his life was important in determining Gibbon's later distaste for all strong emotions, particularly in religion. His father, horrified that his son had debarred himself from Oxford and largely from English society, sent him to live with a Protestant pastor named Pavillard at Lausanne. After some months of unhappiness before he became fluent in French, Gibbon came to regard Lausanne as his second and ultimately his real home. His reconversion to Protestantism was no mere acquiescence in *force majeure* but the result of long arguments with Pavillard. But this was only a stage in his religious development; he remained fascinated by religion all his life and while continuing to observe the formal requirements of Protestantism when in England, as his reading progressed he became increasingly a sceptic and at most a deist. Totally absorbed in the French culture of the day, for a while he thought and wrote in French rather than in English. At this time he was particularly influenced by Bayle's *Dictionnaire historique et critique*, Pascal's *Lettres provinciales* and la Bléterie's *Vie de l'empereur Julien*. Other intellectual giants of the century whom he read were Locke, Voltaire and Montesquieu. He also continued to read extensively in Greek and Latin literature, acquiring a particular admiration for the spirit of political and intellectual liberty which he found in Cicero. Above all, as a brief but intense love affair with Suzanne Curchod, future wife of the French statesman Necker, was terminated on his father's orders, he came at an early age to find his chief fulfilment in a life of study. When he returned to England in 1758 at the age of 21, he can have had few equals among young men of his age in the breadth and depth of his reading.

From 1760 to 1762 he held a commission in the Hampshire militia and 1763 and 1764 were spent in Europe, where he made his first and only, but decisive, visit to Rome. The next seven years were divided between London and Buriton. As he entered his thirties without a profession, totally dependent on his father, he regarded these years as the worst of his life; but his reading and study had continued undiminished and it was in 1768 that he began serious preparation for the *Decline and Fall*.

Two years after his father's death in 1770 he was at last able to settle in London. The stimulus of independence was immense, not only on the progress of his *History* but on his social and political life. He became an assiduous member of the Literary Club and was a particular friend of Reynolds, Sheridan and Adam Smith. In politics the family tradition was Tory, if not Jacobite, but while at Lausanne Gibbon came to a Whiggish position, influenced primarily by Locke. Through his relation Edward Eliot, who controlled six parliamentary seats, he obtained election for Liskeard in 1774. Gibbon took a relatively independent position, supporting North's ministry but, for example, voting with Wilkes in 1775. However, he never spoke once in his nine years in Parliament and his romantic hopes of shining as a 'senator' came to nothing: 'the great speakers fill me with despair', he wrote, 'the bad ones with terror'.[2] It may be supposed that his long years of solitary study and his consciousness of a diminutive stature made him fear ridicule in the robust atmosphere of the House. In the divisive period of the American War, he believed the government's policy was constitutionally justified, though by 1777 he was for peace. The declaration of war by France brought him to support the government again and in 1779 he obtained a place as a Lord Commissioner of Trade. This brought much criticism from his many friends among the opposition. Finally Eliot withdrew his support when Gibbon voted against Dunning's resolution. However, in 1781 the ministry got him a seat at Lymington; when North fell the next year, Burke's Economical Reform Bill which abolished many offices, including Gibbon's, was passed. The following year Gibbon withdrew to Lausanne, permanently as it turned out, except for brief visits to London. He never regretted the move and was probably well aware that he was regarded as a figure of fun in London society, as Boswell and Horace Walpole show: at Lausanne on the other hand he was one of the most respected residents. There was a final evolution in his political views: he developed a fear and hatred of the French Revolution as early as 1790, calling the revolutionaries 'the new barbarians', and was full of enthusiasm for Burke's *Reflections on the French Revolution*. He blamed the *philosophes* for 'exposing an old superstition to the contempt of the blind and fanatic multitude' without any recognition of how far his own work might have done the same. His death occurred suddenly during a brief visit to England in 1794.

Although Gibbon read some works of history in his youth, it was many years before he came to think of writing history himself. His principal reading had been the traditional humanist study of the Greek and Latin classics and their commentators. Between 1758 and 1761 he worked on several drafts of his first published work called *Essai sur l'étude de la littérature*, of which a major theme was a defence of the classics against their attackers among the *philosophes*. At the same time he had been influenced by Montesquieu's seminal *Considérations sur les causes de la grandeur des romains et de leur décadence* and the *Esprit des Lois*, where the fertility of the general ideas put forward without the arrogance or, for that matter, the errors which Gibbon found in Voltaire was particularly attractive to him. Equally important was the revelation of the possibilities of serious historical writing in the spirit of the Enlightenment revealed by William Robertson's *Charles V*, including the section entitled 'View of the progress of society in Europe', and David Hume's *History of Great Britain* (i.e. England under the Stuarts), which had recently appeared.

The perfect composition, the nervous language, the well-turned
periods of Dr Robertson inflamed me to the ambitious hope, that I
might one day tread in his footsteps; the calm philosophy, the care-
less inimitable beauties of his friend and rival [Hume] often forced
me to close the volume, with a mixed sensation of delight and
despair.[3]

This is in part a stylistic judgement but Gibbon was nothing if not an
artist, and the mutual esteem of the three historians is well attested.
Gibbon at first considered a variety of topics: the crusade of Richard I
and Sir Walter Raleigh among others in English history, and a History
of the Liberty of the Swiss; but he rejected the English topics as
exhausted, and the sources for the Swiss project were in German,
which Gibbon never learnt. His next idea, and one more appropriate to
his intense love of Latin literature, was for a *Recueil géographique sur
l'Italie*, which was to be a collection of all available material on ancient
Italy as a background to classical literature. Here he found that
seventeenth-century scholarship had done most of the work, but he
benefited from a further intensive session of reading and an acquaintance with numismatics, epigraphy and even archaeology through the
recent discoveries of Herculaneum.

In October 1764 Gibbon visited Rome. His celebrated description[4]
of an evening when he sat meditating amid the ruins of the Capitol
and formed the idea of his great work is unfortunately suspect as it
exists in several versions with variations in detail, and is not in his
contemporary Journal; but the visit was certainly a highly charged
experience and it is not improbable that the idea of describing at least
the decline and ruin of the monuments of ancient Rome did occur at
that time. The evolution of his ideas into his immense concept of a
complete history of the decline and fall of the Roman Empire is not
known. A brief revival of the Swiss project, inspired by a friend who
would translate the sources, came to nothing after criticism from some
other friends, but Hume praised the effort and above all persuaded
Gibbon to write in future in English, not French. Finally, by 1768 he
knew what he was going to do and began to assemble his material;
the hiatus caused by two years of trouble over his father's disordered
estate was more than compensated for by his feeling of independence.
Systematically, those *érudits* of the sixteenth and seventeenth centuries
whom he had long admired and defended against the fashionable
philosophes were read and re-read. The most important among these
were the Jansenist Le Nain de Tillemont (1637–98) who had collected
the sources for the first six centuries AD in his *Histoire des empereurs*
and to whom Gibbon constantly acknowledged his debt; the
Antiquitates Italiae medii Aevi and *Annali d'Italia* of Muratori; the
Annales Ecclesiastici of Cardinal Baronius; and a range of Protestant

Church historians whom he listed, and judged, at the beginning of Chapter 47, the most important of whom was Mosheim.

Volume I of the work was published at the beginning of 1776. It covered the history of the empire from AD 180 (the death of Marcus Aurelius) to the achievement by Constantine of sole power (324) and included two of his most famous chapters – 15 and 16 – on the rise of Christianity in the Roman Empire. Reaction was almost entirely favourable except from churchmen who objected to these chapters. Gibbon received a splendid letter from Hume. The doyen of Scottish letters expressed gratified surprise that such a production should come from an Englishman whose countrymen 'for almost a whole generation have given themselves up to barbarous and absurd faction'; he praised the dignity of style, the depth of matter and the extensiveness of Gibbon's learning, correctly foresaw the clamour which the chapters on Christianity would provoke and ended by saying that 'in all events you have courage to despise the clamour of Bigots'.[5] Volumes II and III appeared with equal acclaim in 1781; they covered the fourth century AD, with the triumphant establishment of Christianity in spite of the reaction of Julian the Apostate, to whom three chapters (22–4) were devoted, the collapse of Roman government in the western provinces and the establishment of the barbarian kingdoms. The final chapter (38) concluded with some 'General Observations on the Fall of the Roman Empire in the West'. The remaining three volumes were largely written at Lausanne and published together in 1788. Volume IV centred on the epoch of Justinian and the narrative continued to the victory of Heraclius over the Persians in 628. Conscious that at this point he was entering upon an era of history fraught with difficulties of presentation because of its geographical and temporal extent, and in any case likely to be unfamiliar to most of his readers, Gibbon began Volume V with an outline of what the last two volumes contained, and one of the chapters most heavily criticised in modern times (48), containing a brief summary of all the Byzantine emperors from Heraclius to the Latin conquest of Constantinople in 1204. Subsequent chapters departed from a chronological arrangement, and dealt with a number of individual topics, for instance, the Iconoclast Controversy, Mohammed and the rise of Islam (50). The scene became ever wider as Gibbon turned to the Crusades, to Genghis Khan and Tamurlane, the rise of Ottoman power and finally the capture of Constantinople in 1453 (68). Even then he had not finished; a *coda* (as it were) of three chapters gives an account of the history of the city of Rome from the twelfth to the fifteenth centuries and a discussion of the destruction of its ancient monuments. Thus Gibbon returned to the starting point of his ideas of 1764.

It has been observed that Gibbon applied the mind of the eighteenth century to the learning of the seventeenth.[6] What are the implications of this statement? Gibbon's own immense learning was obvious to all and his reading in the vast folios of seventeenth-century erudition was unparalleled. In his own lifetime this heritage, much of it admittedly pedantic, laborious to read and downright tendentious, was actively despised by most of the leading spirits of the age. It was not that these men despised history but rather that the idea of the 'philosophic historian' was paramount. Such historians were more interested in general ideas about human society and its progress than in amassing detailed information. They were interested not only in political history but also in the history of religion, commerce, law and civilisation. There are few general ideas about human society in the *Decline and Fall* which cannot be found in the works of leading French writers of the time; and Gibbon always considered himself, like Hume and Robertson, a philosophic historian. However, he objected to the extremely cursory attitude to historical evidence manifested by some of these writers (though not his Scottish friends) and took some pleasure in picking on Voltaire's errors in historical knowledge. This was not mere pedantry; it seemed to Gibbon that the general ideas of philosophic historians deserved to be supported by detailed evidence.

Gibbon had as clear-cut a point of view as the most committed Marxist. All readers are impressed by the Olympian height at which he moves, by his total mastery of his material and by his supreme self-confidence; equally striking is the expression on almost every page, directly or by implication, of judgement on men, events, religion, manners and the nature of civilisation itself. The standards of the judgements are those of the 'man of sense' of the Enlightenment. Particularly frequent and important are the demonstrations of the evils of despotic government, which he believed to be intimately connected with political, moral and cultural decline, the evils of religious fanaticism and the irrationality of much human behaviour. The decline of Rome for Gibbon began with the suppression by the emperors of the political liberty of the Roman Republic, and every stage of it towards the final 'triumph of barbarism and religion' stemmed from this first cause. Conversely political liberty was the greatest good not only in itself but because it led to the advance of civilisation as had been shown in ancient Greece, the Roman Republic and in Europe since the Renaissance. 'In all the pursuits of active and speculative life, the emulation of states and individuals is the most powerful spring of the efforts and improvements of mankind.' Political liberty as understood by Gibbon was that of the 'mixed constitution' so admired in classical antiquity and which seemed to have achieved its modern form in the revolution of 1688: 'a martial nobility and stubborn commons possessed of arms, tenacious of property and collected into constitutional

assemblies form the only balance capable of preserving a free constitution against the enterprises of an aspiring prince'.[7] In most
European states this happy situation did not exist but an 'emulation
of states' existed in the 'Republic of Europe' and had the same effects,
in contrast to the position of the Roman Empire, isolated from other
civilised powers except Persia.

Gibbon went further than most English writers of the Enlightenment in his hostility to manifestations of organised Christianity and
some of his most ironic and contemptuous passages are devoted to the
cult of images, belief in miracles and, above all, to monks of all
descriptions. Yet he never displayed the destructive virulence of
Voltaire and other French writers towards the church of his own
day, which he attacked chiefly for ignorance and indolence. The difference was no doubt due to his English environment; the capacity of
the church in England to persecute actively had disappeared. Even
those of his readers, no doubt the majority, who were sincere if conventional Christians would find acceptable his irony at the expense of
monks and images, long since effectively banished from England.
Even Chapters 15 and 16 soon found assent after the first shock.
Chapter 15 was the first attempt to explain in human terms the rise
of Christianity and its appeal to Roman society, and whatever Gibbon
said about the later ages of Christianity he never attacked Jesus or
the Christians of the apostolic age. Chapter 16 was a critical survey
of the persecution of the early Christians, and if it ended with the
conclusion that 'it must be acknowledged that the Christians, in the
course of their intestine dissensions, have inflicted far greater severities
on each other than they had experienced from the zeal of the infidels',[8]
this had to be accepted as true, however unpalatable.

Gibbon's conviction that the decline of Rome began with the end
of republican liberty involved him in an inconsistency when he took
the death of Marcus Aurelius (AD 180) as his starting point, and wrote
a well-known sentence 'if a man were called to fix the period in the
history of the world, during which the condition of the human race
was most happy and prosperous, he would, without hesitation, name
that which elapsed from the death of Domitian to the accession of
Commodus'.[9] This passage and the generally favourable description of
the Roman world at that date might lead one to suppose that Gibbon
gave his assent to the currently fashionable idea of benevolent despotism as the best form of government, but this would be incorrect;
Gibbon stressed that this favourable situation depended on the un-
predictable will of one man, and that all the evils of despotism had
been already present in the first century AD under 'the dark unrelenting
Tiberius, the furious Caligula, the feeble Claudius, the profligate and
cruel Nero'.[10] Further, he gives a notably hostile portrait of the reign
of Augustus as the crafty and subtle founder of imperial despotism,

a view notably at variance with that of the majority of English writers of the eighteenth century, who derived their image of Augustus from Virgil, Horace and Livy rather than, as Gibbon did, from Tacitus and Dio. At the end of his life he regretted that he had not in fact begun his *History* with Augustus. The reason for his chosen date appears to be the contrast which the long period of internal peace and success on the frontiers would present with the centuries of turmoil which followed.

As for Gibbon's terminal date, about which he was not certain when he began his work, a minor German scholar named Cellarius had established in 1688 the convention of regarding the capture of Constantinople by the Turks as marking the end of the Middle Ages, and its adoption by Montesquieu in the *Considérations* was doubtless decisive for Gibbon. Even though he was well aware that the 'rebirth of taste and science' in Italy preceded this event, and that the Roman Empire had long been reduced to the compass of a single city, the dramatic and formal significance of the capture was inescapable for a writer with an artistry.

At the end of the third volume, in Chapter 38, Gibbon appended his 'General observations on the Fall of the Roman Empire in the West'; no similar passage concludes the work as a whole. It is thus partly, though only partly, due to Gibbon that even today the 'fall of the Roman Empire' in the minds of most educated persons means the fall of the Western Empire to the Germanic invaders. It is 'our' empire the West is interested in, not the Eastern. Gibbon's last three volumes show that his vision was incomparably wider than that but he no doubt correctly judged his readers' interest. However, his observations are only a few pages long and offer no detailed analysis of possible causes; in fact they constitute a piece of writing of no great originality. The key passage reads:

The decline of Rome was the natural and inevitable effect of immoderate greatness. Prosperity ripened the principal of decay; the causes of destruction multiplied with the extent of conquest; and as soon as time or accident had removed the artificial supports, the stupendous fabric yielded to the pressure of its own weight. The story of its ruin is simple and obvious; and instead of inquiring *why* the Roman empire was destroyed, we should rather be surprised that it had subsisted so long. The victorious legions, who, in distant wars, acquired the vices of strangers and mercenaries, first oppressed the freedom of the republic, and afterwards violated the majesty of the purple. The emperors, anxious for their personal safety and the public peace, were reduced to the base expedient of corrupting the discipline which rendered them alike formidable to their sovereign and to the enemy; the vigour of the military government was relaxed and finally dissolved by the partial institutions of Constantine; and the Roman world was overwhelmed by a deluge of barbarians.[11]

This obviously does not go very far, and the handful of occasions on which Gibbon refers in the narrative to the causes of the fall of the empire are simple statements about the decline of the army. In fact a close analysis of causes of the sort we would expect was alien to Gibbon's genius, which was primarily in narrative history and secondarily in the organisation of apparently intractable matter, like Roman law, into readable prose. And it is in the narrative that we can see other 'causes' of the decline and fall working themselves out. Gibbon makes constant use of the fashionable contrast between the Noble Savage and his complement, the decadent civilised man – 'the Caledonians, glowing with the warm virtues of nature, and the degenerate Romans, polluted with the mean vices of wealth and slavery'.[12] He amplified the use made of this theme in Tacitus' *Germania*, a fundamental document in the history of primitivism as an idea. He held that climate had something to do with it and developed a trick of style when he needed periphrases for the various peoples of northern Europe: – 'the fierce giants of the north', 'the hardy children of the north', 'the shepherds of the north', 'the hostile tribes of the north' – are a selection; and frequently they are directly or implicitly compared with the 'soft' inhabitants of the south (or the east). Yet on several occasions he attacks the idea in trenchant terms: 'Such were those savage ancestors whose imaginary virtues have sometimes excited the praise and envy of civilized ages' and (the Germans) 'passed their lives in a state of ignorance and poverty which it has pleased some declaimers to dignify with the appellation of virtuous simplicity'.[13] When it came to it Gibbon was firmly against Rousseau and with Voltaire, and for him the Noble Savage was a literary device.

Yet there remained the theme of the 'corruption' of civilisation. Those other enemies of the Roman Empire, the Persians, were, unlike the Germans, 'long since civilized and corrupted'; the senatorial nobility of Rome was 'luxurious and unwarlike', the urban masses 'an unwarlike populace enervated by luxury'.[14] There was an intimate connection between a wealthy civilisation and despotic government since 'our designs and our possessions are the strongest fetters of despotism'. In addition to lowering the effectiveness of the Roman army, emperors followed 'the timid policy of reducing whatever is eminent, of dreading every active power and of expecting that the most feeble will prove the most obedient'.[15] These ideas were commonplace in classical literature and were the subject of active discussion among the *philosophes*. When it comes to the role of Christianity in the decline of the empire the situation is more complex. Gibbon believed the two were intimately connected but rarely indicated definite causes and effects. Emperors began to insist on conformity with their chosen creed and to distribute favours to their ecclesiastical advisers; this 'introduced new causes to tyranny and sedition': public order and even loyalty were disturbed by conflicts between Christian sects – 'the most implacable enemies of the Romans were in the bosom of their country'.¹⁶ In general, the caustic manner in which he writes of the various theological controversies, and such chapters as 17 and 18 in which he has a hostile judgement on nearly every feature of the reign of Constantine, suggest that Christianity was not only a symptom of the decline of the empire but also an aggravation of it.

Yet the 'General observations' conclude with Gibbon's demonstration why civilised, Christian Europe of the eighteenth century was probably immune from the fate of the Roman Empire. This was in part due to the progress of science as applied to warfare; any possible barbarian enemies 'before they can conquer must cease to be barbarous', that is, master modern techniques of warfare, while such mastery would be accompanied by 'an improvement in the arts of peace and civil policy'. At the same time, the effects of truly despotic government in modern Europe would be limited by the division of Europe into a number of independent states, and 'we may therefore acquiesce in the pleasing conclusion that every age of the world has increased and still increases the real wealth, the happiness, the knowledge, and perhaps the virtue, of the human race'¹⁷.

Gibbon's account of Byzantine civilisation has been the most heavily criticised part of his work. The key chapter is 48, which sketched the emperors from Heraclius to the Latin conquest of 1204 concentrating almost exclusively on the most deplorable and vicious events in the series of some fifty emperors (Gibbon's own calculation). The contrast with the first three volumes which covered only three centuries is obvious. It was not that sources were unavailable: most of the literary texts had been published with commentaries in a *Corpus Historiae Byzantinae* begun as early as 1645, and for ecclesiastical history he had his Baronius and Mosheim. In fact Gibbon was doing no more than give historical flesh to what was already a commonplace: Voltaire had said that the history (i.e. the historiography) of Byzantium contained nothing but declamation and miracles and was a disgrace to the human mind. Montesquieu had described Byzantium in the last chapter of the *Considérations* as nothing but a tissue of rebellions, seditions and treachery, and found it difficult to explain why it had lasted so long. Gibbon was as unfavourable:

the story of the Eastern Empire must continue to repeat a tedious and uniform tale of weakness and misery . . . a dead uniformity of

abject vices which are neither softened by the weakness of humanity
nor animated by the vigour of memorable crimes.[18]

Any positive achievements are attributed to a handful of exceptional
individuals. The preservation of Constantinople from Arab sieges is
said to be due chiefly to the fortunate secret of how to manufacture
'greek fire', though in a passive sense, like the rest of Europe, it was
also saved by 'the luxury and arts, the division and decay, of the
empire of the caliphs'.[19] Gibbon had little conception of the importance
of the conversion of the Slavonic peoples to Christianity through Constantinople, although he had been positive on the importance of the
conversion of the Germanic peoples in the West. His view of the Greek
Church was as low as his view of the imperial government.

The prostrate Greeks were content to fast, to pray, and to believe
in blind obedience to the patriarch and his clergy. During a long
dream of superstition the Virgin and the saints, their visions and
miracles, their relics and images, were preached by the monks and
worshipped by the people.[20]

Gibbon was unable to relate this religious phenomenon to the capacity
of the Byzantine state to survive, although he attributed much of the
success of the Arabs to the religious fervour of Islam.

It is obvious from his last two volumes that Gibbon was far more
interested in the Orient in general than in Constantinople. But since
it was historically true that great convulsions like the rise of Islam,
the movements of the Turkish tribes and of the Mongols, and the
Crusades, all affected the destinies of Constantinople, he was able to
seize the opportunity to range geographically as far as the borders of
China. Gibbon showed a width of interest which must put the majority
of historians to shame. He brought himself abreast of all the advances
in Arabic studies which had been made through translations into
English and French in the seventeenth and eighteenth centuries in
order to deal with the most important element in his story, the life of
Mohammed and the rise of Islam. He showed his instinct for historical
criticism in recognising that most of this material was late and affected
by untrustworthy legend, but was not in a position to judge how exceptionally difficult a historically valid account of Mohammed and the
beginnings of Islam was to prove. In his general interpretation, Gibbon
was once again in the mainstream of the Enlightenment, which
tended towards a favourable view of Mohammed and Islam, though
it was in difficulties over their dreaded 'fanaticism'. Islam was believed
by critics of Christianity to be a religion whose founder made no
claims to divinity, which had no organised priestly hierarchy or cult

of images and which retained its earlier traditions uncontaminated by theological speculation. Later chapters on the Seljuks, Ottomans and Mongols have passages and attitudes which verge on the romantic, though Gibbon rarely held them up against the image of a decadent Constantinople and was aware of the cataclysmic effects of the Mongol invasions. Gibbon's treatment has another interest; naturally it lacks the knowledge acquired by and through the success of Western imperialism, but by the same token it lacks any of the prejudices (or guilt) which these successes brought to Western attitudes.

Gibbon founded no historical school and in many ways his work was soon to be outdated by the improvements in historical methods of the nineteenth century. Even the techniques of source criticism, for various reasons of particular importance in the study of ancient history, which were being developed in Germany in his own lifetime, were unknown to him. Yet the *Decline and Fall* remained a standard history for a century for reasons other than its standing as a work of literature. The nineteenth century in Western Europe had little interest in Byzantine history. Gibbon's brilliant but totally hostile account has been blamed for this, but unfairly. After all, he was equally unflattering about the mediaeval period in the West in so far as he dealt with it, but this did not inhibit the rapid growth of mediaeval studies in the nineteenth century. Perhaps the unchallenged successes of European imperialism diverted attention from Gibbon's 'awful revolution', the prime example of an empire's fall. But such was Gibbon's accuracy and mastery of his sources (even if it lacked the benefits of source criticism) that between 1909 and 1914 the foremost British Byzantinist, J. B. Bury, still found it eminently worthwhile to produce an edition of the *Decline and Fall* in seven volumes, with notes and appendices indicating where Gibbon's account could be corrected. Bury himself wrote a *History of the Later Roman Empire from Arcadius to Irene* (1889) and a *History of the Later Roman Empire from the Death of Theodosius to the Death of Justinian* (1923). Since that date, and especially since 1945, the later Roman period has been the subject of a great deal of research particularly in the fields of its administration, economy and social history, now comprehensively dealt with in A. H. M. Jones's *The Later Roman Empire 284–602: A Social, Economic and Administrative Survey* (1964, 3 vols). Gibbon's innovatory attempt to integrate religious with secular history received a setback in the nineteenth century when church history as a specialisation became the preserve of theological faculties, and though the situation in recent times has changed – particularly through the work of P. R. Brown – the later Roman world still lacks its R. W. Southern.

The question of the causes of decline and fall of the Roman Empire, so blandly dismissed by Gibbon, has naturally been the subject of intense debate. Since the debate has in some measure been a response to the crisis of modern Western European empires, it is not surprising that it has not always been illuminating.

Well over a dozen alleged causes of the decline and fall have been seriously discussed by scholars over the last half-century.[21] Theories of climatic deterioration and exhaustion of the soil leading to economic collapse have remained unproven; manpower shortage has been found attractive, but cannot be supported by any evidence as to how far, if at all, the population in AD 400 was lower than in AD 100. In contrast to such general explanations – which would perhaps have attracted Gibbon himself – was J. B. Bury's denial of any general explanation whatever. '[The success of the barbarians] is accounted for by the actual events and would be clearer if the story were known more fully. The gradual collapse of the Roman power in [the western] section of the Empire was the consequence of a series of contingent events. No general causes can be assigned that made it inevitable' – at the least a sober warning against the neglect of the accidental and unforseeable in history.

More frequent have been analyses of internal weaknesses in the empire, some of which were mentioned, if only briefly, by Gibbon, or were implicit in his general view of despotic government. The empire had been won by military might and since the time of Augustus had been defended by the most professional army that had ever existed or was to exist for many centuries. Gibbon believed that the quality of the army had declined because of specific imperial policies and thought that the recruitment of Germans was particularly deleterious. Modern views have tended to show that German recruits were both effective and loyal, at least to the end of the fourth century. Reasons for their recruitment are not given in the ancient sources, though the Romans had always utilised the military strengths of their subjects and neighbours where possible. In the fourth century recruitment from outside the empire appears to have been due, in part, to the fact that the state lost revenue if too many peasants were drawn from the land into the army. The economic difficulties of the empire have been much to the fore in modern discussion; its resources, primarily agricultural, appear to have been barely sufficient to sustain the army and the administration as well as a vastly expensive court, and other non-producers such as the senatorial and city aristocracies and, increasingly, the church. Whether the taxes, which weighed most heavily on the poor, and the widely attested corruption of the administration led to widespread disaffection and revolt is another matter. There were a few revolts of an apparently social character, mostly caused by local and temporary shortages of food, and some instances of collaboration with invaders, but no general and effective movements. More significant was a lack of loyalty in a positive sense. Gibbon noted the total lack of resistance to the invaders in Gaul, not just among the peasants but among social élites. Decline of public spirit was, in his view, due to the deadening effect of despotic government; but it has been argued[22] that the landed aristocracy at least not only sabotaged imperial efforts to maximise revenues and check corruption but quickly saw advantages in collaboration with barbarian rulers, who would be bound to rely on the existing administrative structures controlled by this class.

However, one crucial point about all explanations was emphasised by N. H. Baynes, Bury's successor as the leading British Byzantinist; their impact must be shown to be more damaging in the western part of the empire than in the east. In fact, most of the negative aspects of imperial government can be observed in both parts. Indeed, Christianity, singled out by Gibbon as a major source of internal weakness, was far more significant in the east than in the west. It is obviously true that the greatest single flaw in Gibbon's picture is his undifferentiated view of imperial despotism, unchanged, it might seem, from the first to the last Constantine. It was no doubt reasonable on this view to wonder why the Western Empire had lasted so long but blindness not to ask why Constantinople survived another thousand years. The notion of 'decline' has itself been questioned especially in, France, where some have argued that it is a misleading application to Roman history of a term originally used in the Renaissance of a particular phenomenon in Latin literary culture; the second century AD which Gibbon made his starting point can be regarded as a period of economic and intellectual stagnation, while success in overcoming the crisis of the third century led to a transformation of Roman society under Diocletian and Constantine as full of promise in the Latin half of the empire as in the Greek east which was to become the Byzantine state; as Piganiol wrote, the empire did not die a natural death; it was murdered.[23]

It is not after all surprising that most scholars have abandoned or never begun the search for what Momigliano called 'the D.Phil. candidate's dream of sleeping beauty – the true cause of the fall of the Roman Empire'.[24] It may be noted that sophisticated, as opposed to vulgar, Marxists find it equally difficult to reach accord on the precise modes whereby the slave-owning society of the Roman Empire was superseded by feudalism, to use Marxist categories. Hence the popularity of a sociological approach, describing the transformation of the Roman world over a period of several centuries covering the period of the barbarian kingdoms; this approach stems ultimately from the debate provoked by the Belgian historian H. Pirenne,[25] who maintained that the true 'end of the ancient world' came not with the Germanic invasions but with the conquests of Islam in the seventh and eighth centuries.

Gibbon's work is still widely read, not merely because of the stimulus provided by his approach or even because it is a vital document of the Enlightenment, but because it is a work of literary genius. Gibbon was quite consciously creating a work of art and was intensely pre-occupied with the stylistic problems involved in writing history which were, and are, formidable.

> The style of an author should be the image of his mind: but the choice and command of language is the fruit of exercise: many experiments were made before I could hit the middle tone between a dull chronicle and a rhetorical declamation; three times did I compose the first chapter and twice the second and third before I was tolerably satisfied.

When he came to write the second and third volumes he felt more confident: 'I was now master of my style and subject: and while the measure of my daily performance was enlarged, I discovered less reason to cancel or correct', and 'it has always been my practise to cast a long paragraph in a single mould, to try it by my ear, to deposit it in my memory; but to suspend the action of my pen till I had given the last polish to my work'.[26] In his artistic preoccupation Gibbon was following the traditions of ancient historians from Thucydides to Tacitus and beyond. This is not the place to analyse the major features of Gibbon's style, but to make two points; to call it the apotheosis of the grand manner is true but insufficient. An essential feature is the irony which illuminates countless pages. It serves a double purpose; first, to maintain that position of judgement in a manner more accept-able than mere priggish moralising; but, more important, to arrest the reader. Without the irony, the beautifully structured sentences, elaborate Latinate vocabulary and sonorous cadences would be ultim-ately soporific. With it, the reader is constantly amused, provoked or challenged; he is made conscious that his own intelligence, his own reason, is being put to the test by a master. The assumption is always that a man of reason will accept the point; if he is provoked, let him parry the thrust with his own learning, if he can.

NOTES: CHAPTER 2

1 *Memoirs*, ed. G. Bonnard (1966), pp. 46 ff.
2 Gibbon to John Baker Holroyd, 15 February 1775, quoted in *The House of Commons, 1754–90*, ed. L. B. Namier and J. Brooke, Vol. II, p. 494.
3 *Memoirs*, p. 99.
4 ibid., p. 136.
5 Printed in *Memoirs*, pp. 167 ff.
6 G. M. Young, *Edward Gibbon* (1932), p. 72.
7 *Decline and Fall*, Vol. I, p. 59. References to *Decline and Fall* are to the Everyman edition of 1910, reprinted 1976.

 8 *Decline and Fall*, Vol. II, p. 68.
 9 ibid., Vol. I, p. 78.
10 ibid., Vol. I, p. 79.
11 ibid., Vol. IV, p. 105.
12 ibid., Vol. I, p. 126.
13 ibid., Vols III, p. 393; I, p. 213.
14 ibid., Vols I, p. 208; I, p. 313; III, p. 241.
15 ibid., Vol. II, p. 110.
16 ibid., Vols II, p. 311; II, p. 456.
17 ibid., Vol. IV, p. 112.
18 ibid., Vol. V, pp. 72 ff.
19 ibid., Vol. V, p. 75.
20 ibid., Vol. V, p. 488.
21 Some of the views are conveniently summarised in *Decline and Fall of the Roman Empire: Why Did It Collapse?*, ed. D. Kagan (1962).
22 E. A. Thompson, 'The settlement of the Barbarians in Southern Gaul', *Journal of Roman Studies*, Vol. XLVI (1956), pp. 65–75; 'The Visigoths from Fritigern to Euric', *Historia*, Vol. XII (1963) pp. 105–26.
23 *L'Empire chrétien* (1947), p. 422.
24 *Studies in Historiography* (1966), p. 49.
25 The fullest account of his views is in his posthumous *Mohammed and Charlemagne* (English translation, 1939).
26 *Memoirs*, pp. 155–6, 159.

NOTE ON FURTHER READING

The most convenient edition of the *Decline and Fall* is in the Everyman series (1910, reprinted 1976), though the modern notes are seriously deficient. J. B. Bury's edition (1909) contains many useful notes and appendixes. Unfortunately neither edition conforms to Gibbon's original division into volumes. A definitive edition of the *Memoirs* is that of G. Bonnard (1966). Gibbon's correspondence was edited by J. E. Norton and published in three volumes in 1956 as *The Letters of Edward Gibbon*. Gibbon's *Journal to January 28th, 1763*, ed. D. Low (1929) and *Journey from Geneva to Rome: his Journal from 20 April to 2 October 1764*, ed. G. Bonnard (1961) contain much important material on Gibbon's intellectual formation. The most substantial biography of Gibbon is D. M. Low's *Edward Gibbon, 1737–1794* (1937). More recent is J. M. Swain, *Edward Gibbon the Historian* (1966). G. M. Young's *Edward Gibbon* (1932) is an attractive brief study but is not annotated. An excellent study of the *Decline and Fall* as a work of literature is H. L. Bond, *Literary Art of Edward Gibbon* (1960). The bicentenary of the publication of Volume I was marked by the publication of *Edward Gibbon and the Decline and Fall of the Roman Empire*, ed. G. Bowesock and others (1977): it contains a number of important essays on Gibbon's intellectual background and historiographical approach. A useful paper on 'Gibbon's contribution to historical method' is included in A. Momigliano, *Studies in Historiography* (1966).

3 *Leopold von Ranke*

Leopold von Ranke was born in Thuringia in 1795 of a line of Lutheran pastors, though his father was a lawyer; educated at the Schulpforta, a boarding school where Bismarck was later a pupil, and at Leipzig University, where he read theology and classical philology. His life was uneventful. His first post was at the Gymnasium of Frankfurt-am-Oder (1818–25); his first book, published in 1824, brought him fame and appointment as Professor of History at Berlin; he had friends and acquaintances in the university and in the literary circle of Varnhagen von Ense. His second book, *Die Osmanen und die Spanische Monarchie* (1827), was part of a project he never completed; instead he made his first tour of foreign archives (1827–31), when he met Gentz and Metternich. Between this and his second tour (1834–7) he edited the *Historisch-politische Zeitschrift* and published much in it himself. He did not renew his early social connections but became the friend of Frederick William, King of Prussia, and later of Maximilian of Bavaria. Promoted to an established chair at Berlin in 1834 and remained professor until 1871. At the age of 48 married Clara Graves, an English-woman whom he met in Paris; his great-nephew was Robert von Ranke Graves, the poet. He was ennobled in 1865. Began to revise his chief works and republish them in the fifty-four volumes of *Sämmtliche Werke* in 1865: these collected works came out between 1867 and 1890. The last volume to be edited by Ranke himself was Volume 45. He died in 1886.

In 1876 Ranke's *A History of England, principally in the seventeenth century* had just been published in English translation. Bishop Stubbs, lecturing on the progress of the Modern History Honours School in Oxford during the ten years of its existence, ventured to compare it – to its disadvantage – with the history departments in certain German universities. He would not dare to compare any English historian with the German author who was in his audience's mind. Leopold von Ranke was 'not only beyond all comparison the greatest historical scholar alive, but one of the very greatest historians that ever lived'.[1]

Indeed, he wrote a great deal about a great geographic area and a great length of time. He had great narrative skill and told the history of five great states through the actions and thoughts of a relatively small number of great people. Considering all the facts he included and the standard of his time, the pace of his narrative was quick. One can always tell when something happened but he did not over-burden his page with dates. He arranged his materials skilfully so that he could make a point in a short reflective passage – he used them sparingly – when the reader was ready for it, if he had not already made it by the very arrangement itself. He lit up his narrative with characterisation which at its best, in the study of Catherine de Medici, for example, in the French History, was written with a novelist's free-dom and insight. He even sometimes stole the imaginative writer's advantage by first telling what a poet might have imagined, about Bothwell's motives for murdering Darnley, for example, before he claimed to abide by the more rigid standards of the historian. He purported to know the exact words of a speech or conversation or the precise train of thought in the mind of a statesman. His style gave drama to his narrative, for he confronted one abstract principle with its opposite or faced an historical figure with his enemy or victim. The character study of Admiral Coligny followed that of Catherine de Medici and he waited to describe both until he had reached 1570 and the massacre of St Bartholomew's Eve. He often built up the story of a statesman's or general's policy to the point when the reader expected a great triumph: in the next sentence he told of his death and told it in some half-dozen words.

But Bishop Stubbs chiefly meant, if one may judge by what Stubbs normally thought most important, to pay tribute to Ranke's initiative and assiduity in searching for historical documents and to his faith-fulness in refraining from saying more than he had evidence to support. Ranke did not present the evidence for and against a par-ticular interpretation in a modern analytic way. He was a narrative historian in the grand manner. He told his story, however, after he had drawn his conclusions about what happened from contemporary records. Some of these, if they had not been used before, he would then publish in full or in extract and discuss in a documentary appendix. Ranke's young man's boast – in the preface to the first work he published – that he would relate history as it really happened, *wie es eigentlich gewesen*,[2] was not quite so foolish as, detached from its context, it seems. He meant that he would report what the documents he read told him, and relate the narrative objectively, as interesting in itself.

Of course he could not stand outside the period in which he lived and he did not, as Burckhardt did, acknowledge an ambition to do so. The *Historisch-politische Zeitschrift* which he edited in 1832–4 had arisen out of the Prussian king's wish for a periodical which should link the past with the present and it contained political as well as historical matter.[3] Ranke wrote much on what we should call contemporary history. The work published in Volumes 43 to 50 of Ranke's collected works (*Sämmtliche Werke*) on Serbia and Turkey, Prussian history 1793–1813, the restored monarchy in France and the revolutions of 1830 was all on the borderland between history and politics. He was a frequenter of courts and a supporter of monarchs. The contents of his narrative was determined by the prevalent ideas of the public for which he was writing and of which he was part. The Prussian victory over France in 1870–1 was reflected in his writing and in his revision of what he had already written before it was published in his collected works. Yet there is still a difference between Ranke's attitude and, say, Machiavelli's use of Livy or the Younger Pitt's alleged use of Thucydides: he did not go to history as a guide to human motives or as a key to how human beings might be governed. He wrote history because he enjoyed history; but as a pious Lutheran he enjoyed it as a pious man, not as a rationalist, would.

I propose to divide what follows into the three main grounds I have indicated for Stubbs's admiration: first, the grand structure of Ranke's work as a whole; next, the thought which runs through it, that is, the consistency of his interpretation of history; finally, the sources he used.

Ranke's subject was Europe: he called it the world. A significant event in European history he called an event of world historical importance. His last (unfinished) work he called *World History*, but it was a history of Europe from the last centuries of the Roman Empire to the high Middle Ages. Ranke's several great histories relate to events which ended in the European state-system of the mid-nineteenth century. He set out, however, to write not the history of states but of peoples. The relationship between state and nation[4] became a problem which confronted him more seriously the further his work proceeded. He did not blur the problems, as a less 'objective' historian writing at the time of the unification of Germany might have done. He wrote of the French *state* under Louis XIV when that word seemed appropriate and of the French *nation* when, in the fourteenth and fifteenth centuries, that seemed the appropriate word. He never tried to tidy away the untidiness of history. Moreover, although he began with the intention of writing about the peoples of Europe, in the last parts of his work he found himself writing about the concentration of power in the hands of great individuals like Louis XIV or Cromwell. He seemed in his last years to be fascinated by this phenomenon. In the *Books of Prussian History* – in its revised form a post-1870 work –

he wrote of supreme power and nationality as standing in the most varied relationship one to another, varying between the extremes of mutual support and mutual conflict. He did not, however, begin with the individual, but with the nation. Thus his first book, a *History of the Latin and Teuton Peoples* (*Geschichten der romanischen und germanischen Völker*), came into his mind as a complete whole, virtually as it was finally printed.

It was so coherent because it was held together by the idea that Europe was a cultural unit marked by its Christian character or, rather, by its Latin Christian character. The Europe of which Ranke wrote excluded, as well as all Asia and Africa and America (except for the effect upon Europe of its discovery), the Slavs, the Letts and the Magyars as foreign, or so he thought, to Latin civilisation. It included six great nations: three – the Italian, French and Spanish – in which the Latin element predominated and three – the German, English and Scandinavian – in which the Teuton element prevailed. The material of the first book was provided by the conflict of these peoples in the Italian Wars at the turn of the fifteenth to the sixteenth century. The structure built upon this foundation seemed intended to comprise separate histories of each of these peoples, but the Spanish history was only touched upon and the Scandinavian never written at all. His unexpected preoccupation with Prussian history deprived the structure of its symmetry in the end.

Ranke believed that historical understanding required the longest possible perspective. It was a common belief in the early nineteenth century. The narrative in each of the great histories is only detailed for the sixteenth and later centuries, but it begins with the emergence of a nation from the chrysalis of the Roman Empire, if not earlier. In his first book it is short and generalised for the early centuries and perspective is sometimes achieved by casting back. For example, Maximilian I, Emperor of the Holy Roman Empire, is introduced by writing:

He was ruler of Austria and the Netherlands. Some six hundred years before maybe, in the Danube Valley, between the Alps and the Bohemian mountains, round about Krems and Melk, the mark of Austria had just been founded . . .[5]

The detailed narrative begins with Charles VIII's invasion of Italy in 1494 and ends in 1514–15 just before the defeated Louis XII's death and just after the death of Pope Julius II. Ranke had no hesitation in writing of the Italian 'nation' and related Julius II's actions to an aim to free Italy from the foreigner and to assert the Italian nation's right to live its own life. The result had been to establish an Austro-

Spanish ascendancy in Europe such as seemed likely to unite the six nations into a single political combination. The unity of the Roman and German peoples was exemplified as never before. The unity broke up, as break up it must, to release the nations to diverge along their separate individual historical roads. So Ranke confronted the principle of unity with that of diversity.

In 1832, after his first tour of archives when he visited Vienna, Modena, Venice and Rome, Ranke published his next large work *Zur Deutschen Geschichte von 1555 bis 1618*. In his collected works this is Volume 7 and follows the six volumes of *Deutsche Geschichte im Zeitalter der Reformation* which it would seem to complete if its rhetorical style did not show its earlier composition. It is better thought of as part of the foundation of the structure of Ranke's work, since it enabled him to develop his thought about nationality. The materials which Ranke arranges in his narrative relate to the religious Peace of Augsburg, the harmony of the Holy Roman Empire during the generation which followed when, so he maintains, a Protestant cast of mind coloured the whole German nation even including the Catholic aristocracy and Catholic churchmen; the cultural flowering and urban prosperity which accompanied it; the end of the harmony with the onset in the 1570s of the Counter-Reformation; the disputes in which the Reichstag was, for reasons which he explains, the arena, relating to the secularisation of ecclesiastical property. Nuremburg, Augsburg, Donauwörth, the names succeed each other in the narrative until they lead into the Bohemian Succession question and the outbreak of the Thirty Years' War. From these materials Ranke draws the conclusion that, since the unity of Europe in the Middle Ages had been sustained by the partnership between the temporal and spiritual powers, when the church withdrew from this partnership the unity of Europe broke up and diversity reasserted itself in the way in which each nation solved the old problem of relations between temporal and spiritual powers. He believed that nationality played a chief part in determining the differences between these solutions.[6] The greatest distinction between mediaeval and modern times was created by the disappearance of ecclesiastical territory and property on which the political power of the mediaeval episcopal hierarchy had been founded.[7]

Ranke modified this conclusion after he had written the German, French and English histories but the importance of the Reformation, which it thus highlighted, provided the foundation on which he built the structure of the following German, French and English histories. Ranke first visited the archives and libraries in Venice, Florence, Rome, Frankfurt, Dresden and other German cities as he was later to visit those of Paris, London and Oxford. The first fruit of this tour was *The History of the Popes* in three volumes, published between

1839 and 1840. I have used the title of the English translation by Sarah Austin published in 1840 and reviewed by Macaulay in the *Edinburgh Review* for October 1840, because this work made Ranke's international reputation secure. This was Ranke's substitute for a full history of the Italian people. He believed, as he tells us in the preface to a biographical study of Savonarola, that each nation had periods or aspects of its history which were of universal significance and that it behoved the historian to give prominence to these.[8] It was through the papacy from earliest times to the beginning of the nineteenth century that Italian history had this universal significance.

The *Deutsche Geschichte im Zeitalter der Reformation* (1839–47) Ranke considered his most important work and deliberately put it first in his collected works. He begins with Carolingian times but this characteristically long perspective ends in the disorders of the fifteenth century. 'Those things to which the Middle Ages had given birth and raised up to maturity everywhere fell into conflict with each other and in this universal conflict destroyed each other.'[9] But out of chaos arose the powers which rearranged things in a new order. These powers were the kings who made themselves the focal points of their nations and gave them self-awareness and a consciousness of their own creative energy (*Kraft*). In Germany the Reichstag, rather than the Emperor, played this part, so that the detailed narrative begins with its effort to give Germany a new constitution between 1490 and 1519. The movement failed and Volume 1 ends with Germany pulled in two opposite political directions. After the election of Charles of Austria, Spain and the Netherlands as Holy Roman Emperor there existed Austrian and anti-Austrian directions in Germany. They were given irrepressible force by their coincidence with the religious divisions (between papal and Catholic on one hand and Lutheran on the other) signalled by the decisions of the Diet of Worms. The material for Volume 2 was provided largely by the Knights' War and the Peasants' Revolt of 1522 and 1525. Ranke showed a surprising modernity in his discussion of the ingredients in a revolutionary situation. In a modern way he shows how the established order in Germany was no longer acceptable and, striking a nineteenth-century note, he shows how the elemental forces (*die elementaren Kräfte*) upon which the state rested rose up against it.[10] A new thread in Ranke's thought comes into this volume when he describes the 'germanising of Prussia' by the secularisation of the Order of Teutonic Knights. The material for the third volume is the arming of the Catholic princes and of the Schmalkaldic League among the Protestant minority, within the political framework of the later Italian Wars, the renewed Turkish onslaught upon Europe and the development of Protestant Churches outside Germany. Ranke breaks off in 1534 leaving deeply engraved on the reader's mind the impression of the diverging paths along which Germany, France and

England were by then proceeding. The fourth volume opens with Emperor Charles's attack on Tunis, then part of the empire of the Ottoman Turks with whom Francis I of France was allied. This alliance marked the withdrawal of the military force of a great kingdom from the system of Latin Christian unity which had so far prevailed in Europe. It was the more striking in that it was taken by an old-style Catholic and not a new-style Protestant ruler. Enough has been said of this work to show the varied themes to which Ranke's dominant idea could lead.

Ranke had been writing at the same time the nine books of Prussian history, published between 1837 and 1848. They continued the German history in that, in order to find his long perspective, Ranke traces the rise of Prussia and tells its history under the Great Elector. This is, however, a rather general account, and when Ranke revised the history to make twelve books it was expanded. The real hero of the work is Frederick William I and Ranke finds that his material, as he interprets it, causes him to build in a direction he did not originally intend. Prussia proved an exception to his theory of the growth of peoples from the shell of the Roman Empire. It derived its national coherence from simply having filled the empty space left by the struggle of the four Great Powers to achieve a balance of power among themselves. Frederick William I understood and seized this opportunity. The nation bore the imprint of his genius and his three guiding principles of military strength (conserved, not used), a healthy economy and a Protestant rule of life. Ranke, who believed an essential continuity existed between the reign of Frederick the Great and that of his father, fits the psychology of the early struggle between them into an arrangement of materials which leads to this conclusion. He is able to justify Frederick the Great's seizure of Silesia in a narration of events which still allows Frederick to adhere to his father's principles. Ranke could not continue in this vein. In the collected works he published, as a substitute for the continuation, three studies, one written earlier and two after 1870: *Maria Theresa, her State and her Court in 1755, The Origins of the Seven Years War* and *The German Powers and the League of Princes 1780–90.* Frederick the Great, with some stretching of the material, is made to appear as the defender of the German nation against an assertive Austrian Empire. After the accession of Frederick William IV to the Prussian throne in 1840, Ranke's thinking took a new turn. He was increasingly committed to the view that the German nation had found its full expression in the cultural and political achievement of Prussia. Before he came to assemble his collected works he did not believe that this was *military* achievement. He was never entirely comfortable with the conclusion forced upon him by the Prussian victories at the end of his life. He had already in 1840, as he was writing the Prussian history, found that it did not fit snugly into the theory of six nations emerging from an original Roman and Teuton unity.

It is as if the structure of his work has an extra wing thrown out in an unexpected direction. The main building, nevertheless, continued. The five volumes of *Französische Geschichte*, chiefly in the sixteenth and seventeenth centuries, were published between 1852 and 1861. The long perspective is set by a history of the formation of the French nation beginning in the first century BC. The formation of the French kingdom under the Capetians follows. The Crusades are treated as the great unifying force which made of the French kingdom a truly national one. Throughout the rest of the history, which continued to the meeting of the French Assembly of Notables in 1787, Ranke drew attention to the interplay of forces which made for the concentration of power and those which encouraged its dispersal. Three-quarters of the first volume are given to the Religious Wars of the second half of the seventeenth century, for 'the foundations of the Bourbon monarchy were laid in the storms of general war'.[11] It is an exciting volume and, with the massacre of St Bartholomew's Eve as its climax, a violent and dramatic one.

Ranke's materials are now dictating to him a history of the French kings and the French state and increasingly so, as he moves on through the periods of Henry IV, Richelieu, Mazarin, the Fronde and Louis XIV. They oblige him to show how the feudal, aristocratic and national forces, which he believed would have dispersed power, were defeated. There was, however, another theme which Ranke could also discern in the preliminary material of Volume 1. This enabled him to keep alive the idea of the French nation at least to the end of the reign of Henry IV. This preliminary material covered the Hundred Years' War against the English. The war was a fresh unifying force to the nation, but it was also the occasion, because of the rise of towns, for the differentiation of an urban popular element from the feudal and hierarchic. It was no coincidence that the Maid of Orleans came from the workers (*den Arbeitern des Landes*).[12] Through the balancing of these two forces, France avoided both the formation of republics and the setting-up of tyrannies. Henry IV, who balanced them most successfully, was Ranke's model of kingship. Part of the first volume and nearly a third of the second are devoted to him and the first chapter of this volume is the most dramatic of all, even when much of it deals with finance. Ranke skilfully leads the reader to the conclusion that Henry was the kind of king with whom the nation, in its popular as well as aristocratic elements, could identify the state.

The personae of the drama which follows to the height of Louis XIV's power (1672–86) are few for the scope of the history which Ranke tells through them, and the institutions they represent. The scope extended over the whole continent, for a third theme, which has been present from the beginning, is the pressure upon France of events outside France. When Ranke reached Louis XIV at the height of his power he could show that the king had established control even here. So at the climax of the history Ranke gives a definition of absolute monarchy and explains how 'all the elements characteristic of the Latin-Teuton peoples . . .' (and he catalogues them) 'which have stood side by side from ages ago in their manifold relationships and filled long spaces of time with their conflicts' are used by Louis to enlarge his power until it is entire and complete. Ranke ends the account: 'his concept of himself was a concept of all the common interests of France: his ego had become the state itself'.[13] Characteristically Ranke gives a hint of catastrophe even here and the next volume begins with the War of Spanish Succession and the disintegration of the greatness of both king and state. It is striking that Ranke's idea of the development of the European nations has served just far enough to give coherence to the structure of his work and no further. He has not forced the materials of French history into a pattern which they will not fit.

Ranke's last great book, *A History of England, principally in the seventeenth century*, was published in seven volumes between 1859 and 1868. Though it, too, had grown out of the idea of the book of 1824, it has a shape of its own – one dictated by English events, notably the establishment of an independent Anglican Church and a parliamentary constitution combining monarchical and popular elements. The first volume begins with the Celts and the Roman occupation, but its theme is the foundation and defence of the Anglican Church, treated as an assertion of the English national will to be free of foreign rule. The second volume is dominated by the union with Scotland and the alliance with Spain. France, Spain, Scotland and Ireland almost conceal the struggle over the prerogative which should dominate the third volume, for it ends with the execution of King Charles. The fourth volume is more interesting. It begins with the assertion that a republic has been founded and shows that this meant an attempt to realise the sovereignty of the people. The climax of the volume is the result of the failure of this attempt; for out of it sprang the enormous power of Oliver Cromwell. Characteristically it is only now, when the reader's interest has been caught, that Ranke tells something of Cromwell's life.[14] He then shows how his power was derived from his being constitutionally the executive, how he used Parliament as his instrument further to extend it – he does justice to Parliament's reform of the law – and how it came to be rooted in his military strength and in his ability to command wealth. Yet the 'world historical significance' of the Cromwellian period lay, not here, but in the trading wealth and sea power won by his Navigation Act and the wars with Holland. Ranke shows how the great power of Cromwell passed away and under Charles II, when absolute monarchies were developing everywhere else in Europe, gave place to a sharing of power between king and Parliament. Trading-wealth and sea-power, however, remained and led Ranke to interpret the last years of the seventeenth century in a way which did justice to England's position in relation to Europe better than any other historian has done. Charles II had chosen a continental policy of subservience to Louis XIV, though he hoped only to go as far with that relationship as would enable him to control the parliamentary opposition. In fact, Charles II had the worst of both worlds and neither his policy nor that of James II could have been maintained in the face of a national way of thinking in maritime and trading terms. So the policy of 1668, briefly pursued when Charles was over-ridden, a policy of alliance with Holland and Austria to defend the liberty of the continent against the ascendancy of Louis XIV was the one which eventually carried consequences and was historically important. The period of George I and George II, of Walpole and the Seven Years' War, was little more than an epilogue to the history of England conceived of in this way.

Ranke brings this set of volumes to the edge of his own lifetime. There is nothing quite like the architecture of Ranke's work in all the history of historical writing. One realises this as again and again one reads analogies and comparisons sweeping across centuries of time and the whole geography of Europe.

Ranke wrote several biographical studies. The first, 'Don Carlos', was an essay published in the *Wiener Jahrbuch* for 1829.[15] He shows psychological insight of a high order in analysing the frustrated affection of the father, Philip II of Spain, and the frustrated ambition of the son, Don Carlos, poorly endowed both in physique and brain and coveting strength and intelligence. Among other studies those on Savonarola and Wallenstein stand out. *The History of the Popes* is a series of biographies. Yet it is far more; for as Ranke sweeps through the centuries from the early church to the French Revolution he gives coherence to his long narrative by showing how the single endeavour to establish, sustain or recover the secular power of the church bound all their lives together. To do this he has virtually to recount the history of international relations, at least from the papacy of Alexander VI onwards. This he does and still succeeds in transferring from his own mind's eye, where they lived with great clarity, to that of the reader, a succession of sharply differentiated individuals. Even among so many, the study of Cardinal Contarini is notable. Ranke believed that he, whose 'life evolved with the regularity with which Nature brings forth her harvest in the cycle of the seasons',[16] almost succeeded in bringing about reconciliation between Catholics and Protestants before the rigidities of the Counter-Reformation closed in. Characteristically, the study of Contarini is balanced by a similar digression on Ignatius Loyola, the founder of the Jesuit Order. The volumes have importance for Ranke's interpretation of history because they illustrate best of all the interplay of character and circumstance. Ranke interpreted history consistently as interplay between these two or, expressed differently, between freedom and necessity. In the preface to Volumes 40 and 41 of the collected works, a book of biographical studies, Ranke wrote that 'freedom and necessity both contend against each other and penetrate each other. Freedom appears more in personalities; necessity in the life of communities.'

It is hard to understand what Ranke means by such phrases as 'the nature of things' or 'the necessity of things' (*die Nothwendigkeit*, or *Natur der Dingen*, or *Sachen*). They are used with a moderate, but significant, regularity. Sometimes he uses 'necessary' simply to describe the means appropriate to an adopted aim. There are three examples on pages 62 and 72–3 of the first volume of the German History. The sense of Ranke's usage here is that the Germans were struggling for national self-dependence and military resistance to the French was the necessary, that is, the appropriate, means to achieve it. The most interesting example of this use occurs in the volume of Prussian History devoted to Frederick William I. Ranke wrote that the military strength (*Kriegsmacht*) of Prussia during his reign was not a matter of arbitrary choice (*Willkür*) but a necessity (*sondern eine Nothwendigkeit*).[17] Since Prussia owed her very existence, in Ranke's view, to the balance of strength between four Great Powers, not to mention the northern balance between Russia and Sweden, the only appropriate means to maintain herself was to arm herself sufficiently to be a military threat to any power who tried to break the balance.

On other occasions, the necessity which constricts the free will of individuals is simply something which follows from the psychology of men or the character of things. Charles V, for example, though he had defeated the pope and yet did not become 'the Caliph of the western world', still fought on, for 'it is not in the nature of men to be content with limited gain'.[18] Again, 'it lay in the nature of things that the victorious Catholic army after the battle of Moncontour would above all seek to subdue this stretch of land',[19] that is, Poitou with its strategical position in relation to La Rochelle and Navarre. Ranke's contrasted treatment of three historical characters best illustrates this kind of use. Ranke wrote of Berchtold of Mainz (the spokesman of the Reichstag when it was attempting to reform the empire) that he appeared to be a colourless figure, because he was one of those whose stance was not adopted as an act of will or from an inclination of mind, but from an insight into the inner necessity of things. Like Philippe le Bel of France he was 'in alliance with the nature of things'.[20] He acted along the grain of the wood. Elizabeth of England was very far from being a colourless character. She was by no means dominated by the character of men and things which made the situation in which she lived. Yet her life is hardly explicable as a series of actions dictated by willed choices or inclinations of mind. Ranke concluded from the narrative of her last years that it could be understood only as a kind of fusion between free choice and determined choice. 'Every life of great historical importance', he wrote, 'has a determined content.'[21] The content of Elizabeth's was her success or failure in coping with the problems of her reign. Her very personality was absorbed in the great events of which the defeat of the Armada was the climax. A continuous reading of Ranke's narrative of the reign of the third figure, Louis XIV, leaves the impression that he has not once found it meaningful, in writing the third of one volume and the two-thirds of the next devoted to him, to use the words necessary or necessity in relation to him. Indeed, when Louis annexed Strasbourg Ranke described him, not unexpectedly, as flying in the face of the nature of things. The history of the reign of that king was a history of the moulding of France by the will of one man. This the reader is reconciled to by the catastrophe which follows when a human being so over-reaches his limitations.

Ranke, however, sometimes used *Nothwendigkeit* to suggest a driving power in events, an inner logic in history which made what had happened inevitable, simply because it *had* happened. In Volume 4 of the German History there is a good example. Ranke wrote: 'all doctrinal prejudice apart [i.e. his prejudice as a Lutheran], from the merely historical standpoint it seems to me that it would have been best for the national development of Germany' if the Protestant princes had succeeded in taking her their way. 'The movement of the Reformation had arisen from the deepest and most characteristic spiritual drives of the nation.'[22] This ground for his initial assertion Ranke then elaborated: a Protestant victory would have drawn together the frontiers which were widest apart, for Protestant principalities lay on all the frontiers; it might have given Germany its widest possible extent by including the Protestant Netherlands; it would have identified the nation with constructive cultural forces instead of with the destructive personal policy of Charles V. It is only a short step to conclude from this that a Protestant victory would have caused in the sixteenth century the united Germany which was 'inevitable' in the nineteenth.

Ranke's moderation stands in the way of anyone who wishes to fasten on him a crude doctrine of historical inevitability. In the French History he wrote: 'historical science often flatters itself by referring to the unbroken continuity of something which it has observed growing from its beginning to an inner necessity, as its cause'.[23] 'It flatters itself' suggests that inevitability may after all be an illusion.

Yet 'it lay in the nature' of the French situation, since this included the personality of Catherine de Medici, that the delicate balance of forces upon which religious peace depended could not be preserved. It was thus inevitable that violence should break through the frustrations inherent in the balance. Again in the English History Ranke is clear that England's taking on the burden of defending Europe against the ascendancy of Louis XIV was not simply the deliberately and arbitrarily chosen purpose of William III. It was but the last consequence of a long series of events. In that sense it was inevitable.

Ranke's religion also prevented his adopting any crude doctrine of historical inevitability. In 1824 he wrote that he believed he saw, 'at least from a distance, the direct guidance and the visible working of God in history'. On page 3 of Volume 1 of the collected works he wrote:

> there exists no human activity of real intellectual significance which does not, in its origin, stand in a relationship, whether recognised or not, to God and to divine things. No nation worthy of the name but does not raise its political life to a higher level by religious ideas; no nation worthy of the name but constantly occupies itself with religion, constantly seeks to develop it and to give it more valid and public expression.

He wrote of things which God had brought into the world in his chosen time by his chosen instruments. Yet if Ranke would not escape from the task of explaining human actions by historical inevitability on one side, neither would he escape it on the other by a crude belief that events happened as they did because such was God's purpose for the world. He has too strong a religious sense to claim to penetrate the mystery of God's purpose for the world.

In short, Ranke's interpretation of history as the interplay of character and circumstance amounts to the recognition of three things and a summons, in the end, to jettison the abstract and to consider simply what can be established as having happened without looking for a single explanation which will fit everything.

Ranke in his early years was much under the influence of Immanuel Kant. The first thing he recognised was no more than the distinction Kant made between the particular and the general.[24] It is intelligible to assert that the general climate of area A is warmer and drier than that of area B, although on any particular day it might be cold and wet in area A and fine and dry in area B. So on any particular occasion an historical character might deflect the general trend without, in historical time, succeeding in making any difference to the ultimate outcome. The individual might thus still act freely and the general outcome yet accord with God's plan for the world. In the rhetorical peroration to an essay on the Great Powers written in 1833 Ranke indicates that the reader should leave the matter there.

The second thing which Ranke recognised was the moral energy or power for growth (*die Kraft*) which existed in communities as well as individuals. This word is an important part of the vocabulary of Johann Gottfried Herder, the philosopher of nationality and the national characteristic under whose influence Ranke also fell. Ranke believed that the elemental forces (*Kräfte*) of a nation came to the surface in civil war or revolution as was mentioned above. He also used this word to describe the internal logic by which events seemed at times to follow each other as if the historical process had a vitality of its own. Again this train of thought ends in Ranke in the view that mortals must tolerate the mystery of world history (*das Geheimniss der Weltgeschichte*) which elsewhere he calls a divine mystery (*ein göttliches Geheimniss*).

Finally there is a sense in which Ranke recognised that something became inevitable through the simple accumulation of events tending in the same direction. This may best be illustrated from what he wrote about the relationship between nation and state. In the German History he defines a state as an organised *congeries* of powers. In the French History the state is also an organisation of power, but of a rather different kind. The nation by distinction is composed of people who have much in common and are capable of composing a living community with a power for growth and change (*eine Kraft*) peculiar to itself. In *A Political Conversation* (*Ein politisches Gespräch*) the character who speaks for Ranke himself is made to say 'Nations have a tendency to be states, but I do not know of one which really is so' and to indicate that the French state does not include all Frenchmen – some live in English Canada – any more than the English state includes all Englishmen. The conversation develops to show how states have come into being by a train of events to which the nature of things, good fortune and human genius have all contributed. Ranke is clear that states are not the products of temporary contracts for the convenience of property-owners. Indeed, they may be 'spiritual substances, original creations of the human mind, even one might say thoughts of God'.[25] He says much the same of nations. Once again Ranke is content to leave the abstract problem of *why* a particular train of events should have brought a state into being and yet not made it square with the nation; and, as an historian, simply to present his reader with the events as they have happened.

Finally attention should be drawn to Ranke's parallelism with Hegel. Ernst Simon explained, in a supplement (no. 15) to the *Historische Zeitschrift*, the personal aloofness of the one from the other, although Hegel was already a controversial figure in Berlin University when Ranke arrived there and was soon in the opposite camp. Ernst Simon also showed how superficial, if compelling, were the resemblances between the thought of the two men and yet how deeply philosopher and historian ultimately differed. Parallelism is the suitable word in so far as they followed lines which never met. Hegel was a speculative philosopher concerned with generalisation; Ranke, an empiricist and historian concerned with particular individuals and events. Yet both were agreed in their dislike of the cloudiness of the Romantics. Their parallelism is striking. Ranke wrote, in connection with the evolution of modern Europe from mediaeval Europe, that no human achievement or human idea embodied the infinite or perfect. All must die. But equally all contained within themselves an element of the infinite and perfect. It was this which enabled each achievement or idea to give birth as it died to the achievement or idea which succeeded it. It is as if one heard an echo of Hegel's idea of the infinite and the perfect represented by the *Weltgeist* or world spirit in which, through time and eternity, every created thing that had lived, lived now or would live had its share.

Ranke wrote in the *History of the Latin and Teuton Peoples*: 'the life of Europe is lived through the energy of great opposing principles'. Throughout his histories he constantly makes plain the great polarities: between, for example, the unity of Germany and its fragmentation; between the concentration of power and its dispersal; between absolute monarchy and systems where power was shared by the king with those in the neighbourhood of the king; between monarchical and republican rule; between aristocratic forces based on land and popular forces based on towns. It is as if one heard a muffled echo of the Hegelian dialectic between thesis and antithesis. But it is an imperfect parallel. So, too, is the synthesis which Ranke perceives, imperfect. It is not a compromise. It is at least a constructive middle way attained with effort. Equally it is not a speculative or philosophic truth. A last illustration is provided by Ranke's writing of mediating actions (*vermittelnde Thätigkeiten*), particular actions by means of which new general forces are brought into play and change is eventually brought about.[26] Both Henry IV of France and Elizabeth of England are described by Ranke as individuals who were the mediating channels along which general principles were made active in the history of their times and countries. 'The greatest thing', he wrote, 'which a human being can do is, indeed, to defend in his particular concerns a general principle.'[27] When this happened a personal existence was enlarged into a world historical factor. It is only proper to conclude by pointing out that Ranke was a better historian for refraining from forcing events into any pattern. His interpretation was consistent, but it does not fit the logical coherence of any philosophic system.

Ranke's school and university education gave him a command of the classical languages. He acquired, then or later, Italian, French, English and some Spanish. He was, therefore, able to use the writings of the respected and established authorities on the history of each of the countries about which he wrote. For example, his first chapter on Louis XIV refers to Pelisson's history of the reign, 1749, to Bailly's financial history of France, 1839, and to a work coming out at almost the same time as his own, Henri Martin, *Histoire de France* in nineteen volumes, 1855–60. He uses of course standard works of reference, such as Dumont, *Traités de paix*. Secondly, Ranke was widely read in the literature of each country of which he wrote. This is obvious, for example, in sections devoted to Rabelais, Montaigne and the writers of Louis XIV's reign in the French History. But he also uses as historical evidence literature of a more polemical kind, sermons and pamphlets, and, especially in the chapters of the German History about the period just before the Reformation, popular songs and broadsheets. In the volume covering the French Religious Wars he appropriately pays much attention to political theorists. Thirdly, Ranke made full use of the great collections of documents of all kinds being published in the nineteenth century. There is room for only a few examples. For Germany there was the *Monumenta Germaniae Historica*, for Italy the *Archivio storico italiano*, for France such things on Louis XIV as G. B. Depping, *Correspondance administrative,* P. Clément's publication of material on Colbert or Mignet's *Négociations relatives à la succession d'Espagne*. For England under Cromwell there were the Carte and Clarendon papers and he did not omit the most recent, Carlyle's *Letters and Speeches of Oliver Cromwell*. He exhausted the available material in memoirs and biographies. A comparison of Ranke's footnote references with the titles listed in a nineteenth-century bibliography of memoirs relating to the reign of Louis XIV shows this.

Finally Ranke made his own important contribution to the discovery and publication of historical material. Lord Acton called him the real initiator of the 'heroic' study of records.[28] It is for this that he is chiefly known. In the archives of the German state capitals Ranke principally read and made extracts or copies from the records of the Reichstag and other imperial institutions. More of the business of the Diets was conducted by formal correspondence than oral debate, so that these records contained more than an account of business discussed and decisions reached. It is not surprising that the Diets lie at the centre of Ranke's German History. When he came to write the history of Prussia Ranke had Frederick the Great's own writings and a great deal of correspondence from him and from his father. In the Italian cities Ranke found his richest treasures in the great houses of the old families. He wrote his *History of the Popes* without access to the Vatican archives. He believed this was no disadvantage, as he wrote in the preface, because in Italy the archives of the states were virtually scattered through the private collections of the families whose members had run their affairs. This means, however, that Ranke was reading a particular kind of record: principally letters, and among the letters, principally those of ambassadors or envoys abroad reporting home what was going on, or alleged to be going on, in the capitals, where they were stationed. Ranke did not use the kind of record made by the actual process of government except in one part of it: that relating to foreign affairs. It is significant that when he gives figures for the size of the English navy or the volume of English trade he has taken them from a secondary source and not from Admiralty or Customs and Excise records. Much of what he published in the documentary appendixes to his histories consisted of hitherto unknown letters or diaries. It is not surprising then that wars, diplomacy, the struggle for power between contending factions and above all the thoughts, motives and actions of political figures should dominate what he wrote. Yet Ranke so arranged his materials that the reader has the impression, not that he is being told the history of a few powerful persons, but that he is being told the history of whole nations *through* their thoughts and actions.

Alfred Dove, who edited the last volumes of Ranke's collected works from his papers, tells us that Ranke was inspired to go to original documents by his perception that the King Louis in Sir Walter Scott's *Quentin Durward* was quite a different man from the King Louis of the historian Commines. Ranke became famous for his critical attitude to the original sources. He is said to have inherited this from the German historians of classical Rome, Niebuhr and Mommsen. Ranke asked the same questions as they asked. 'How did this document come into existence?' 'How has it come down to us?' 'How is the trustworthiness of the evidence it provides influenced by the answers to be given to these questions?' But he is more inclined in his critical discussions to point out the differences between two accounts of the same event, or between the 'legend' and the fact he can 'prove', and to explain why he prefers to believe one rather than the other or to reject both and to preserve an open mind. In his documentary appendixes with their critical commentaries he is sceptical, doubtful and probing. The narratives which arise from his reading and inferences are assured, unhesitant and leave no apparent gaps. His character studies are drawn with a firm and unbroken line.

NOTES: CHAPTER 3

1 William Stubbs, *Two Lectures on the present state and prospects of Historical Study, delivered on 17th and 20th May 1876* (1878), p. 34.

2 *Geschichten der romanischen und germanischen Völker* in *Sämmtliche Werke,*
   Vols 33 and 34, p. vii.
3 See *Sämmtliche Werke,* preface by A. Dove to Vols 49 and 50, pp. v–xii, for
   an account of the *Historisch-politische Zeitschrift.*
4 *Ein politisches Gespräch* in *Sämmtliche Werke,* Vols 49 and 50, pp. 314–39,
   translated by T. H. von Laue as 'A Dialogue on Politics', in *Leopold von
   Ranke: The Formative Years* (1950), pp. 152–80.
5 *Geschichten der romanischen und germanischen Völker* in *Sämmtliche
   Werke,* Vols 33 and 34, p. 69.
6 *Sämmtliche Werke,* Vol. 7, p. 101.
7 ibid., Vol. 7, p. 147.
8 ibid., Vols 40 and 41, p. 183.
9 ibid., Vol. 1, p. 55.
10 ibid., Vol. 2, pp. 124 and 147.
11 ibid., Vol. 9, p. 3.
12 ibid., Vol. 8, pp. 37 and 43; Vol. 9, ch. 1.
13 ibid., Vol. 10, pp. 199–209.
14 ibid., Vol. 17, pp. 97–100.
15 ibid., Vols 40 and 41 for *Historisch-biographische Studien;* Vol. 23 for
   Geschichte Wallensteins.
16 ibid., Vol. 37, p. 101.
17 ibid., Vol. 27, p. 17.
18 ibid., Vol. 1, p. 148.
19 ibid., Vol. 8, p. 208.
20 This phrase comes from the French History in *Sämmtliche Werke,* Vol. 8,
   p. 33, but Berchtold of Mainz is discussed in the German History, ibid., Vol.
   1, p. 81.
21 See the English History, ibid., Vol. 14, p. 323.
22 ibid., Vol. 4, p. 247.
23 ibid., Vol. 8, p. 57.
24 In the opening paragraph of *Idee zu einer allgemeinen Geschichte in welt-
   bürgerlicher Absicht,* I. Kant, *Werke,* ed. E. Cassirer (1922), Vol. 4, p. 151.
25 T. H. von Laue, *Leopold von Ranke: The Formative Years,* pp. 166–9,
   translates it this way.
26 The three illustrative passages come, respectively, from *Sämmtliche Werke,*
   Vol. 1, p. 55; Vol. 33, p. 323; Vol. 1, p. 237.
27 ibid., Vol. 14, p. 324.
28 See 'German schools of history', in *Historical Essays and Studies* (1907),
   pp. 352–8, and 'The study of history', in *Lectures on Modern History* (1906),
   pp. 18–20.

NOTE ON FURTHER READING

There was an ambitious project to republish all Ranke's writings (*Gesamt-
ausgabe Leopold von Rankes Werke*) edited by Erich Marcks, F. Meinecke
and H. Oncken in the 1930s. Only the *Deutsche Geschichte im Zeitalter der
Reformation* and the *Neun Bücher Preussischer Geschichte* appeared in it.
Otherwise only short works such as *Die Grossen Mächte* (1955) or the
lectures delivered before Maximilian of Bavaria have been recently republished (*Über die Epochen der neueren Geschichte*). English translations
of the *History of the Popes,* part of the *German History 1555–1618* and of
the English History are to be found in libraries and are a better way of

discovering Ranke the historian than the short essays which tell one more about his political ideas. Two of these have been translated and published with a biographical introduction in Theodore H. von Laue, *Leopold von Ranke: The Formative Years* (1950). The two essays, to use the titles he gives them, are 'A dialogue on politics' and 'The Great Powers'. The best study of Ranke in English is in Peter Gay, *Style in History* (1975). It has a full list of books and articles on Ranke. Leonard Krieger's *Leopold Ranke* is a long book published by the University of Chicago Press in 1977 and confusing to someone who has not read a great deal of Ranke for himself. It provoked a notable review by John Kenyon in the *Times Literary Supplement* of 6 January 1978. The attention of anyone who reads German should be drawn to Friedrich Meinecke, *Ranke und Burckhardt*, a lecture delivered and published in Berlin in 1948.

4 Thomas Babington Macaulay

Thomas Babington Macaulay was born at Rothley Temple, Leicestershire, in 1800; his evangelical family moved to Clapham not long after his birth. Educated at a private school and Trinity College, Cambridge, becoming a fellow in 1824; the following year, published the first of many contributions to the radical *Edinburgh Review*. Practised at the bar and from 1828 to 1832 was a commissioner for bankruptcy. In 1830 became MP for Calne, a borough disfranchised by the 1832 Reform Act, which he supported; subsequently became MP for Leeds. Spent the years 1834–7 in India as a member of the Supreme Council, significantly influencing its educational and legal provisions for Indians. In 1839 became MP for Edinburgh, a seat he held until 1847; Secretary at War in the Melbourne government, a post he lost in 1841. The years 1842 and 1843 saw the publication of *Lays of Ancient Rome* and *Critical and Historical Essays*, while in 1848 he brought out the first two volumes of his *History of England*. Became MP for Edinburgh again in 1852 but suffered a heart attack shortly afterwards; gave up his seat in 1856. His *Speeches* were published in 1854 and the third and fourth volumes of his *History* in 1855. Created Baron Macaulay of Rothley in 1857 and died in December 1859.

Professor J. H. Plumb once observed that 'men write history for many reasons; to try to understand the forces which impel mankind along its strange course; to justify a religion, a nation, or a class; to make money; to fulfil ambition; to assuage obsession; and a few, the true creators, to ease the ache within'.[1] Most, if not all, of these motives are discernible in Macaulay.

To making money he perhaps assigned a higher priority than did Professor Plumb, who discreetly relegated it to the middle of his list. Macaulay certainly wanted his *History of England* to sell. The first public hint of the idea of writing it is expressed in a review of Sir James Mackintosh's *History of the Revolution in 1688*, of which he wrote:

We find in it the diligence, the accuracy, and the judgment of Hallam, united to the vivacity and the colouring of Southey. A history of England, written throughout in this manner, would be the most fascinating book in the language. It would be more in request at the circulating libraries than the last novel.

While working on the first two volumes of his own major work, he wrote to a friend: 'I shall not be satisfied unless I produce something which shall for a few days supersede the last fashionable novel on the tables of young ladies.' He took pains to make his *History* readable. 'What labour it is to make a tolerable book,' he once noted, 'and how little readers know how much trouble the ordering of the parts has cost the writer.' To Macaulay the art of narration was 'the art of interesting the affections, and presenting pictures to the imagination'.[2] He strove to bring his own narrative to life, with eye-witness accounts presented in vivid sentences. Although he was writing about the past he contrived to make it seem like the present, keeping the reader in suspense about the outcome of battles, trials and parliamentary debates. The story-telling skill of Sir Walter Scott's historical novels intrigued him, and he hoped to produce similar effects in his own writing. He also wanted his *History* to be as popular and, judging by its sales, he succeeded. Volumes 3 and 4 sold 26,500 copies in the first ten weeks following their publication and earned for their author a cheque for £20,000 from his publishers.

Yet he did not write solely to make money. Popularity meant more to him than sales. When he learned that a group of workers had attended readings of his *History* and that at the last meeting they had moved a vote of thanks to him 'for having written a history which working men can understand', he was delighted, noting privately: 'I really prize this vote.'[3] Nor did he seek commercial success because he needed the money. During the years when he was a fellow of Trinity College, Cambridge, a commissioner for bankruptcy and a regular contributor to the *Edinburgh Review*, his annual income was around £900, a comfortable sum in those days, even though his father's trading ventures to Sierra Leone did not pay off and he was obliged increasingly to care for his beloved sisters. It is true that after losing his fellowship in 1831 and ceasing to be a bankruptcy commissioner in 1832 he went through a sticky financial patch, but the appointment to the Supreme Council of India brought with it the handsome salary of £10,000 a year and, after his return from India, he never wanted for money. Remaining a bachelor himself, while his sisters made good marriages, he was, on the contrary, a wealthy man of independent means; so much so that he was able to decline the offer of the Regius Professorship of History at Cambridge, which carried a salary of £400 a year.

Following the appearance of the first two volumes of the *History*, he was far more concerned to fulfil ambition than to make money, being very anxious to complete the story he had set out to narrate. He declined the Regius chair primarily because he wanted the liberty to finish his work. Originally he had hoped to span the period from the accession of James II in 1685 to a point within living memory, probably down to the Reform Act of 1832. As the scale of the work grew, he had to contract this ambition, but still hoped to reach the accession of George I. In fact, he never quite completed the reign of William III. He also wanted his work to last and to gain for its author immortal fame. In 1850, when he was worried that it might not get the recognition that he thought it deserved, he entered in his Journal: 'but corragio! And think of AD 2850.' Whether people will still be reading his work in a thousand years is unknowable; but it is indisputable that they are being widely read over a hundred years after his death, and there are even signs of a revival in his popularity.[4]

One reason why his *History of England* still commands respect is that it was based upon a prodigious amount of research. Something of the range of his sources is indicated in the programme he mapped out for the third and fourth volumes:

> I must visit Holland, Belgium, Scotland, Ireland, France. The Dutch archives and French archives must be ransacked. I will see whether anything is to be got from other diplomatic collections. I must see Londonderry, the Boyne, Aghrim, Limerick, Kinsale, Namur again, Landen, Steinkirk. I must turn over hundreds, thousands, of pamphlets. Lambeth, the Bodleian and the other Oxford libraries, the Devonshire papers, the British Museum, must be explored, and notes made: and then I shall go to work.[5]

When he did come to write, he had at his disposal a greater stock of manuscript and printed authorities than had been used by any previous historian of late seventeenth-century England. 'The wonderful industry, the honest, humble toil of this great scholar' gained the admiration of Thackeray: 'he reads twenty books to write a sentence; he travels a hundred miles to make a line of description'.[6]

Such labours suggest the extent to which Macaulay wrote history to assuage obsession. He was obsessed with the past. Almost everything he wrote was concerned with history, from ancient Rome to the France of the restored Bourbons. He was above all preoccupied with Stuart England. Even when addressing himself to such contemporary questions as parliamentary reform or Indian education, he is to be found drawing on seventeenth-century English history, alluding to Cromwell's franchise reforms in speeches on the former, urging the 'learned native' to study Milton, Locke and Newton in his minute on the latter.

In his insistence that Indians should be educated in English, he betrayed a desire to justify a nation which also pervades his historical writings. Thus, in the Minute on Indian Education, he boasted: 'the claims of our own language it is hardly necessary to recapitulate. It stands pre-eminent even among the languages of the West.' Similar sentiments inform his essay on Mackintosh, in which he claimed that the English were 'the greatest and the most highly civilised people that the world ever saw'. He was convinced that history demonstrated the superiority of nineteenth-century England over other nations. Such attitudes have led him to be regarded as an insular, boastful Englishman. Thus the Dutch historian Pieter Geyl found the attitudes expressed in his *Essays* to be 'exclusively and intolerantly English'.[7] There is a great deal of truth in this, yet Macaulay did not hold that England was innately superior to other countries. On the contrary, he argued in his essay on Machiavelli, that throughout the Middle Ages Italy had enjoyed a cultural supremacy in Europe, during centuries when the English were backward if not barbaric; he found much in the United States of America of his own time which he considered to be preferable to England; and he was even prepared to imagine that the day might come when London would be 'dwindled to the dimensions of the parish of St Martin's, and supported in its decay by the expenditure of wealthy Patagonians and New Zealanders'.[8]

This view of the fate of nations reflects his understanding of the forces which impel mankind along its strange course. It seems at first sight to be a cyclical view of history.[9] Yet on closer examination, much of what Macaulay wrote on the causes of historical change cannot be reconciled with such an interpretation. Towards the end of his essay on Southey's *Colloquies on Society*, he expressed his view of progress as follows:

We know no well-authenticated instance of a people which has decidedly retrograded in civilisation and prosperity, except from the influence of violent and terrible calamities, such as those which laid the Roman empire in ruins, or those which, about the beginning of the sixteenth century, desolated Italy. We know of no country which, at the end of fifty years of peace and tolerably good government, has been less prosperous than at the beginning of that period. The political importance of a state may decline, as the balance of power is disturbed by the introduction of new forces. Thus the influence of Holland and of Spain is much diminished. But are Holland and Spain poorer than formerly? We doubt it. Other countries have outrun them. But we suspect that they have been positively, though not relatively, advancing. We suspect that Holland is richer than when she sent her navies up the Thames, that Spain is richer than when a French king was brought captive to the foot-stool of Charles the Fifth.

History is full of the signs of this natural progress of society. We see in almost every part of the annals of mankind how the industry of individuals, struggling up against wars, taxes, famines, conflagrations, mischievous prohibitions and more mischievous protections, creates faster than governments can squander, and repairs whatever invaders can destroy. We see the wealth of nations increasing, and all the arts of life approaching nearer and nearer to perfection, in spite of the grossest corruption and the wildest profusion on the part of rulers.

There are, of course, obstacles in the path of uninterrupted progress which Macaulay here makes explicit – violent and terrible calamities such as war or intolerably bad government. But these are not inevitable. Societies did not struggle up the wheel of history to reach the peak of progress before plunging inevitably down to the bottom again. Instead of comparing history to the rotating of a wheel, Macaulay preferred a metaphor inspired by the sea. In his essay on Mackintosh he observed:

We said that the history of England is the history of progress; and, when we take a comprehensive view of it, it is so. But, when examined in small separate portions, it may with more propriety be called a history of actions and re-actions. We have often thought that the motion of the public mind in our country resembles that of the sea when the tide is rising. Each successive wave rushes forward, breaks, and rolls back; but the great flood is steadily coming in. A person who looked on the waters only for a moment might fancy that they were retiring. A person who looked on them only for five minutes might fancy that they were rushing capriciously to and fro. But when he keeps his eye on them for a quarter of an hour, and sees one sea-mark disappear after another, it is impossible for him to doubt of the general direction in which the ocean is moved. Just such has been the course of events in England. In the history of the national mind, which is, in truth, the history of the nation, we must carefully distinguish between that recoil which regularly follows every advance and a great general ebb. If we take short intervals, if we compare 1640 and 1660, 1680 and 1685, 1708 and 1712, 1782 and 1794, we find a retrogression. But if we take centuries, if, for example, we compare 1794 with 1660 or with 1685, we cannot doubt in which direction society is proceeding.

Macaulay therefore had a tidal rather than a cyclical view of history. Moreover, although in reality the sea starts to go out after it has come in, he did not envisage that the great tide of Progress would one day recede.

The great dynamic of this flux, the moon, as it were, that exerted its pull on the waves of history, was politics. Macaulay saw the history of England in terms of a political struggle between the forces of Progress and those of Reaction. This is implicit in the short intervals he chose to demonstrate that the tide could appear to be ebbing. To him, 1640 was an advance on 1660 because in the former year the Long Parliament met to put an end to Stuart tyranny, while in the latter Charles II was restored; the accession of James II in 1685 was a recession following the highwater mark of the Exclusion crisis in 1680; in 1708 the Whigs were in the ascendant while in 1712 the Tories were in power; in 1782 the Rockingham Whigs formed a ministry, while in 1794 Habeas Corpus was suspended. Yet even under the Younger Pitt, Englishmen were better off than they had been under Charles II or his brother James.

To Macaulay, politicians were the agents of progress or of reaction, and as such were heroes or villains in the epic struggle for English liberty. It is usual to observe that his heroes were generally Whigs, while most of his villains were Tories. An examination of his portrait gallery for Charles II's reign, however, shows that his selection was not quite so crude. He has in fact very little to say in favour of the politicians of either side under the Merry Monarch, and hardly any time for the Earl of Shaftesbury, leader of the first Whigs, despising his apostasy and his demagogy. His main hero during that period, as Professor Hamburger has demonstrated, was not a Whig at all, but Lord Halifax, the Trimmer.[10] Macaulay mistrusted extremists of either party, deploring the religious excesses of both Archbishop Laud and the Puritans under Charles I, censuring the intolerance of the Tories towards dissenters and the bigotry of the Whigs towards Catholics under Charles II; and ridiculing the republicanism of Algernon Sydney along with the divine right absolutism of the later Stuarts. It seems that his tidal theory of history led him to fear that the more extreme the action, the more violent would be the reaction. His own predilection was for moderation, which is why he admired a man like Halifax.

At the same time, it cannot be denied that the moderation he most admired was that of the moderate Whig rather than that of the moderate Tory. He identified himself enthusiastically with those post-Revolution Whigs who had shed their religious excesses, and who approached politics pragmatically. This he reveals most clearly in his portraits of the Whig leaders who were known as the Junto, and above all in his praise of Lord Somers, 'the greatest man among the members of the Junto, and in some respects the greatest man of that age'.[11] Macaulay was utterly convinced that men like Somers had guided England's destiny along the path of moderate reform from the meeting of the Long Parliament, from which he felt that 'whatever of political freedom exists in Europe or in America has sprung', to the passing of the first Reform Act, which he saw as a moderate compromise between oligarchy and democracy. And he was in no doubt that such men were to be found in the ranks of the Whig Party. He thus saw the Whigs as the agents of progress in the seventeenth century, recounting to the electors of Edinburgh in 1839 that:

> it was that party which forced Charles I to relinquish ship-money. It was that party which destroyed the Star Chamber and the High Commission Court. It was that party which, under Charles II, carried the Habeas Corpus Act, which effected the Revolution, which passed the Toleration Act, which broke the yoke of a foreign church in your country, and which saved Scotland from the fate of unhappy Ireland.

Although when discussing English history he tended to concentrate on high politics, and above all on the struggle between the Whigs and their opponents, Macaulay was not a narrow political historian. 'We must remember', he once observed, 'how small a proportion the good or evil affected by a single statesman can bear to the good or evil of a great social system.'[12] He was as much concerned with society as with governments, and strove in his *History of England* to relate how the seventeenth-century conflict between Crown and Parliament had been superseded in the eighteenth century by a struggle between 'a large portion of the people on the one side, and the Crown and the Parliament united on the other'. This was why he originally planned to narrate events from the revolution of 1688 to the Reform Act of 1832: to begin with 'the Revolution which brought the Crown into harmony with the Parliament' and to end with 'the Revolution which brought the Parliament into harmony with the nation'.[13]

Nor was progress entirely political. Although the conflict between Crown and Parliament held up the advance of constitutional monarchy in the seventeenth century, while the struggle between Parliament and people postponed the advent of representative government until the nineteenth century, they also created tensions between progress and reaction in many other spheres. 'The history of our country during the last one hundred and sixty years', he claimed at the outset of his *History of England*, 'is eminently the history of physical, of moral, and of intellectual improvement.' By physical, he meant material, and the role of his famous third chapter was to show how backward England had been at the accession of James II, and how between 1685 and 1848 every sector of the economy had expanded, the population had increased and the standard of living had improved. Though he tended to dwell on material progress, he also insisted that the nineteenth century was more humane than the seventeenth. Men were less cruel, not meting out the savage punishments which their ancestors had inflicted upon those convicted of crime. They also knew more, for instance, about the physical sciences, and could use this knowledge to better their condition.

Ultimately he accounted for this progress by drawing a parallel between developments in science and in society. 'Our creed', he proclaimed, 'is that the science of government is an experimental science, and that, like all other experimental sciences, it is generally in a state of progression.' 'In every experimental science', he insisted, 'there is a tendency towards perfection. In every human being there is a wish to ameliorate his own condition. These two principles have often sufficed, even when counteracted by great public calamities and by bad institutions, to carry civilisation rapidly forward.'[14] His formulation of these principles as fundamental laws owed a lot to the philosophy of Francis Bacon, and not a little to the utilitarianism of Jeremy Bentham and the economics of Adam Smith.

Macaulay's respect for Bacon's contribution to civilisation was expressed in the longest of his essays. According to the historian, previous philosophers had engaged in pure speculation, while Bacon was concerned with the application of philosophy to improving the lot of mankind. This distinction he developed by comparing the reactions of a Stoic and a Baconian to such calamities as the smallpox, firedamp in a mine and shipwreck: the Stoic offers consolation to the victims, while the Baconian recommends vaccination, a safety lamp and a diving bell. 'It would be easy', Macaulay concluded, 'to multiply illustrations of the difference between the philosophy of thorns and the philosophy of fruit, the philosophy of words and the philosophy of works.' The fruit which Bacon planted yielded Utility and Progress.

Bacon's Utility differed from that of the later Utilitarians, as far as Macaulay was concerned, because it was based upon inductive reasoning, and not, like theirs, upon *a priori* deductions. His preference for induction, and his scepticism about the value of deductive systems, made him a critic of utilitarianism. He was also opposed to the democratic trend of their politics. Thus, in his essay on the utilitarian theory of government, he attacked their assumption that good government could on principle only come from a democratic representative assembly, by applying Bacon's method and examining the constitutions of all those countries in which good government could be said to exist; from which he concluded that Denmark was well governed even though ruled by an absolute monarch. Yet although he was not a utilitarian himself, he was greatly influenced by the principle of utility, and incorporated the Benthamite precept – that government should aim at the greatest happiness of the greatest number – in the penal code which he drew up for India when he was on the Supreme

Council. It is also clear that he agreed with both the utilitarians and the classical economists that the pursuit by individuals of their own happiness was beneficial rather than detrimental to the progress of society.

His acceptance of the *laissez-faire* theories in *The Wealth of Nations* also made him advocate free trade, and he was reluctant to allow the government to interfere in the economy. He concluded his review of Southey's *Colloquies* with a statement which Adam Smith himself might have written:

> Our rulers will best promote the improvement of the nation by strictly confining themselves to their own legitimate duties, by leaving capital to find its most lucrative course, commodities their fair price, industry and intelligence their natural reward, idleness and folly their natural punishment, by maintaining peace, by defending property, by diminishing the price of law, and by observing strict economy in every department of the state. Let the Government do this: the People will assuredly do the rest.

He was prepared, however, to support a Bill restricting the working hours of young people to ten a day, on the grounds that, although 'the science of political economy teaches us . . . that we ought not on commercial grounds to interfere with the liberty of commerce', the measure was interfering with it 'on higher than commercial grounds'.[15]

Being an active politician rather than an academic historian, Macaulay regarded history as an eminently useful study. Properly studied, it could teach lessons from which the wise statesman could profit. Since government and society could progress at different speeds, the rulers of a country should adjust their policies to the rate of progress which its citizens were setting, or risk calamity. It was precisely because the Stuarts in seventeenth-century England and the Bourbons in eighteenth-century France had not appreciated the progressive mood of the public mind in each country, and had not made timely reforms, that they had been overtaken by revolution. Similarly, he argued in his speeches on the Reform Bill that it was a necessary measure to avert, not rebellion, so much as 'extensive and persevering war against the law'. 'All that I know of the history of past times,' he argued, 'all the observations that I have been able to make on the present state of the country, have convinced me that the time has arrived when a great concession must be made to the democracy of England.' His knowledge of past times led him to believe that:

> History, when we look at it in small fragments, proves anything, or nothing . . . [but] it is full of useful and precious instruction when we contemplate it in large portions, when we take in, at one view,

the whole lifetime of societies. I believe that it is possible to obtain some insight into the law which regulates the growth of communities, and some knowledge of the effects which that growth produces. The history of England, in particular, is the history of a government constantly giving way before a nation which has been constantly advancing.[16]

These beliefs led Macaulay to call himself a Whig. They put him in the company of Edmund Burke and Sir James Mackintosh, both of whom he greatly admired, who believed in preserving the essence of English institutions by responding intelligently to change. Enshrined in his *History*, these principles led to his reputation as the outstanding exponent of the Whig interpretation of history.

Macaulay's reputation as an historian has never fully recovered from the condemnation it implicitly received in Herbert Butterfield's devastating attack on *The Whig Interpretation of History*.[17] Though he was never cited by name, there can be no doubt that Macaulay answers to the charges brought against Whig historians, particularly that they study the past with reference to the present, class people in the past as those who furthered progress and those who hindered it, and judge them accordingly.

The unbroken line which Macaulay claimed to see stretching from the Magna Carta to the Reform Act existed only in his own mind. The men who debated the Petition of Right in 1628 or the Bill of Rights in 1689 were not trying to promote a process which would lead to Victorian liberalism; indeed, they would have abhorred the very concept, even if they could have understood it. They were discussing issues relevant to their own generations, valid in their own times. Too often Macaulay denies the past its own validity, treating it as being merely a prelude to his own age. This is especially noticeable in the third chapter of his *History of England*, when again and again he contrasts the backwardness of 1685 with the advances achieved by 1848. Not only does this misuse the past, it also leads him to exaggerate the differences. For example, he paints far too primitive a picture of agriculture in the 1680s, which was experiencing great improvement, and gives a misleading impression of the state of communications by concentrating upon the roads, when water transport by sea and navigable rivers, which he largely ignores, was relatively easy.

The dramatic change which he believed to have occurred between 1685 and 1848 was due to the triumph of those who were progressive over the reactionaries. In the world of politics, this meant the victory of Whiggism over Toryism. Yet, as Butterfield observed, to ask the question 'to whom do we owe our liberty?' is to be fundamentally unhistorical.[18] The changes which occurred between the seventeenth and the nineteenth centuries cannot be ascribed to the efforts of one set of men without oversimplification and distortion.

It is also to impose values on men in the past, to praise the progressive and to blame the reactionary. Macaulay did not hesitate to sit in judgement, as we have seen, and to reward his heroes and condemn his villains. This is exactly Butterfield's Whig historian who 'tends to regard himself as the judge when by his methods and his equipment he is fitted only to be the detective'.[19]

Although he liked to think of himself as a judge in the court of history, it has been said that Macaulay treated evidence more like a barrister. When he cross-examines witnesses, there can be no doubt in the reader's mind whether he is acting as counsel for the defence or for the prosecution. Titus Oates, one of his greatest villains, has his very appearance made to tell against him, with 'his short neck, his legs uneven, the vulgar said, as those of a badger, his forehead low as that of a baboon, his purple cheeks, and his monstrous length of chin . . . those hideous features on which villany seemed to be written by the hand of God'. Such crudity has led Macaulay to be accused of drawing caricatures rather than characters. Curiously, he seems to have done this quite consciously, once writing that 'the best portraits are perhaps those in which there is a slight mixture of caricature'.[20]

At the same time, it is wrong to assert that Macaulay's portraits are all in black and white. He took pains to present the virtues even of a rogue, and he painted the virtuous warts and all. The first glimpse we get of John Churchill, Duke of Marlborough, whose treachery is to be denounced several times in the severest terms, stresses his handsome appearance, his dignity, his admirable judgement and his professional skill. Lord Wharton, on the other hand, whose dedication to the Whig cause earned Macaulay's approval, if not admiration, makes his appearance as 'the greatest rake in England'. Macaulay delighted in such paradoxes and stressed the contradictions in men's characters to such an extent that Sir Leslie Stephen complained that 'these contrasts are actually painful'.[21] Moreover, although he tried to strike a balance by this technique, the scales are always weighted heavily. He usually presents the virtues of a rogue and the vices of a hero first, to get them out of the way. Thus, the introduction of Marlborough continues: 'unhappily the splendid qualities of John Churchill were mingled with alloy of the most sordid kind'; while he makes the transition from Wharton's vice to his Whiggism by saying: 'the falsest of mankind in all relations but one, he was the truest of Whigs'. The defects of his method stand out most starkly in his portrayal of James II and William III, the principal villain and hero respectively of the *History of England*, of whom it has been said that they are 'God and Satan; the great history is a kind of *Paradise Lost* and *Paradise*

Regained'.[22] Both kings kept mistresses, but while in the case of James this is a mortal sin, in William it is a peccadillo. More seriously, both presided over the harsh suppression of disaffection, with the Bloody Assizes in James's reign, and the Glencoe massacre in William's. James's treatment of the Monmouth rebels in 1685 is condemned as one of the darkest crimes against humanity in history; William's acquiescence in the massacre of the Macdonalds is excused on the specious grounds that he did not really appreciate what he was authorising. Yet James was faced with a deliberate attempt to deprive him of his throne, while William was confronted only with token resistance. The so-called 'Bloody Assizes' did at least deal with an utterly unlawful rebellion by legal means; the Glencoe massacre dealt with a technical breach of the law with brute force and treachery.

One danger about judging men in the past is that one man's hero can be another man's villain. Macaulay treated both Marlborough and William Penn, the prominent seventeenth-century Quaker, with disdain because of their alleged assistance to what he regarded as the forces of reaction. His preconceived notion of Penn led him to misread evidence, to the distress of Quakers in his own day, some of whom actually visited him to try to set the record straight. It was no use. Macaulay, completely convinced that he was right, could not be dissuaded.[23] To Sir Winston Churchill, his ancestor Marlborough was a saint rather than a sinner, and in his biography of the duke he attempted to rescue him from Macaulay's denigration. Churchill was so incensed by the historian's treatment of one episode in Marlborough's career that he was driven to write: 'It is beyond our hopes to overtake Lord Macaulay. The grandeur and sweep of his story-telling style carries him swiftly along, and with every generation he enters new fields. We can only hope that Truth will follow swiftly enough to fasten the label "Liar" to his genteel coat-tails.'[24]

This accusation brought G. M. Trevelyan, Macaulay's great-nephew, to the defence of his ancestor.[25] 'I have stated elsewhere that I think Macaulay was wrong in his reading of Marlborough,' he wrote to the *Times Literary Supplement*:

> Indeed I think it is the worst thing in his History, and I have no wonder that Mr Churchill's family piety has aroused him to take revenge. All the same, he has no right to call Macaulay a 'liar'. A 'liar' is not a man who misreads another man's character, however badly, or who sometimes accepts inadequate evidence; if that were so, almost all historians would be 'liars'. A 'liar' is a man who makes a statement that he knows to be false.

Trevelyan then proceeded to show that Macaulay really believed what he wrote about Marlborough. And there can be little doubt that he did. Indeed, he was never guilty of suppressing or distorting evidence to make it support a proposition which he knew to be untrue. Trevelyan concluded:

I do not think Mr Churchill makes enough allowance for the 'pioneer' historians of a hundred years ago. They had not the machinery we moderns have, the masses of published documents, the Historical Manuscripts Commission volumes, the learned periodicals, and whole libraries of monographs and studies of particular points. A pioneer historian who had to find the straw for his own bricks, and was moreover 'cock-sure' by temperament, could make ghastly mistakes without being a 'liar'.

It is not surprising that the development of history as a profession since Macaulay died should have left his method and many of his conclusions unacceptable today. What is in fact striking is the extent to which his *History of England* at least has survived subsequent research. Although it is often dismissed as inaccurate, it is hard to pinpoint a passage where he is categorically in error, though there are occasions where his bias leads him into errors, as in his treatment of Marlborough and Penn, and others where he relied too much on his phenomenal memory and did not go back to check his sources. Several of his citations of Pepys's *Diary*, for instance, seem to be based upon recollection, so that, given Macaulay's aptitude for embroidery, Pepys's stories gain something in the re-telling. Yet despite such flaws his account of events has stood up remarkably well. Professor J. P. Kenyon, in a recent account of the debates in the Convention in 1689, noted that 'as is often the case, Macaulay had it exactly right'.[26] His interpretation of the Glorious Revolution also remains the essential starting point for any discussion of that episode, as Professor J. R. Jones acknowledged in his book *The Revolution of 1688 in England*, which appeared in 1972.[27]

What has not survived, or has become subdued, is Macaulay's confident belief in progress. It was a dominant creed in the era of the Great Exhibition. But Auschwitz and Hiroshima destroyed this century's claim to moral superiority over its predecessors, while the exhaustion of natural resources raises serious doubts about the continuation even of material progress into the next.

And yet, though pessimism may abound as we move towards the close of the twentieth century, there is still ground for hope, if only from the progress of scientific knowledge on which Macaulay pinned so much. Perhaps this is why, paradoxically, the great prophet of progress should be enjoying a revival at this time. His philosophy of the past led him to predict the future, and when we read his predictions they generate reassurance rather than despair. 'It may well be', he predicted at the end of his third chapter,

> in the twentieth century that the peasant of Dorsetshire may think himself miserably paid with twenty shillings a week; that the carpenter at Greenwich may receive ten shillings a day; that labouring men may be as little used to dine without meat as they now are to eat rye bread; that sanitary policy and medical discoveries may have added several more years to the average length of human life; that numerous comforts and luxuries which are now unknown, or confined to a few, may be within the reach of every diligent and thrifty working man.

Who, reading this passage, can deny that he was right? Or, that the man who wrote it did so, not just for fame or fortune, but because he was one of the 'few, the true creators', who write history 'to ease the ache within'?

NOTES: CHAPTER 4

1 *Studies in Social History*, ed. J. H. Plumb (1955), p. xiii.
2 *The Works of Lord Macaulay*, ed. Lady Trevelyan (8 vols, 1875), Vol. 5, p. 154.
3 G. O. Trevelyan, *The Life and Letters of Lord Macaulay* (hereafter GOT), (2 vols, 1878), Vol. II, p. 239.
4 One indication is the number of editions and studies of his writings published in the 1970s, for some of which see the Note on Further Reading, and T. B. Macaulay, *Napoleon and the Restoration of the Bourbons*, ed. J. Hamburger, published for the first time in 1977.
5 GOT, Vol. II, pp. 222–3.
6 GOT, Vol. II, p. 220.
7 P. Geyl, *Debates with Historians* (1955), p. 30.
8 GOT, Vol. II, p. 31.
9 See J. Hamburger, *Macaulay and the Whig Tradition* (1976), p. 25: 'one can discern an implied cyclicalism in Macaulay's observations on historical change and even in the language he uses'.
10 ibid., especially chs 5 and 6.
11 T. B. Macaulay, *History of England*, ed. T. F. Henderson (1907), p. 648.
12 *The Works of Lord Macaulay*, Vol. 5, p. 156.
13 GOT, Vol. II, p. 14.
14 Macaulay, *History of England*, p. 73.
15 T. B. Macaulay, *Speeches on Politics and Literature* (1909), p. 329.
16 ibid., p. 59.
17 See below, p. 173–7.
18 H. Butterfield, *The Whig Interpretation of History* (1973 edn), p. 37.
19 ibid., p. 79.
20 T. B. Macaulay, *Essays and Lays of Ancient Rome* (1893), pp. 50–1.
21 L. Stephen, *Hours in a Library* (3 vols, 1909), Vol. II, p. 338.
22 G. R. Potter, *Macaulay* (1959), p. 31.

23 Sir Charles Firth, *A Commentary on Macaulay's History of England* (1938), pp. 269–73.

24 Sir Winston Churchill, *Marlborough, his Life and Times* (4 vols, 1933), Vol. I, p. 129.

25 G. M. Trevelyan, *England under Queen Anne* (3 vols, 1930–4), Vol. III, pp. xi–xiii.

26 J. P. Kenyon, 'The Revolution of 1688: resistance and contract', in *Historical Perspectives*, ed. N. McKendrick (1974), p. 47, n. 14.

27 Professor Jones even claimed that 'most professional historians . . . assumed that the general lines of re-interpretation established over a century ago by T. B. Macaulay were still valid, so that a few factual amendments, or minor modifications of his judgements, were the most that a new study could expect to achieve'. See *The Revolution of 1688 in England* (1972), p. ix.

NOTE ON FURTHER READING

'When you sit down to read Macaulay', advised Lord Acton, 'remember that the Essays are really flashy and superficial . . . It is the History that is wonderful.' Certainly any assessment of Macaulay's achievement as an historian must start and end with the *History of England from the Accession of James II*, the most scholarly edition of which is that edited by Sir Charles Firth in six volumes (1913). For a convenient abridgement, with a brilliant introductory essay by the editor, see Lord Macaulay, *The History of England*, edited and abridged with an introduction by Hugh Trevor-Roper (Penguin, 1979). Nevertheless, the *Essays* should also be consulted, most readily in *Critical and Historical Essays by Thomas Babington Macaulay* (Everyman edn, 2 vols, 1907). Together these present a bulky assignment and students daunted by this might prefer to sample judicious extracts from them, and from his other writings, selected by G. M. Young in *Macaulay: Prose and Poetry* (1952), and by John Clive and Thomas Pinney in *Thomas Babington Macaulay: Selected Writings* (1972). Those encouraged to go beyond the historian to the man should start with G. O. Trevelyan, *The Life and Letters of Lord Macaulay* (2 vols, 1876), though this has been partly superseded by John Clive, *Thomas Babington Macaulay: The Shaping of the Historian* (1973), and *The Letters of Thomas Babington Macaulay*, ed. Thomas Pinney (4 vols, 1974, proceeding). For criticisms of the History, see Sir Charles Firth, *A Commentary on Macaulay's History of England* (1938); of Macaulay's style, Peter Gay, *Style in History* (1975), pp. 95–138; and of his political philosophy, Joseph Hamburger, *Macaulay and the Whig Tradition* (1976).

5 *Alexis de Tocqueville*

Alexis de Tocqueville was born 1805, of an aristocratic Norman family; educated at the Lycée in Metz where his father was prefect under the restored Bourbons; trained in the law, became a magistrate at Versailles. Visited the USA in 1831 to study the penal system. Married an Englishwoman, Mary Mottley. Published *Democracy in America* (Volume I in 1835, Volume II in 1840). Elected to Académie Française in 1841. Member of Chamber of Deputies from 1839 and of the Constituent Assembly of the Second Republic in 1848. Foreign Minister in Barrot's government, June to October 1849. Withdrew from political life after *coup d'état* of 2 December 1851 and lived mainly on the family estate at Tocqueville. Published *L'Ancien Régime et la Révolution* in 1856 and died in 1859.

There are people who maintain that the past is to be studied for its own sake and think it unscholarly to investigate the past in the hope of throwing light upon the present. Alexis de Tocqueville was not among these pedants. He grew up in a France indelibly marked by the revolution of 1789, a France in which men's political and social attitudes were largely fashioned by their views of that revolution. Tocqueville's own family had felt its impact: his maternal great-grandfather, Malesherbes, was one of the defence lawyers at the king's trial before the Convention; his father was imprisoned and would have been guillotined had not the Thermidorian reaction supervened to halt the Terror. Though his father was *maire* of a commune under the empire, he regularly referred to Napoleon as 'l'usurpateur'; he returned to the service of the Bourbons after 1814 and retired in 1830 rather than take the oath to Louis-Philippe. In Alexis de Tocqueville's formative years the effects of the revolution were omnipresent and its interpretation was a matter of debate. We have seen in our lifetime a generation of young Germans growing up after the Second World War, possessed with curiosity about the Third Reich and the path that led to war. Similarly, between 1918 and 1939, many young people, growing up under the shadow of the First World War, were anxious to know how it had come about and how such conflicts could be prevented in future. To these Tocqueville may well appear a kindred spirit.

Tocqueville's claim to greatness as an historian rests upon a single work, his last. *L'Ancien Régime et la Révolution*, published in 1856, was intended as the first volume in a history of the entire revolutionary and Napoleonic period. But his reputation as a political and social thinker had been made twenty years earlier. He served as a magistrate under Charles X and, unlike his father, took the oath to the Orléans monarch in 1830. Soon after that, however, he obtained leave to visit the United States, ostensibly to investigate the American penal system. Out of that visit emerged not only the penal report but also the two volumes of *Democracy in America*, which appeared in 1835 and 1840. At a time when the government and society of the United States were little studied in the Old World and few Europeans visited the New, Tocqueville's analysis aroused interest in England as well as in France and opened up questions of general and major importance: the nature of liberty, the relationship between liberty and equality, the relationship between the individual and the community and the best way of ensuring the participation of the citizen in government and administration.

Though Tocqueville had already come to believe that the nineteenth century would witness the inexorable advance of democracy, he did not start out with any predisposition in its favour. He saw in America a democratic society and set out to analyse its features. He combined a capacity for keen and unwearying observation with a flair for generalisation from the evidence which he accumulated. He was always ready to modify his views as new evidence came to light; nevertheless the essential arguments of *Democracy in America* are all present in embryo in a letter written from the United States to his friend Chabrol.[1] In this he pointed out that America was so fortunately situated that individual interests were not contrary to the general interest: her geographical position gave her security, so that a large military establishment was not needed, taxation was light, and the power of central government relatively weak; there was a strong tradition of local initiative and local self-government. The material of *Democracy in America* came largely from personal contacts and interviews. Though Tocqueville frequently writes about 'the American', he does not name a single individual American in the two volumes.

Twenty years later, in *L'Ancien Régime et la Révolution*, Tocqueville's material came from documents rather than from personal testimony, but he uses it in the same way. He shows the same capacity for generalising from an accumulation of evidence and the same concern for fundamental questions – the sometimes conflicting relationship between liberty and equality; the perception that democracy may mean the tyranny of a majority; and the recognition that a democratic state may be free or unfree.

It is significant that Tocqueville visited America before he ever visited England. He has been criticised for failing to perceive that the American was an Englishman transplanted; and James Bryce, himself an expert on America, thought that a previous acquaintance with English life would have saved Tocqueville from some erroneous conclusions. *Democracy in America*, however, earned Tocqueville a reputation in England; on his second visit there in 1835 he had the entrée to leading political and literary circles and gained the friendship of men like Nassau Senior, John Stuart Mill and George Cornewall Lewis.

If Tocqueville the historian owes something to Tocqueville the sociological investigator, he also owes much to Tocqueville the politician. After his resignation from the magistracy his ambition seems to have been focused on active political life rather than on literature. As a deputy in the Chamber from 1839 onwards, as a member of the Constituent Assembly of the Second Republic in 1848 (and of the committee which drafted its new constitution) and briefly as Minister for Foreign Affairs in 1849, Tocqueville was preoccupied with the relationship between political theories and political practice. Dr J. P. Mayer, the editor of the definitive edition of Tocqueville's collected works, points out that Edmund Burke, who shared that preoccupation, is the author whom Tocqueville quotes most frequently: indeed he goes so far as to describe *L'Ancien Régime* as a commentary on Burke's *Reflections on the Revolution in France*.[2] But though critical of the Revolution, Tocqueville did not share Burke's attitude of total hostility: he could look back to 1789 as a year of imperishable memory – of generosity, enthusiasm, manliness and greatness of spirit; a time when Frenchmen, undeterred by their lack of political experience, were confident that they could solve the problem of reconciling liberty with order.[3] Moreover, Tocqueville's analysis of the old regime is both more detailed and more profound than Burke's.

Tocqueville's active political life came to an end with the *coup d'état* of 2 December 1851, of which he strongly disapproved. Indeed, he tried to rally English opinion against Louis-Napoleon by the time-honoured method of writing to the editor of *The Times*. His *Souvenirs*, written mainly during a stay in Italy in 1850–1, record his personal involvement in the affairs of the Second Republic. They reveal a different facet of his literary skill. The *Souvenirs* are concerned less with the analysis of society than with the interaction of persons and their response to political and social crises. They contain a splendid gallery of pen-portraits, sometimes etched in acid, but never wilfully malicious. He shows conspicuous distrust of Thiers, who in his opinion bore greater responsibility than Guizot for the failure of the Orléans monarchy and whose vanity he found insufferable.[4] The language of the *Souvenirs* is lucid, direct and often quietly ironic; the romantic phrase-making which sometimes occurs in *Democracy in America* has been pared away and the polished use of antithesis, so characteristic of *L'Ancien Régime*, is already in evidence. The *Souvenirs* also contain the key to Tocqueville's view of history:

> I have come across men of letters who have written history without themselves participating in public affairs, and politicians, who have been concerned only with producing events without thinking of describing them. I have always noted that the former were always inclined to find general causes for everything, whereas the latter, living in the midst of disconnected daily events, were prone to imagine that everything had to be attributed to individual incidents and that the devices which they never tired of manipulating were the mainsprings of the world. It is to be presumed that both are equally mistaken.[5]

Tocqueville's conclusion, that the February Revolution of 1848 sprang from general causes impregnated by accidents, could well be applied to many other historical events.

After leaving political life, Tocqueville planned to write an historical study of the French Revolution and the Napoleonic Empire, similar in scale and plan to Montesquieu's *Considérations sur les causes de la grandeur des Romains et de leur décadence*. His early ideas for the work centred on the personality and achievements of Napoleon; but he soon became aware that the revolutionary and Napoleonic era could be explained only by reference to the period that had preceded it. The chapter or two on the old regime which he had planned[6] grew into a volume, *L'Ancien Régime et la Révolution*, the only part of his magnum opus to be completed. Fragmentary drafts for the later parts of the work were found among his papers after his death.[7]

Writing the history of the revolution of 1789 was a major industry in nineteenth-century France. Before Tocqueville, Mignet, Thiers, Lamartine and Michelet had made their contributions; Louis Blanc, living in England after the collapse of his national workshops scheme in 1848, was bringing out his version during the 1850s. Authors might hold differing points of view; their respect for and use of their sources also differed widely; but all had sought essentially to write a narrative of events. Tocqueville is said to have been repelled by Thiers's history – which was far from being a conscientious study based upon documentary evidence – and scandalised by Lamartine's *Girondins*.[8] Georges Lefebvre pointed out that Tocqueville does not once quote from any earlier history of the revolution.[9] In the foreword to

L'Ancien Régime (written, like most good forewords, after the rest
of the volume) Tocqueville claimed that he had written 'without prejudice but not without passion. It would be futile to deny that my own
feelings were engaged.'[10] The ideal of objectivity in history – if it is
an ideal – is unrealisable: totally objective history would also be totally
dead history. The most dangerous historian is the one who believes,
and encourages his readers to believe, that he is totally objective. It
is because Tocqueville's own feelings were engaged that his book has
power to grip the reader; and it is because Tocqueville admits this
engagement that he can give his reader a genuine insight into the old
regime.

It must be remembered that Tocqueville's feelings were not un-
ambivalent. By birth and instinct he was an aristocrat, aware of the
virtues and graces possible in an aristocratic society and regretful of
the pressures which had led to its decline. But he was, in C. B. A.
Behrens's phrase, a 'repentant aristocrat',[11] conscious of the follies,
errors and vices of the class from which he had sprung. He was also
a man supremely concerned with, and devoted to, liberty. A paper
dated 1841, found after his death, and headed 'My instinct, my
opinions', declares: 'Liberty is the greatest of my passions. That is
the truth.'[12] Unlike many nineteenth-century liberals, he did not see
liberty in purely individual terms; individualism could too easily
become selfishness and a society of individuals would lack all cohesion.
Freedom of association was to him always a vital aspect of liberty:
in the United States he had seen communities of free men who
recognised no master, but lived in order and peace and accepted
responsibility for their own lives.

He brought to the study of eighteenth-century France the techniques which he had used in studying contemporary society in the
United States. He had built up his knowledge of America (and subsequently of England) by personal contacts, generalising from a mass
of fragmentary evidence and modifying his generalisations as further
discoveries made it necessary. Seymour Drescher's study of Tocqueville and England has shown how his views of English society and
institutions changed as his knowledge of the country deepened.[13]
Tocqueville's thought was always a living, growing thing, responding
to new facts that presented themselves to his attention. All writers
start with some presuppositions: their greatness depends on their willingness to jettison those which evidence shows to be untenable.

Unlike most of his predecessors in the field, Tocqueville was determined to get beyond the purely literary evidence – memoirs, letters,
pamphlets, polemics – of which there was already an abundance in
his day, and to work from the documentary archives. His first concern
was with society rather than with the state. He does not provide in
L'Ancien Régime a narrative history of the later Bourbons. He does

not deal in personalities: the brilliant portrait sketches of the *Souvenirs* are absent and he makes no attempt to assess the character of such people as Louis XVI or Turgot. He seldom mentions dates and does not assign definite chronological limits to the *ancien régime*. What he sets out to do is to present a broad view of the France that existed before the revolution of 1789. Unlike many historians of that revolution, he did not begin with the *philosophes* and the ideas of the Enlightenment: they indeed have a place in his book but we come to them only in Part III. Tocqueville was not unsympathetic to the *philosophes*, but he did not regard their ideas as the cause of the revolution of 1789 any more than he regarded the economic crisis of the 1840s as the cause of the revolution of 1848. Causation in history could not, in his view, be attributed to a single factor.

His starting point was administration, which he regarded as the essential framework of society. He pointed out that a foreigner who had access to the files of the Ministry of the Interior would know more about French society than Frenchmen themselves could possibly know.[14] Although many criticisms of the old regime made by eighteenth-century writers were available to French readers, they had at their disposal no detailed studies of the actual working of the administration, comparable with those which existed for earlier periods of the monarchy. Tocqueville did not ask what laws had been enacted but how they were applied, how they affected Frenchmen of all classes in all parts of the kingdom. He wanted to find out how public business was transacted; what were the relations between government officials and the public; what were the relations between different social classes – above all, what was the position of those sections of the population who could not make themselves heard or seen.[15]

Tocqueville drew upon both central and local archives. He studied the public Acts and the records of the Ministry of the Interior, the *procès-verbaux* of such provincial estates as still existed in the eighteenth century, and the archives of the *généralités*, the areas administered by the *intendants* whose key position in the old regime he was quick to recognise. Finding in Paris few records of the *généralité* of the Ile-de-France of earlier date than 1787, he spent a long time in the local archives at Tours, where he profited from the interest and sympathetic co-operation of the archivist, Grandmaison.[16] Since problems of land tenure were central to his study, he investigated the *terriers* (land registers) of many private estates; and, according to Lefebvre, he was the first historian to consult the deeds of sale of national property after 1790, in order to throw light on land ownership before 1789.[17] He also worked through the *cahiers de doléance* of 1789 – those grievance-lists brought to Versailles by the deputies of the three orders in the Estates-General – preserved in manuscript in the national archives. Only after absorbing these materials did Tocqueville turn to the works of eighteenth-century authors and commentators.

In the foreword, Tocqueville explained that he had decided not to clutter up his pages with footnotes. Such notes as he has are put at the end of the book and are brief explanatory essays rather than simple references. He offered, however, to supply detailed references to any reader who might require them and there can be no doubt that he could have done so in abundance.[18] Seventeen large bundles of documents relating to *L'Ancien Régime* were found in his study after his death.[19]

Tocqueville assumed initially that the highly centralised political and administrative structure of the France which he knew was the legacy of Napoleon: he soon realised, however, that centralisation was a feature of the old regime – the only part of that regime to survive it, since it was the only part that could be adapted to the social system created by the revolution. But Tocqueville made other assumptions which were confirmed, not undermined, by the documentary evidence: that the work of the revolution was still incomplete and that its influence was all-pervasive in the France of his time. He observed the pursuit of political equality in the revolutionary era, and the attack upon privilege; he understood that it must lead to a similar pursuit of economic equality, as had already become perceptible by 1848. The long-term history of the revolution was the history of the coming of democracy and there were many chapters of that history still to be written. Tocqueville never equated democracy with liberty: he believed that democratic societies might be free or unfree. He thought that the free democratic society that he had seen in America was made possible, at least in part, by the weakness of the central government (a weakness which he probably overestimated). He saw French society under Napoleon I as one in which men were equal but not free, and he was a severe critic of the Napoleonic Empire, as he probably would have been of twentieth-century dictatorships. From the 1830s he believed that administrative decentralisation such as he had seen in America and England was essential to a genuinely free society. Equally perceptively, he understood as early as 1848 that universal suffrage and popular plebiscites did not necessarily produce a free society.

L'Ancien Régime is primarily a study of France, but Tocqueville argued that the problems of France were shared by most of Europe in the eighteenth century, since they had similar political and social institutions. 'He who has seen and studied only France, I dare assert, will never really understand anything of the French Revolution.'[20] He used both England and Germany for purposes of comparison. He spent some time in Germany in 1853 and towards the end of his life he was studying the German language and contemplating extended work in the German archives. Many of the notes to *L'Ancien Régime* bear witness to his German researches: he there discusses the code of

Frederick the Great, the position of the peasants in Germany and the contrast between the agrarian system of the Rhineland and that of the rest of Germany.[21] In his European outlook he is the precursor of Albert Sorel, whose monumental *L'Europe et la Révolution Française* began to appear in 1885. The European connections of the French Revolution loomed larger in Tocqueville's mind than the Atlantic ones. There is little exploration in his work of the effects of the American War of Independence either upon French thought or even upon the French Treasury.[22] It was left for historians of our own time, R. R. Palmer in the New World and Jacques Godechot in the Old, to put forward the concept of an Atlantic Revolution in the eighteenth century.[23]

The general plan of *L'Ancien Régime* is strikingly simple. Part I, the briefest of the three, sets out to define and summarise the achievements of the revolution. Initially, Tocqueville thought that this would require a single chapter;[24] eventually, he found that he needed five. Part II is a more detailed analysis of the structure of French society under the old regime. Part III which, unlike the others, has some narrative content, examines the train of events which immediately preceded the revolution. It is here that Tocqueville takes into account the work of the *philosophes* and economists, the development of anti-clerical feeling, the desire for governmental reform and the difficulty of effecting reform without precipitating revolution. The clarity of Tocqueville's plan is emphasised by his practice of using brief explanatory sentences as chapter headings: for instance, 'Why feudal rights had become more hateful to people in France than in any other country' (Part II, Chapter 1) or 'Why the French people desired reform rather than liberty' (Part III, Chapter 3). Within this framework, he writes with superb conciseness and clarity of language, so that *L'Ancien Régime* in the original may be understood and enjoyed by those who have only a moderate knowledge of French. It is precisely this conciseness and clarity, however, which make the work a challenge to translators. Few can match the lapidary qualities of Tocqueville's style: 'How the people were roused by attempts to relieve them of their burdens' (Part III, Chapter 5) is far less eloquent than 'Comment on souleva le peuple en voulant le soulager.'[25]

In the first part, Tocqueville builds up a general picture of eighteenth-century Europe with broad brush-strokes on a large canvas. He makes assertions which he proposes to illustrate and hopes to prove later in the work. We need to remember that Tocqueville's intention was to write a comprehensive study of the revolutionary and Napoleonic era, and that Part I of *L'Ancien Régime* was designed as an introduction to the whole. He claimed that, when he was writing, the time was ripe for judging the revolutionary period and seeing it in perspective: 'We are now far enough away from the Revolution to be little affected by the passions that blinded its makers, yet near enough to enter into and understand the spirit which carried it through.'[26] With a characteristic use of antithesis, he points out that never were great events 'better prepared and less foreseen'[27] – prepared by a chain of historical developments but unforeseen by most of those who lived through them. Among those whom he regards as having misunderstood the import of the events of 1789 were Arthur Young and Edmund Burke. The former, who happened to be in France in the summer of 1789, thought that the revolution might well result in an increase of aristocratic privilege. The latter, though antagonistic to the revolution from its inception, thought that it would destroy for a long time to come France's capacity to make war.[28]

Tocqueville's assertion that the revolution was 'a political revolution which developed after the fashion of religious revolutions'[29] rested upon his awareness that the doctrines of the revolution transcended frontiers and had a potentially universal human appeal. Just as the religious reformers of the sixteenth century had been able to evoke a widespread response in a continent which shared a common ecclesiastical system and suffered under its abuses, so the French Revolution could awaken sympathies in other parts of a continent which, as Tocqueville showed, largely shared a common social and administrative system. The most remarkable thing about the age was that so many peoples had reached a stage of development which made them receptive to the revolutionary ideology. The chief work of the French Revolution was not to destroy religious beliefs or to do away with all authority: it was 'to abolish those political institutions, usually described as feudal, which for several centuries had held undivided sway in the majority of European countries'.[30] Its objective was to replace these institutions by a simpler and more uniform system, based on equality. Since those institutions marked for destruction affected the entire social fabric, the changes made by the revolution appeared more sweeping than they actually were. In the long term, as Tocqueville shows, the revolution made fewer changes in France than had been supposed; and this circumstance drew Tocqueville's attention to the problem of continuity in history, which was one of his constant concerns.

If, at the end of the eighteenth century, Europe was, as Tocqueville believed, ripe for revolution, why was it in France rather than elsewhere that the actual outbreak occurred? This is the question that underlies the detailed analysis of the French administrative system that fills Part II of *L'Ancien Régime*. Explaining his plans to a friend, Tocqueville wrote: 'I shall point to facts, and I shall follow their import, but my principal business will not be to narrate them.'[31] In the opinion of Georges Lefebvre, Tocqueville achieved an historical synthesis that is near to perfection: he likens *L'Ancien Régime* to the view from a mountain top, in which the details of the landscape are clearly shown in relation to the whole, and considers the work as 'the finest that had been written on the Revolution up to that time.'[32]

The basic argument of Part II reveals Tocqueville's awareness of the irony of history: France was the scene of revolution not because it was backward but because it was progressive; what survived of the feudal system became the more intolerable as the system itself crumbled into decay. In France the peasant was no longer bound to the soil and personal servitude had almost disappeared, in marked contrast to the position in most of the German states. Moreover, in France, well before the revolution, the peasants were acquiring land and becoming small proprietors. The division of the soil of France into small properties, so characteristic of Tocqueville's day, had already been noted a hundred years previously. Agricultural societies had complained of the fragmentation of land-holding; Turgot had commented that holdings were becoming too small for subsistence; and Necker described France as 'an immensity of small properties'.[33] Tocqueville demonstrated that although much land changed ownership during the revolution, most of it was bought by people who owned some land already.[34] But the peasant proprietor under the old regime naturally resented those seignorial rights that had survived (and which Tocqueville catalogued in detail in a final note).[35] The political powers of the nobility had largely disappeared; their financial privileges had remained and sometimes increased. The French peasant's passionate devotion to the soil was something that Tocqueville knew from his own experience. To the peasant who, by dint of careful saving, had become the owner of a small plot of land, the burdens of taxes, tolls, tithes, game laws and feudal obligations seemed unjust and unbearable.

Tocqueville saw in the centralising tendencies of the royal administration the main solvent of feudal society. The royal council and the controller-general occupied the key positions at the centre of the governmental system; the *intendants* and their subordinates, the *subdélegués*, were the key men in the provinces. He quotes the alleged remark of the financier John Law to the Marquis d'Argenson: 'Do you know, this kingdom of France is governed by thirty intendants.'[36] This royal administration had taken over a large part of the apportionment and collection of taxation, the maintenance of law and order, the raising of the militia, the execution of public works and the relief of famine and distress. Only in the field of justice did the *noblesse* retain vestiges of their ancient powers; and even here increasing use was made by the government of 'exceptional' courts which put the administration in a virtually unassailable position. In the towns, a 'deceptive diversity' of constitutional arrangements concealed an underlying similarity:[37] urban offices were acquired by purchase (the sale of offices being one of the main expedients used by the Crown to try to solve its financial problems), civic spirit was lacking and the government could think of no remedy but further centralisation and more interference in the minutiae of local affairs. The administrative tutelage in which the central government held France under the Second Empire was no new thing.

How, asked Tocqueville, had this come about? It was a piecemeal process, a matter of patience, skill and gradualness. 'When the Revolution began, practically nothing of the old administrative system of France had been destroyed but another substructure had been added to it.'[38] Even the critics and opponents of the existing regime wanted to strengthen the central power so that it might deal with the abuses which they denounced. Those with grievances hoped for redress by petitioning the Crown and its agents. Among these petitioners, Tocqueville noted, the nobles were distinguishable only because 'they begged in a loftier tone' and were even prepared on occasion to address an *intendant* as 'Monseigneur' rather than 'Monsieur' if they thought it would improve their chances of success.[39]

Lefebvre, a Marxist, noted Tocqueville's awareness of the workings of economic forces in the eighteenth century and of the conflicting interests of different classes.[40] Himself an aristocrat, Tocqueville had an aristocratic preoccupation with land as against other forms of property. His social analysis is powerful when he deals with those who lived on and by the land – admittedly the majority of the population. He observed the impoverishment of many of the *noblesse* and the great disparity of wealth within the order. He paid less attention to the growing importance of commerce and industry and to the diversity of groups and interests within the bourgeoisie. Further, his definition of class did not rest upon a purely economic basis.

Among the consequences of administrative centralisation, Tocqueville singled out the predominance of Paris in France, something which had no parallel in Europe. In 1789, according to Arthur Young, provincials dared not even form opinions until they knew what was thought in Paris. But the ascendancy of Paris was not confined to the fields of government and ideas; it was also an ascendancy in commerce and manufactures. The growth of the capital in size and population had continued in spite of repeated efforts by Louis XIV and his successors to restrict it. In this population the working class formed a significant element. 'So', Tocqueville points out, 'Paris had become the master of France; and the army which was to make itself master of Paris was already assembling.'[41]

That there was discontent in eighteenth-century France was clear. Tocqueville saw, at all levels of society, a spirit of criticism of the administration, and among government servants a profound mistrust of those outside the ranks of officialdom who tried to interfere in governmental matters. He noted the constant concern of the central government with petty detail and its constant quest for trivial statistical information. He saw the likeness to the administrative system of the Second Empire; the officials of the two eras seem, he says, 'to clasp hands across the chasm of the Revolution which separates them . . . Prefect or intendant, the style is the same.'[42] The eighteenth-century system, however, combined severity of rules with laxity in their application. It would be impossible to reach a just estimate of the system simply by studying its legislation. The execution of the law was subject to wide variation: the government rarely broke the laws but it frequently allowed them to be bent.

Partly for this reason, Tocqueville could devote a whole chapter to explaining what kinds of liberty were to be found in France under the old regime and how they affected the character of the revolution.[43] Beneath the surface of conforming, a spirit of individualism survived, and Tocqueville finds evidence of it in the *cahiers* of 1789 – not just in those of the third estate but also in those of the clergy and nobility. But the spirit of liberty showed itself irregularly and intermittently, and to make an effect under the old regime you had to have 'a place from which you could be seen and a voice capable of making itself heard'.[44]

Why did the French Revolution occur when it did? This is Tocqueville's concern in Part III. Here he considers the importance of the literary movements of the eighteenth century and of the growth of religious scepticism. French writers did not turn their backs on politics and retreat to pure philosophy as their German contemporaries tended to do, nor did they engage in active political polemics like their counterparts in England. They were free, however, to indulge in abstract political speculations: consequently, 'every public passion was disguised as philosophy'. Political life was diverted into literary channels. The nobles themselves, while clinging to their immunities and privileges, gave currency to ideas of building a new society on a foundation of pure reason – without realising that such ideas might become a basis for violent political action. 'So', with a curious blindness, 'the upper classes of the old regime furthered their own downfall.'[45] In the *cahiers* of 1789, the nobles' main fear was of royal encroachment on their position; Louis XVI, for his part, as Burke noted, saw the aristocracy as the main threat to royal power. In none of the *cahiers* of the three orders does there appear to be any apprehension of the imminence of revolutionary violence.[46]

Tocqueville held that the economists – the physiocrats – had more to contribute to an understanding of the revolution than the *philosophes*. The physiocrats were more firmly attached to reality – though they too were capable of indulging in abstract speculation. They advocated a programme of practical reforms and hoped to use the royal power to achieve them. They scorned the past and its legacies, believed in the perfectibility of man and looked to universal education as the only guarantee against the abuse of power. 'Despotism', proclaimed Quesnay, one of the most prominent among them, 'is impossible if the nation is enlightened.'[47] The desire for reform, in Tocqueville's view, was stronger in France than the desire for liberty. After the accession of Louis XVI in 1774 there seemed a possibility that reform might be achieved.

Yet the prosperity of Louis XVI's reign, which Tocqueville saw as the golden age of the *ancien régime*, probably hastened the revolution. Those parts of France which most fully experienced this prosperity – the Ile-de-France for example – turned out to be prominent centres of revolutionary activity; the more backward areas, like Brittany and the Vendée, were the most conservative. 'The most dangerous moment for a bad government is usually the moment when it begins to reform itself': [48] of all Tocqueville's aphorisms this is probably the most frequently quoted and the most thoroughly vindicated by the course of history.

Since in Tocqueville's mind respect for law and love of freedom went together, he was critical of the royal government for the disdain it showed towards established institutions like the *parlements* and for its arbitrary dealings with private citizens – for instance in seizing private lands for the sake of roadmaking or public works. He saw that the revolution was beginning before the meeting of the Estates-General on 5 May 1789 and that the administrative reforms of 1787 had thrown public life into confusion and had repercussions on the private life of virtually every Frenchman. France was in no condition to withstand the shocks of 1789.

It is not surprising that more recent writers have been able to point out errors and, more frequently, omissions in Tocqueville's work.[49] He assumed that administrative practice in other *généralités* was similar to that in Touraine and the Ile-de-France which he had studied in detail. His assertion that the seignorial *terriers* deteriorated after the mediaeval period has been contested by Georges Lefebvre.[50] He failed to appreciate that by the eighteenth century the *intendant* was not necessarily a 'man of humble birth' and that the royal administration was being to some extent penetrated by the aristocracy: indeed, in the second half of the century the nobility was closing its ranks against outsiders and probably increasing its political importance. He over-estimated the prosperity of Louis XVI's reign and did not allow for the financial consequences of French involvement in the American War of Independence. Nor, indeed, did he take account of the financial difficulties created by the European and colonial commitments of the French monarchy and the frequent wars of the seventeenth and eighteenth centuries. Lefebvre criticises Tocqueville for giving too much space to the nobility and too little to the third estate.[51] Within the third estate, moreover, he pays disproportionate attention to the peasantry at the expense of the bourgeois and artisan elements. The reader might get the impression that France passed directly from royal centralisation to a more efficient and ruthless revolutionary and Napoleonic centralisation: the decentralising work of the Constituent Assembly and the division of France into departments in place of the historic provinces is hardly mentioned. No doubt these changes, and the reaction in favour of centralisation after the outbreak of European war in 1792, would have been considered more fully if Tocqueville had lived to carry out his entire project.

All these are minor blemishes. Tocqueville's work remains required reading for any serious student. Pierre Goubert, writing in 1969, called it 'one of those rare books that bear the stamp of genius'. He put it at the head of the list of six books which he regarded as all that were recommendable on the *ancien régime*.[52] C. B. A. Behrens recognised it as the basis of most subsequent attacks on the old regime.[53] It has been a framework of reference for researchers making detailed studies of different localities: they have frequently been able to add to Tocqueville's picture, sometimes to amend it; but no one has ever effaced it.

Tocqueville's sense of the continuity of history pervades the whole book. The peasant he knew in his own Normandy was essentially the same as the peasant of the old regime: his status had changed, but his temperament and his passion for the land had not.[54] The office-hunting bourgeois was as familiar a figure under Napoleon III as under the Bourbons – only he no longer had to pay cash to secure an appointment.[55] Tocqueville shows us the roots of that mistrust of groups and associations intermediate between the individual and the state, for so long a characteristic of French history. Across the great divides of history there is far more traffic than a superficial observer would expect. Tocqueville discerned clear lines of continuity in France – despite its 'nine or ten constitutions established in perpetuity during the last sixty years'.[56] What is true of France could well be true of other countries – of Russia before and after 1917, for example, or of Germany between 1870 and our own times.

Tocqueville saw clearly the links between the old regime and the age in which he lived and worked. The further his researches went, the clearer the links became and the more he became convinced that the French Revolution was not yet over and done with and that its effects were still being worked out in France and Europe. The past to him was an aid to understanding the present and to discerning the probable character of the future. Much of his writing suggests that he viewed the advance of democracy as inevitable and irresistible:

J. P. Mayer dubbed him the 'prophet of the mass age'.[57] But he did not take a determinist or indeed a pessimistic view of history. He believed that the course of history presented mankind with a series of choices. Whether the future democratic age would be free or unfree would depend on how men chose.

NOTES: CHAPTER 5

Reference is made throughout to the complete edition of Tocqueville's works, edited by J. P. Mayer and published under the auspices of the *Commission Nationale pour l'édition des Oeuvres d'Alexis de Tocqueville*, (1951 onwards). *L'Ancien Régime et la Révolution* is printed in Volume II; Tocqueville's notes and sketches for his planned later volumes are bound together in a separate volume labelled II.2. For the convenience of English readers, references are also made to the Fontana edition, *The Ancien Régime and the Revolution* (translated by Stuart Gilbert, with an introduction by Hugh Brogan, 1966). When quotations from Tocqueville appear in the text, however, the translations are my own. I am grateful to my former colleague, Mr H. L. Sutcliffe, for some helpful suggestions.

1 Antoine Redier, *Comme disait Monsieur de Tocqueville* (1925), p. 98.
2 J. P. Mayer, *Prophet of the Mass Age* (1939), pp. 154–5.
3 *Oeuvres*, Vol. II, p. 247 (Fontana, p. 225).
4 ibid., Vol. XII, p. 237.
5 ibid., Vol. XII, p. 83.
6 ibid., Vol. II.2, pp. 15–16, critical note by A. Jardin.
7 They are printed in *Oeuvres*, Vol. II.2.
8 *Comme disait Monsieur de Toqueville*, p. 257.
9 *Oeuvres*, Vol. II, p. 17, foreword by Georges Lefebvre.
10 ibid., Vol. II, p. 73 (Fontana, p. 28).
11 C. B. A. Behrens, *The Ancien Régime* (1967).
12 *Comme disait Monsieur de Tocqueville*, p. 48.
13 S. Drescher, *Tocqueville and England* (1964), chs 3 and 4.
14 *Oeuvres*, Vol. II, p. 70 (Fontana, p. 25).
15 ibid., Vol. II, p. 70 (Fontana, p. 24).
16 ibid., Vol. II, p. 71 n. (Fontana, p. 25 n.).
17 ibid., Vol. II, p. 18, foreword by Georges Lefebvre.
18 ibid., Vol. II, p. 76 (Fontana, pp. 31–2).
19 ibid., Vol. II.2, p. 11, critical note by A. Jardin.
20 ibid., Vol. II, p. 94 (Fontana, p. 49).
21 ibid., pp. 268–71, 267–8, 271–2 (Fontana, pp. 244–9, 243–4, 249–50).
22 R. Herr, *Tocqueville and the Old Regime* (1962), p. 25.
23 See, for example, R. R. Palmer, *The Age of the Democratic Revolution* (1959), and J. Godechot, *Les Révolutions, 1770–99* (1963), translated as *France and the Atlantic Revolution* (1965).
24 *Oeuvres*, Vol. II.2, p. 16, critical note by A. Jardin.
25 ibid., Vol. II, p. 226 (Fontana, p. 199).
26 ibid., Vol. II, p. 82 (Fontana, p. 36).
27 ibid., Vol. II, p. 79 (Fontana, p. 33).
28 ibid., Vol. II, p. 80 (Fontana, p. 34).
29 ibid., Vol. II, p. 87 (Fontana, p. 41).
30 ibid., Vol. II, p. 95 (Fontana, p. 50).

31 ibid., Vol. II, p. 19, cited by Lefebvre in his foreword.
32 loc. cit.
33 ibid., Vol. II, p. 100 (Fontana, pp. 53–4).
34 ibid., Vol. II, p. 102 (Fontana, p. 55).
35 ibid., Vol. II, pp. 312 ff. (Fontana, pp. 306 ff.).
36 ibid., Vol. II, p. 110 (Fontana, p. 65).
37 ibid., Vol. II, p. 116 (Fontana, p. 72).
38 ibid., Vol. II, p. 127 (Fontana, p. 85).
39 ibid., Vol. II, p. 137 (Fontana, p. 97).
40 ibid., Vol. II, p. 23, foreword by Lefebvre.
41 ibid., Vol. II, p. 142 (Fontana, pp. 101–2).
42 ibid., Vol. II, pp. 130, 131 (Fontana, pp. 88, 90).
43 ibid., Vol. II, pp. 168 ff. (Fontana, pp. 132 ff.).
44 ibid., Vol. II, p. 175 (Fontana, p. 141).
45 ibid., Vol. II, pp. 196–7 (Fontana, pp. 163–4).
46 ibid., Vol. II, p. 197 (Fontana, p. 165).
47 ibid., Vol. II, p. 210 (Fontana, p. 180).
48 ibid., Vol. II, p. 223 (Fontana, p. 196).
49 R. Herr lists the main errors in Tocqueville, ch. X, pp. 120 ff.
50 Oeuvres, Vol. II, p. 18 n., foreword by Lefebvre.
51 ibid., Vol. II, p. 28.
52 Pierre Goubert, The Ancien Régime (English translation, 1973), pp. 24, 25.
53 ibid., p. 41.
54 Oeuvres, Vol. II, p. 106 (Fontana, pp. 60–1).
55 ibid., Vol. II, pp. 154–5 (Fontana, pp. 116–7).
56 ibid., Vol. II, p. 125 (Fontana, p. 83).
57 J. P. Mayer, Prophet of the Mass Age (1939).

NOTE ON FURTHER READING

The Fontana translation, *The Ancien Régime and the Revolution*, has a useful introduction by Hugh Brogan and is convenient for English readers, but Stuart Gilbert's version is at best a paraphrase and sometimes a distortion of the original. J. P. Mayer, *Prophet of the Mass Age* (1939), links Tocqueville's life and work lucidly and convincingly. Tocqueville the political thinker, rather than Tocqueville the historian, is the subject of Jack Lively's *Social and Political Thought of Alexis de Tocqueville* (1962). Richard Herr in *Tocqueville and the Old Régime* (1962) is concerned with the genesis and import of his historical work. H. J. Laski's essay in F. J. C. Hearnshaw (ed.), *The Social and Political Ideas of Some Representative Thinkers of the Victorian age* (1933), is still worth reading. Seymour Drescher concentrates upon one aspect of Tocqueville's career in his *Tocqueville and England* (1962). In Preston C. King's *Fear of Power* (1967), Tocqueville finds himself in the strange company of Proudhon and Georges Sorel – the common denominator being their hostility to centralised government. R. H. Soltau, *French Political Thought in the Nineteenth Century* (1931), puts Tocqueville into his political and intellectual context.

6 *Karl Marx*

Karl Marx was born in 1818 in Trier in the Prussian Rhineland, of Jewish parents, recently converted to Protestantism; educated at the Trier High School and the universities of Bonn and Berlin; received his doctorate from Jena in 1841. Failing to secure a university post, became editor of the *Rheinische Zeitung* and shortly after the suppression of this newspaper married Jenny von Westphalen, leaving Germany for Paris. There developed his theory of historical materialism and began his life-long collaboration with Engels. Expelled from France, lived in Brussels between 1845 and 1848, where he wrote *The German Ideology, The Poverty of Philosophy* and *The Communist Manifesto*, his best-known work written for the Communist League. After its publication in 1848, returned to Germany to edit the *Neue Rheinische Zeitung* and play an active part in the unsuccessful revolution of that year; in the following year arrived in England as a refugee and lived in London for the rest of his life. After 1848 wrote *The Class Struggle in France* and *The Eighteenth Brumaire of Louis Bonaparte*, his most brilliant contributions to contemporary history. Constantly short of money, despite the help of Engels and paid journalistic work for the *New York Daily Tribune*, amassed material for his great work on economics; only the first volume of *Capital* appeared in his lifetime, in 1867. Between 1864 and 1872 played a leading role in the First International but poor health increasingly limited his intellectual and political activities. Marx died in 1883 and was buried in Highgate cemetery.

History was Karl Marx's weakest subject according to his teachers at Trier High School, a verdict which some later critics would consider valid for his entire career. Treitschke, a Saxon historian turned Prussian apologist, wrote:

Marx completely lacked a scholar's conscience which is the hallmark of a genuine man of learning. In his works there is no trace of the humility of the true researcher who, aware of his own ignorance, approaches his material with an open mind in order to learn. For Marx what has to be proved is known before the research starts.[1]

This has been reiterated more recently by A. J. P. Taylor, who argued:

Marx never made a discovery in the scientific sense. He never had an illumination which turned his previous ideas upside down. He decided beforehand what he wanted to discover and then sure enough discovered it.[2]

But the same historian can write that, because of *The Communist Manifesto*, 'everyone thinks differently about politics and society, when he thinks at all'.[3] Edmund Wilson, author of the now classic *To the Finland Station*, made similar comments about another of Marx's works: [4]

Never, after we have read *The Eighteenth Brumaire*, can the language, the conventions, the combinations, the pretensions, of parliamentary bodies, if we have had any illusions about them, seem the same to us again . . . The old sport of competition for office, the old game of political debate, look foolish and obsolete; for now we can see for the first time through the shadow-play to the conflict of appetites and needs which, partly unknown to the actors themselves, throws these thin silhouettes on the screen.

There are particular difficulties in attempting to define Marx's role in the development of historical studies. For him, historical study was of fundamental importance, but it was inextricably bound up with other disciplines and it would be misleading to concentrate exclusively on this aspect of his career. Several commentators have seen three phases in Marx's intellectual development: a philosophical phase up to 1845; a political phase up to 1850 when he lived in Brussels and in Cologne during the revolutions of 1848 and 1849; and an economic phase from 1850, when he received his ticket for the Reading Room of the British Museum until his death over thirty-two years later. This is an over-simplification, because Marx avidly read economic works during his 'political phase' and played a very active political role in the First International between 1864 and 1872 during his 'economic phase', but it does reflect the general development of Marx's interests.[5] Central to any study of Marx the historian must be the middle phase, in which historical materialism was elaborated and *The German Ideology* and *The Communist Manifesto* written, but his achievements in this field can only be understood by reference to the earlier period, and any attempt to discuss Marx without mentioning his masterpiece *Capital* of 1867 would be like a biography of Nelson omitting Trafalgar.

Associated with this problem is the question of Marx's philosophy of history, the framework in which he developed his view of man and society. This has been variously described as 'dialectical materialism', which is perhaps too esoteric; 'the economic interpretation of history', which is deplorably platitudinous; 'the materialist conception of history', which is too verbose; and 'historical materialism', which is at least commendably terse. Like most of his contemporaries – and perhaps with more justification – Marx recognised no limits to the range of knowledge available to his powerful mind. 'Historical generalisations', it has been written, 'of the most far-reaching and universal kind were not merely admired but expected'.[6] Saint-Simon, Comte, Taine, Mill, Spencer (and there are hazards in coupling Marx with Spencer) and – most important for understanding Marx – Hegel, are just a few of the nineteenth-century thinkers who produced theories or hypotheses of breathtaking scope, backed by immense erudition and awe-inspiring self-confidence. In their all-embracing systems, they had a tendency to divide history into epochs, each of which portrayed some kind of advance in the general progress of mankind. Writing after the French Revolution and in the midst of the industrial revolution, it was scarcely surprising that their view of history was dynamic, not static, and that as invention followed invention, they believed in progress. They differed, however, in their explanations of what created this momentum. In the past, Aristotle had spoken of the Prime Mover and, more recently, Newton had suggested God, while Hegel wrote of the World-Spirit and the German historian, Ranke, of Guiding Ideas. Marx gave as his explanation the Mode of Production. This may seem a depressing anticlimax, but the use he made of this discovery in the 1840s is an exciting episode in intellectual history and is Marx's basic contribution to historical study.

One of Marx's disciples, his friend and collaborator, Friedrich Engels, poses a third problem in any attempt to evaluate Marx as an historian. From the time of their historical meeting in the Café de la Régence in Paris in the summer of 1844 until the death of Engels in 1895 a unique intellectual partnership flourished, so strong that it survived Marx's death in 1883. It was the most important relationship in Marx's life, his love for his wife and family notwithstanding. The practical experience gained by Engels in his father's mill at Barmen, his work in the seaport of Bremen and, above all, his employment in the family firm of Ermen and Engels at the Victoria Mills in Manchester between 1842 and 1844 gave him an insight into the workings of capitalism which he brilliantly enshrined in various articles and in his classic *The Condition of the Working Class in England in 1844*. Undoubtedly Marx would have mastered economics even if he had never met Engels, but in fact their collaboration began at just the moment when he was struggling to combine Hegelian philosophy and Feuerbachian materialism with the real world of capitalism. The assistance of Engels proved invaluable. As political *émigrés* in Paris and Brussels they became involved in revolutionary socialism and elaborated its theoretical justification in joint works like *The Holy Family, The German Ideology* and the famous manifesto of 1848. Together, they plunged into the revolutionary maelstrom of 1848–9 and, after the triumph of reaction, they both emigrated to England, Engels to resume employment at the Manchester factory and Marx to settle in London as an unemployed, and indeed, unemployable, refugee. The money which Engels was able to send kept the Marx family alive – although three of the children died in the 1850s – but equally important was the encouragement and intellectual stimulus which he provided. To help Marx, Engels willingly wrote articles on Germany and other topics, which were published under Marx's name so that he could receive payment for them. The secret of their authorship was so well kept that as late as 1971 Allen & Unwin republished those articles entitled *Revolution and Counter-Revolution,* wrongly ascribing them to Marx.[7] An equally well-kept secret was the paternity of Frederick Demuth, the illegitimate son of the family servant of the Marx family. To protect Marx, Engels let it be assumed that he was the father, and it was only on his deathbed that Engels revealed the truth.

For twenty years after 1850, Marx and Engels corresponded at least twice a week, and after his retirement from business in 1869 Engels went to live in London and once again became Marx's inseparable companion. After Marx's death, it was Engels who laboriously worked over his friend's manuscripts so that the remaining volumes of *Capital* could be published. The closeness of this long partnership makes it tempting to devise a joint name along the lines of Sellar and Yeatman's 'Williamanmary'. One historian has casually evaded the whole problem by remarking: 'in this essay Marx and Engels are treated like one personality'.[8] Such a statement is both preposterous and understandable. It is preposterous because although the two men in many ways complemented each other, they were far from identical in personality, workpatterns, style and thought processes, and it is understandable because to perform this surgical operation properly is an arduous and exacting task. Engels was such an attractive personality and so obviously devoted to Marx that it seems cavalier to accuse him of misrepresentation. There is little doubt, however, that his facile pen, his gift for oversimplification and his willingness to compromise did Marx a grave disservice. Lacking his friend's subtlety, his philosophical training and exact scholarship, Engels popularised but at the same time debased Marx's thought. It was Engels rather than Marx who was the 'terrible simplifier'.[9]

Those who called and who call themselves Marx's followers do indeed produce the last and most obvious problem. There are perhaps a few score Namierites scattered along the frontiers of historical knowledge and a few Gibbonians may still gather together over their port and Bath Olivers, but Marxists are numbered in hundreds of millions. Some of them write history while many of them make it, but there are serious disagreements among them over both theory and practice. Marxists and non-Marxists can at least agree over one fact: that Marx, like Alexander the Great, died intestate. His legacy, historical or otherwise, has to be fought for.

Marx was more influenced by people than places, but by the printed word most of all. 'He was', wrote Sir Isaiah Berlin, 'a man unusually impervious to the influence of environment: he saw little that was not printed in newspapers or books'.[10] It is therefore pointless to speculate whether his home town of Trier, with its Roman, mediaeval and recent French past, inspired the young Marx with a love of history, and it seems equally fruitless to read too much into his Jewish ancestry. It was, of course, a factor, but reading Marx's *On the Jewish Question* reveals that it was a minor one. Far more important was the influence of his father and his father's friend, Baron von Westphalen. From his lawyer father, who had abandoned Judaism long before his conversion to Christianity, Marx learned about Voltaire and the eighteenth-century rationalists of the Enlightenment, while the baron introduced him to the Romantics and to Shakespeare and Homer. He dedicated his doctoral thesis on Democritus and Epicurus to the baron and, until the later 1830s, it was Romanticism that played a dominant role in his life, not least because of his consuming passion for Jenny von Westphalen. At the University of Bonn, where he went to read law to follow in his father's footsteps, he lived the drunken, duelling life of the Byronic hero, writing poems and accumulating debts. He soon abandoned poetry, although his first published works were poems, but indebtedness remained an ineradicable characteristic. Wisely, his father moved him to the University of Berlin, where he rapidly immersed himself in philosophical studies. In a letter to his father on 10 November 1837 he explained how he had come to realise that jurisprudence and philosophy were connected. He had therefore written a 300-page study of the philosophy of law but, increasingly aware of its 'boring prolixity', had discontinued it. It had, however, he wrote, 'put me into the habit of making excerpts from all the books that I read', a habit that persisted throughout his life. This is the first reference to his famous notebooks, although the first volume to survive dates only from 1839.[11] As philosopher, historian or economist, this was the way Marx did research, copying out long passages from various writers and then adding his own comments and interpretations. In his letter he informed his father that he had been ill, another recurring feature in Marx's life: he once remarked that he was writing *Capital* to pay back bourgeois society for the state of his liver. Typically, Marx decided to convalesce by plunging into Hegel, whose 'grotesque and rocky melody' had initially repelled him. He ended the letter by apologising for his illegible writing and his bad style, two more characteristics which proved permanent.[12] In 1862, when he reluctantly made his only attempt to secure employment in England, he was refused the post of railway clerk because of his handwriting. Indeed, a retired detective in the German Democratic Republic, who taught himself graphology in a Nazi prison, has produced the Müller Primer to assist research students.[13]

At the Doctors' Club in Berlin, Marx endlessly discussed philosophy with the other young Hegelians. One of them, Bruno Bauer, was a university lecturer at Bonn and confidently expected to secure a similar post for Marx, but this prospect was closed when Bauer was dismissed in 1842. Marx was therefore never a professional historian: he never held a university post, nor did he write history as a pastime or as a means of livelihood. He wrote history because he saw it as the indispensable framework for his theories concerning the human emancipation of the proletariat and for his political programme, which sought to implement this in the real world of the class struggle. These theories and this programme Marx worked out between 1842 and 1846; he spent the rest of his life refining and developing them.

Because many of the Young Hegelians had offended the Prussian government by radical criticism of religious doctrines, state employment was out of the question, a gloomy prospect for a graduate like Marx, who finally married Jenny von Westphalen in 1843. He began writing articles for a liberal newspaper, the *Rheinische Zeitung,* and became editor-in-chief in October 1842. So radical were some of the articles that the government suppressed the newspaper in March 1843. He then joined Arnold Ruge as co-editor of the short-lived *German-French Annals.* His most important writing in this period, however, was the *Critique of Hegel's Philosophy of Law,* which he later amended when he moved to Paris. By this time he had become convinced that Hegel's philosophy was upside-down and needed standing on its feet, and he had also studied the materialist writer Ludwig Feuerbach.

Hegel was a system-builder on the grand scale. For him, each branch of human activity, philosophy, music, religion or politics, was an integral part of the portrait of an age, not to be analysed in isolation. The historian must realise that he was portraying an age in motion and must observe the various phenomena against the background of the past and the foreground of the future. This motion was the progressive development of the Idea or Spirit as it moved from one epoch to another: what impelled it forward was the tension between incompatible forces, which led to conflict and the emergence of a new truth or synthesis. The Absolute Idea sought self-realisation in the material world, and Hegel came to believe that it had finally achieved its goal with the development of the Prussian state. As the Idea had been realised in the state, true freedom lay in obedience to the government in Berlin. This conservative conclusion appalled most of the Young Hegelians, so they used Hegel's method of explaining historical change, the dialectic, to reach a radical or even revolutionary conclusion.

Marx was no exception, but he grew increasingly unhappy with idealism. Philosophy had, in his opinion, become detached from reality. It had become necessary to bring it firmly down to earth. This Marx proceeded to do, assisted by his reading of the French materialists and, above all, of Ludwig Feuerbach.[14] In his *Preliminary Theses for the Reform of Philosophy,* Feuerbach had written: 'the true relationship of thought to being is this: being is the subject, thought the predicate. Thought arises from being – being does not arise from Thought.' History was not, therefore, the progressive incarnation of Hegel's Idea. It was, as Sir Isaiah Berlin has so aptly summarised it, 'the sum of existing material conditions' which determined what men did and thought, Feuerbach himself putting it perhaps too succinctly when he stated: 'Der Mensch ist was er isst.'[15] Although later they were to deride him, Feuerbach's influence on Marx and Engels was profound and helped them to find a key to the mystery of human development without abandoning Hegel's dialectic.

Marx's *Critique of Hegel's Philosophy of Right* was rewritten and finally published in the *Franco-German Annals* in 1844. It contained Marx's famous comment that 'man makes religion, religion does not make man'. He went on: 'religion is the sigh of the oppressed creature, the feeling of a heartless world and the soul of soulless circumstances. It is the opium of the people.' After writing this critique, Marx did not pursue the religious question much further. In his opinion, Strauss, Bauer and Feuerbach had effectively killed God, just as Hegel had produced the final, total philosophy. The task ahead was to apply this philosophy, to put thought into action in order to change the world. Marx shared the view of many of his contemporaries that the French Revolution of 1789 had been no more than a 'partial, purely political revolution':

> A part of civil society emancipates itself and attains to universal domination . . . This class frees the whole of society, but only under the presupposition that the whole of society is in the same situation as this class, that it possesses, or can easily acquire, for example, money and education . . . So that one class *par excellence* may appear as the class of liberation, another class must inversely be the manifest class of oppression.

In his previous writings, Marx had spoken of the need for 'human emancipation' as opposed to the merely political emancipation effected in France after 1789 or in the United States after the War of Independence. In the *Critique,* Marx identified the truly emancipating factor as the proletariat:

> As philosophy finds in the proletariat its material weapons so the proletariat finds in philosophy its intellectual weapons and as soon as the lightning of thought has struck deep into the virgin soil of the people, the emancipation of the Germans into men will be completed.[16]

The key concepts of class struggle and proletariat are here outlined but, equally important, Marx had found a mission and a method. It was now essential to analyse scientifically the material basis. In other words, Marx the philosopher had to become an economist in order to develop his theory of human emancipation, and in order to put theory into practice, he would have to become a revolutionary involved in politics. Historical materialism, with its erudite references to history and economics, was not therefore a disinterested search for the truth or a passion for learning for its own sake, but a weapon to confirm a theory of emancipation which had to be translated into reality.

Stimulated by the immense task in front of him as well as by his growing awareness of poverty and suffering, Marx plunged into his research during his months in Paris. Arnold Ruge has left this portrait of Marx:

> He reads a lot. He works in an extraordinarily intense way . . . He never finishes anything – he interrupts every bit of research to research into a fresh ocean of books . . . he always wants to write on what he has read last, yet continues to read incessantly, making fresh excerpts.[17]

Most of this feverish scholarly activity resulted in the compilation of four incomplete manuscripts, often referred to as the 'Paris Manuscripts' and not published in full until 1932. They were to provide the basis for projected works on political economy, law, morals, politics and a general volume pulling all the threads together. In fact, only the first part of his first assignment – political economy – was written up and published during his lifetime. Marx spent nearly forty years pursuing the tactics described by Ruge in an ultimately successful attempt to evade the gigantic commitment he had imposed upon himself in 1844. It is a tactic not unknown to other scholars. He filled his notebooks with passages on the classical economists, on Hegel, on communism, and on what came to be called 'the social question'. The arrival of Engels in Paris in August provided him with a further stimulus.

After being expelled from Paris early in 1845, Marx settled in Brussels where he was soon joined by Engels, both of them becoming full-time revolutionary theorists. They seemed to enjoy their first joint work, *The Holy Family,* a merciless exposure of Bauer and his associates. Their laughter late into the night was said to have kept everyone awake, but their humour has the lightness of touch of bison at play. In this work, largely written by Marx, history is defined as 'merely the activity of man pursuing his own objectives'. This was to be amplified in their next venture *The German Ideology.* Marx had already scribbled down his eleven theses on Feuerbach, including the famous final thesis: 'The philosophers have only interpreted the world in different ways: the point is to change it.' Ironically, this key work could find no publisher until 1932: Marx and Engels consigned it to the 'gnawing criticism of the mice', and apparently the mice obliged.

Had they succeeded in publishing it, the preface to *The German Ideology* would have been as resoundingly impressive as the opening of *The Communist Manifesto:*

Hitherto men have constantly made up for themselves false conceptions about themselves, about what they are and what they ought to be. They have arranged their relationships according to their ideas of God, of normal man, etc. The phantoms of their brains have got out of their hands. They, the creators, have bowed down before their creations.

Even in translation its lack of polish is apparent, but its power is unmistakable. Marx very quickly reveals the kernel of his doctrine:

Men can be distinguished from animals by consciousness, by religion or anything else you like. They themselves begin to distinguish themselves from animals as soon as they begin to *produce* their means of subsistence, a step which is conditioned by their physical organisation. By producing their means of subsistence men are indirectly producing their actual material life.

He then proceeds to define the 'mode of production', which is a 'definite form of activity . . . a definite *mode of life.* As individuals express their life, so they are. What they are, therefore, coincides with their production, both with *what* they produce and with *how* they produce. The nature of individuals thus depends on the material conditions determining their production.' Next, Marx discusses the division of labour and outlines its various stages of development, which are 'just so many different forms of ownership'. This he later calls 'the relations of production', the way in which individuals interact with one another 'with reference to the material instrument, and product of labour'.

These stages of ownership he defines as the tribal, the ancient communal and state ownership, the feudal and, although this is only developed later, the bourgeois capitalist.

The superstructure of society, which includes politics, religion and ideology, is determined by the mode of production:

> In direct contrast to German philosophy which descends from heaven to earth, here we ascend from earth to heaven. That is to say, we do not set out from what men say, imagine, conceive . . . in order to arrive at men in the flesh. We set out from real, active men, and on the basis of their real life-process . . . we demonstrate the development of the ideological reflexes and echoes of this life-process. Morality, religion, metaphysics, all the rest of ideology and their corresponding forms of consciousness, thus no longer retain the semblance of independence. They have no history, no development; but men, developing their material production and their material intercourse, alter, along with this their real existence, their thinking and the products of their thinking. Life is not determined by consciousness, but consciousness by life.

Thus, the upside-down Hegelian philosophy is placed firmly on its feet.

Marx proceeds to underline the dependence of the superstructure on its material base in one of his best-known pronouncements: 'the ideas of the ruling class are in every epoch the ruling ideas, i.e. the class which is the ruling *material* force of society, is at the same time its ruling intellectual force'. Ideas, therefore, have no independent existence, nor are there any universally valid principles or laws. Another of Marx's crucial concepts concerns historical change. 'All collisions in history have their origin . . . in the contradiction between the productive forces and the form of intercourse.' Over a decade later, in the preface to *The Critique of Political Economy*, Marx paraphrased this in the better-known statement:

> At a certain stage of their development, the material productive forces of society come into conflict with the existing relations of production . . . From forms of development of the productive forces these relations turn into their fetters. Then begins an epoch of social revolution. With the change of the economic foundation the entire immense superstructure is more or less rapidly transformed.

In *The German Ideology*, Marx also gives the reader a rare glimpse of his conception of life in the communist epoch when the division of labour has disappeared. He would be able to 'hunt in the morning, fish in the afternoon, rear cattle in the evening, criticise after dinner, just as I have a mind, without ever becoming hunter, fisherman, cowboy or critic'. This is idyllic, rustic and unconvincing.[18]

Having, as they put it, settled their accounts with the German idealists and with Feuerbach, Marx and Engels combined erudition with practical politics by controlling the Communist Correspondence Committee in Brussels and by involving themselves in the League of the Just. Annenkov, a Russian observer, has left an unforgettable account of the meeting of the Correspondence Committee held on 30 March 1846. Wilhelm Weitling, the itinerant tailor and socialist hero of the German workers, had been invited to a discussion. Pencil in hand, Marx listened impatiently to Weitling's rambling speech and then launched his offensive. Rousing the population, Marx insisted, 'without giving them any firm, well thought-out reason for their activity would be simply to deceive them.' Marx equated this with a 'vain dishonest play at preaching which assumed on the one side an inspired prophet and on the other only gaping asses . . .'. Weitling then 'consoled himself for the evening's attacks by remembering the hundreds of letters and declarations of gratitude from all parts of his native land', and declared that his 'modest spadework' was perhaps of greater significance than 'criticism and armchair analysis of doctrine far from the world of the suffering and afflicted people'. Marx was infuriated, banging the table so hard that the lamp jumped about on it. 'Ignorance never yet helped anybody,' he roared, and stalked out.[19]

Marx's confrontation with Weitling was short and direct and the reputation of yet another 'true socialist' lay in shreds. His encounter with Proudhon was a lengthy affair, was largely indirect, and the Frenchman easily survived the onslaught. Proudhon's unwillingness to collaborate with Marx and his warnings against constructing a 'closed system', immune from criticism, had led to a distinct coolness in their relations. When Proudhon published his *Philosophy of Poverty,* Marx replied in 1847 with his *Poverty of Philosophy.* This work was published and, for the first time, Marx's historical materialism was available to readers. Indeed, Marx later recommended this book as an introduction to the understanding of *Capital.* The conflict with Proudhon was suspended, however, because of Marx's increasing involvement in the League of the Just, renamed the Communist League, and because of the outbreak of the 1848 revolutions.

The members of the League were clamouring for a concise statement of their aims and successfully bullied Marx into producing, at great speed, *The Communist Manifesto,* published at the end of February 1848. It was just as well he completed it because the events of the next few months were calculated to distract Marx from any sustained literary effort:

The history of all hitherto existing society is the history of the class struggle. Freeman and slave, patrician and plebeian, lord and serf, guild-master and journeyman, in a word, oppressor and oppressed, stood in constant opposition to one another, carried on an uninter-rupted, now hidden, now open fight, a fight that each time ended, either in a revolutionary re-constitution of society at large, or in the common ruin of the contending classes.

From this famous opening, Marx moves smoothly into an analysis of the conflict between the bourgeoisie and the proletariat, the relation-ship between the proletariat and the communists, and the irrelevance of what he calls reactionary socialism, conservative socialism and critical-utopian socialism. He describes how the bourgeoisie emerged from feudal society and ruthlessly reduced the relationship between men to one of callous cash payment. But the capitalist mode of produc-tion requires ever-increasing numbers of industrial workers, the prole-tariat. Because of the capitalists' relentless quest for profit, the condi-tion of these wage-slaves continually deteriorates, and because of savage competition among themselves the number of capitalists constantly decreases. All other classes, such as the lower-middle class and the peasantry, are forced into the proletariat, until there is confrontation between a small group of men, who own the means of production, and the producers themselves, the proletariat. Inherent contradictions with-in the system, such as recurrent crises of overproduction, make its collapse inevitable. Private ownership of the means of production, which was steadily hampering the productive process itself, will be abolished, and this, in turn, implies the abolition of classes and of the state. Marx defined both class and state as a relationship between exploiters and exploited, so once the source of exploitation, private ownership, was removed, class and state would lose all validity. It was true that in the aftermath of the collapse of capitalism there would have to be what Marx later specifically described as the dictatorship of the proletariat, but this would inaugurate 'an association in which the free development of each is the condition for the free development of all'. With this 'human emancipation', as he had called it in his earliest writings, prehistory comes to an end and a new sort of history com-mences. Unwilling to be classified as a utopian dreamer, Marx disdains to comment on this communist epoch or indicate whether it would have any history at all.

All of these concepts were commonplace amongst intellectuals in the 1840s. Four years later, Marx admitted this:

Long before me, bourgeois historians had described the historical development of the class struggle in modern society, and bourgeois economists the anatomy of classes. What I did that was new was to

prove (1) that the existence of classes is only bound up with particular, historic phases in the development of production (2) that the
class struggle necessarily leads to the dictatorship of the proletariat
(3) that this dictatorship itself only constitutes the transition to the
abolition of all classes and to classless society.[20]

Marx's use of the word 'prove' seems excessive and, indeed, many of
his predictions turned out to be false. The proletariat did not grow
progressively poorer, nor did it exhibit startlingly revolutionary tendencies: that role, both in 1848 and later, was reserved for other classes
or groups like the artisans, the peasantry, the lower-middle classes and
intellectuals like Marx himself. The contradictions within capitalism
were overcome time after time, and Marx's belief that the revolution
would occur in an advanced society like Britain or the United States
was never realised. When so-called Marxist revolutions took place, they
occurred in largely peasant societies like Russia, China, Cuba or Yugo-
slavia, and the scenario was very different from that envisaged by Marx.
His assumption that free trade would spread throughout the world also
proved false, as did his belief that it would assist the cause of inter-
nationalism which would prove stronger than nationalism. Tariff walls
sprang up in the 1870s and the workers of the world did not unite but
fought for the national cause on the battlefields of Europe. Marx's
observations about the iniquities of capitalism in the 1840s were, however, essentially just. His poet friends, Heine and Freiligrath, Disraeli,
and all moderately sensitive observers of the contemporary scene were
in agreement. Ironically, the sources which Marx found most valuable
for his condemnation of capitalism, the Blue Books, the reports of
factory inspectors, the findings of the various Royal Commissions, were
all products of the system itself. Marx saw the textile technology of the
Lancashire mills as mature capitalism in action, whereas he was merely
witnessing an early stage in industrial development. Every historian's
knowledge of the past and the present must be so selective as to rule
out the possibility of correct predictions.[21]

Within two months of the publication of the *Manifesto*, Marx was
back at an editor's desk in Cologne, eagerly awaiting the success of the
revolutions. His autocratic conduct of the *Neue Rheinische Zeitung*
irritated many of his colleagues, while others, like Stefan Born, were
unimpressed by his journalistic abilities:

> Marx is no journalist and never will be. He spends a whole day on
> a leading article that another would write in two hours, as though it
> was concerned with a deep philosophical problem.[22]

In May 1849 the newspaper was suppressed and during that summer the last revolutionary movements were crushed. After his military escapades at Elberfeld and Baden, Engels returned to the family firm in Manchester and Marx settled in London. For a time, Marx believed that the revolutionary tide would rise again. He used a legacy to revive his newspaper and began attempts to re-establish the Communist League. He also gave lectures in Great Windmill Street which, according to Wilhelm Liebknecht, were highly accomplished and popular. Later, he organised the reading programme of his followers, so that 'the scum of international communism might be seen meekly seated at the desks of the reading-room, under the eye of the master himself. Indeed, no social or political movement has laid such stress on research and erudition.'[23]

It was in this period, when Marx began to doubt the imminence of another revolution, that he wrote, in article form, his two masterpieces of contemporary history, *The Class Struggles in France* and *The Eighteenth Brumaire of Louis Bonaparte*. They were a detailed post-mortem on the recent events in France, revealing a subtlety in handling historical material which is not apparent in the more general analyses of Marx's earlier works. Unlike his third great essay in contemporary history, *The Civil War in France*, these are something more than 'history in the service of the revolution' or an attempt at a detailed implementation of historical materialism. Whereas the essay on the Commune in 1871 is an interesting attempt to establish a glorious myth and is more about what Marx wanted to happen than an assessment of actual events, the earlier histories are still used by teachers and scholars. Like Tocqueville's observations, they both deepen and broaden the historical understanding of the reader. They overflow with quotable passages, among them the opening paragraphs of *The Eighteenth Brumaire*:

Hegel remarks somewhere that all facts and personages of great importance in world history occur, as it were, twice. He forgot to add: the first time as tragedy, the second as farce . . . Men make their own history, but they do not make it just as they please; they do not make it under circumstances chosen by themselves, but under circumstances directly encountered, given and transmitted from the past. The tradition of all the dead generations weighs like a nightmare on the brain of the living.

But Marx could also write particularly bad history, especially when in league with a bizarre Russophobe like David Urquart. His peculiar *The Story of the Life of Lord Palmerston* and *The Secret History of the Eighteenth Century* are included in Robert Payne's *The Unknown Karl Marx,* and perhaps it would have been better if they had remained unknown.[24]

In many ways, the last thirty years of his life were a long anti-climax. Domestic problems, financial stringency and increasing illness often made his life a misery. His intention to complete *Capital* in the early 1850s was frustrated by various events and between 1852 and 1857 he abandoned any systematic research on economics. He taught himself English in the same way that he had learned French, by copying out vast passages from the great writers: he wrote – when Engels was not available – dozens of articles for Charles Dana's *New York Daily Tribune,* and in the late 1860s he involved himself fully in the affairs of the First International. Engels, his family, and all his friends were always urging him to complete his great work, but he constantly took evasive action, or his boils and his liver took it for him.

Back in the 1840s Marx had projected a vast work, too enormous perhaps even for a man of his talents and writing in an age which still believed in the attainability of universal knowledge. That he could have employed those talents mercilessly to expose the political system of his host country is evident from scattered remarks in articles and letters. If he had so decided, he could have become another, perhaps greater, Bagehot. They did have their similarities, apart from both publishing their major work in the same year, 1867. 'What is the British constitution?' Marx had asked in 1855. 'Actually the British constitution is just an old-fashioned, antiquated and archaic compromise between the bourgeoisie, which rules *unofficially* but effectively over all the spheres of civil society, and the landed aristocracy which rules *officially*.'[25] This is rather like Bagehot's description of the 'dignified' and the 'efficient' parts of the constitution. Just as Marx had discovered the secret of movement in history, so Bagehot had discovered 'the efficient secret of the English constitution'.[26] Marx placed the mode of production and the role of the proletariat at the centre of his system, and Bagehot placed his emphasis on the Cabinet, which united the executive and legislative powers.

Although he would thoroughly have enjoyed being a political commentator, Marx chose otherwise. He was also eminently suited for the role of contemporary historian, as he proved in his writings on France. He might have concentrated on the philosophy of history, developing on a Victorian scale the theories embodied in *The German Ideology,* or on the formulation of political manifestos and party programmes. But he wanted, above all, to be an economist. Even this, however, was not enough because, as a true Hegelian, there was a constant tension between theory and practice. He did not want merely to be a philosopher or an historian or a writer of political tracts or an economist. As he had written in the eleventh thesis on Feuerbach, philosophers only interpreted the world, whereas the point was to change it. In an indirect way, which would have bewildered him, he achieved just this. In the process, many of his ideas and qualifications were transformed and, indeed, he was himself guilty of many contradictions. In his later years, he suggested that his system could not be applied indiscriminately and was relevant only for the industrialised nations of Western Europe. He hinted that revolution might break out in backward Russia, and that this might be the prelude to a proletarian revolution in the West 'so that both complement each other'. In Russia, and perhaps in other agricultural societies, institutions like the *obschina* or village commune could play a crucial role. Obviously Marx is himself partly to blame for the way in which Marxists have interpreted his teachings, but the Marxists themselves have erred when they extract a rigid determinism from a body of writings so rich in nuances. They also betray Marx when they use his method to take a short-cut through the complexities of history. They have, to a large extent, dehumanised their master, and Marx had a very human face, even when it was contorted in righteous indignation.

NOTES: CHAPTER 6

1 Quoted in W. O. Henderson, *The Life of Friedrich Engels*, 2 vols (1976), Vol. II, p. 403.
2 In the introduction by Taylor to K. Marx and F. Engels, *The Communist Manifesto* (Penguin, 1967), p. 10.
3 ibid., p. 7.
4 E. Wilson, *To the Finland Station* (1941), p. 203.
5 L. Krieger, 'Marx and Engels as historians', *Journal of the History of Ideas*, Vol. XIV (1953), p. 383.
6 G. Lichtheim, *Marxism* (1961), p. 141.
7 D. McLellan, *Karl Marx, his Life and Thought* (1973), p. 286.
8 M. Bober, *Karl Marx's Interpretation of History* (1948), preface.
9 For further development of this theme, consult N. Levine, *The Tragic Deception: Marx contra Engels* (1975).
10 I. Berlin, *Karl Marx* (1963), pp. 17–18.
11 For the Notebooks in the Institute of Social History at Amsterdam, see M. Rubel, 'Les cahiers de lecture de Karl Marx (I: 1840–53)', *International Review of Social History*, vol. 2 (1957), pp. 392–420.
12 This letter is in D. McLellan, *Karl Marx: early texts* (1971), pp. 1–10.
13 D. Riazonov, *Karl Marx and Friedrich Engels* (1973), p. 8.
14 Most authors have to confess that they have not done justice to Hegel and his system and this author is no exception. For someone who has, consult R. Plant, *Hegel* (1973).
15 'Man is what he eats.'
16 References to the *Critique* are from McLellan, *Early Texts*, pp. 115–29.
17 McLellan, *Karl Marx, his Life and Thought*, pp. 104–5.
18 Quotations from *The German Ideology* are from the edition edited by C. J. Arthur (1974), pp. 37, 42–7, 64–5, 89, 54.
19 McLellan, op. cit., pp. 156–7.
20 ibid., p. 187, n. 4.
21 Quotations from *The Communist Manifesto* are taken from the Penguin edition, introduced by A. J. P. Taylor (1967).

22 McLellan, op. cit., p. 198.
23 Berlin, op. cit., pp. 248–9.
24 R. Payne, *The Unknown Karl Marx* (1972), pp. 148–224, 227–323.
25 Quoted in S. Avineri, *The Social and Political Thought of Karl Marx* (1975), p. 42.
26 W. Bagehot, *The English Constitution* (Fontana edn, 1965), p. 65. See also R. Crossman's discussion in the introduction to this edition, pp. 29–33.

NOTE ON FURTHER READING

In order to consult Marx's basic writings, one of the best collections is now the Pelican Marx Library: its six volumes include *Capital; Early Writings; Grundrisse; Revolutions of 1848; Surveys from Exile* and *The First International and After*. The most readable short biography remains Sir Isaiah Berlin, *Karl Marx* (1939) and the best full-scale biography in English is David McLellan, *Karl Marx, his Life and Thought* (1973). Of McLellan's other books, *The Young Hegelians and Karl Marx* (1969), *The Thought of Karl Marx* (1971) and *Karl Marx, Early Texts* (1971) are particularly useful. For Engels, there is the two-volume biography by W. O. Henderson, *The Life of Friedrich Engels* (1976).

On Marx and Marxism in general, always worth reading and re-reading are Edmund Wilson, *To the Finland Station* (1941), C. Wright Mills, *The Marxists* (1963) and George Lichtheim, *Marxism* (1961). An important and sometimes controversial book is S. Avineri, *The Social and Political Thought of Karl Marx* (1968), while M. Bober, *Karl Marx's Interpretation of History* (original edn, 1927; 2nd edn, 1965) is an exhaustive and exhausting treatment of historical materialism. For the development of socialist thought, G. D. H. Cole, *History of Socialist Thought*, 2 vols (1953), and for the historical background to the development of Marx's thought there is a useful summary in W. L. Langer, *Political and Social Upheaval, 1832–52* (1969).

Those who are really keen must either learn German or await the fifty-one volumes of the Collected Works of Marx and Engels to be published by Lawrence & Wishart in the next decade or so. Those eager to pursue themes barely touched upon in this chapter – such as the interrelationship of structure and superstructure, or the 'who educates the educator' problem – can consult the penetrating comments of Max Weber and Antonio Gramsci: R. Aron's *Main Currents in Sociological Thought* (1965) and J. Joll's *Gramsci* (1977) provide a convenient introduction to the thought of these great critics of Marx.

7 *Frederic Maitland*

Frederic William Maitland was born in 1850 into the Victorian intellectual aristocracy, one grandfather being S. R. Maitland, a notable religious publicist and ecclesiastical historian, and the other grandfather, J. F. Daniell, a distinguished physicist and inventor; his father, J. G. Maitland, sometime Fellow of Trinity College, Cambridge, and former barrister, became Secretary of the Civil Service Commission; his wife was Florence Fisher, sister of the historian and politician H. A. L. Fisher, who was to write an interesting memoir of Maitland. Educated at Eton and Trinity College, Cambridge, graduating in 1872 in which year he became a student of Lincoln's Inn; called to the Bar in 1876, became Reader in English Law at Cambridge in 1884, and Downing Professor of the Laws of England in 1888; refused the Regius Chair of Modern History at Cambridge on the death of Acton in 1902. From c.1887 was afflicted with diabetes, a dangerous condition before the discovery of insulin; his health gradually deteriorated and from 1898 he wintered abroad each year; died in Las Palmas, Canary Islands, on 20 December 1906.

For a man whose academic life spanned just twenty-two years, his scholarly output was prodigious, even by the gargantuan standards of the nineteenth century. In 1887 was joint founder of the Selden Society and its presiding genius until his death. Established 'to encourage the study and advance the knowledge of the history of English law' by publication of its basic source material, by the time of Maitland's death the Society had published twenty-one volumes, nine edited by himself (some of joint authorship) and the others by editors chosen and closely supervised by him. Edited other volumes of legal sources, of which *Bracton's Notebook*, 3 vols (1887) and *Memoranda de Parliamento* (Rolls Series, 1893) are of especial importance. His classic book *The History of English Law before the Time of Edward I*, 2 vols, appeared in 1895. It was all the work of Maitland except for one early chapter, despite the attribution of authorship to F. Pollock jointly; much of Maitland's other work was either directly or indirectly an offshoot of this book. His principal articles and reviews were collected by H. A. L. Fisher to form three volumes of *Collected Papers* (1911); Fisher also published a course of lectures Maitland had given at Cambridge in 1887–8, *Constitutional History of England* (1908), valuable evidence of his range and skill as a university lecturer. Two months before his death, Maitland discharged a debt of friendship with the publication of *The Life and Letters of Leslie Stephen* (1906); his portrait of Stephen makes an interesting comparison with that painted by Stephen's daughter, Virginia Woolf, in *To The Lighthouse.*

Maitland found his way to history after several false starts and some disappointments. At school, distaste for compulsory Greek deterred him from the traditional discipline of the classics, though his later scholarship was to be based on outstanding linguistic ability. At Cambridge he began in mathematics before switching to philosophy and politics. On graduation, his dissertation in political science failed to win him a Trinity College fellowship. For eight years thereafter he studied and practised law in London and then, in 1883, he was appointed to a readership at Cambridge established by his former teacher, Henry Sidgwick. In the same year there was published his first book, *Pleas of the Crown for the County of Gloucester . . . 1221,* a study in legal history, but also 'a photograph of English life as it was in the early thirteenth century'.[1]

The law, then, was his bridge to mediaeval history; he has not retraced for us the precise steps he took in crossing it. We have his own authority for the then strong link between the study of the common law and the mediaeval past: 'In his first text-book the student is solemnly warned that he must know the law as it stood in Edward I's day, and unfortunately it is quite impossible to write the simplest book about our land law without speaking of *De Donis* and the *Quia Emptores.*'[2] The adverb 'unfortunately' makes it clear that Maitland was no antiquarian sentimentalist. Indeed he thought the persistence of medieval law into contemporary times caused 'real and deep-seated mischief'. The clearing up of that 'great mediaeval muddle which passes under the name of feudalism' seemed to Maitland an urgent need.[3] Law reform played its part in turning his mind to history. The desire to know the history of the law, for Maitland, went hand in hand with the desire to make it fit for modern needs and to encourage men 'to believe that every age should be the mistress of its own law' free from the tyranny of the past.[4] Nor did Maitland think that study of the statutes of Edward I inevitably made English lawyers good mediaevalists. Usually such study did not impart a knowledge of mediaeval law as mediaeval men knew it but rather, on the assumption that the law was always the same, a knowledge of thirteenth-century law as if it had been devised for men of the twentieth century.[5] Still, whatever the defective historical sense inculcated by this way of thinking, lawyers as a class had contributed more than most to historical scholarship, and it would not be the first time that a 'disappointed barrister' had turned successfully to legal history.[6] But it was neither utilitarian considerations of law reform nor professional failure that was foremost in transforming Maitland from lawyer to historian. It was a deeper, innermost drive: 'intellectual hunger'.[7] Maitland was too reticent a man to reveal more than this hint of his personal thought and feeling.

Maitland's mind retained its philosophical cast[8] but he was not inclined to philosophise about history. There is no great corpus of his reflections to be compiled from the totality of his writings, much less any single source wherein to find his historical credo ready formulated. In this he differs from virtually all the historians of the second half of the nineteenth century. History was a newcomer to the universities and it had its cause to plead at the bar of academic opinion. Maitland wisely left to others in Cambridge (to Lord Acton in particular) the work of educating the 'grey-headed people – classical scholars and such, prone to regard history as an elegant form of trifling',[9] but certain of his basic beliefs are not in doubt.

He took for granted the fundamental importance of law in the life of any society and that was justification enough for the study of its history. He used a quotation from the American jurist, O. Wendell Holmes, whose work he admired greatly, to express the importance of how the history of law 'to the discerning eye [discloses] every painful step and every world-shaking contest by which mankind has worked and fought its way from savage isolation to organic social life'.[10] He would have considered, too, that the study of the development and diffusion of the English common law system, as one of the more remarkable phenomena in modern history, needed no apologia:

> The system which in 1601 prevailed in the southern half of a small island has thence spread outwards until it has become the greatest system that the world has known. This we may say if we think of square miles or if we count heads; but, after a little seemly hesitation, we may say it also when we have distinguished greatness from mere bigness, and have refused to call a legal system great merely because it governs the actions of many men in many lands, or merely because it is our own.[11]

Where he was occasionally persuaded to bring into play his considerable powers of advocacy was in urging the relevance and importance of legal history to other sorts of history:

Think for a moment what lies concealed within the hard rind of legal history. Legal documents, documents of the most technical kind, are the best, often the only evidence that we have for social and economic history, for the history of morality, for the history of practical religion. Take a broad subject – the condition of the great mass of Englishmen in the later middle ages, the condition of the villagers. That might be pictured for us in all truthful detail; its political, social, economic, moral aspects might all be brought out; every tendency of progress or degradation might be traced; our supply of evidence is inexhaustible: but no one will extract its meaning who has not the patience to master an extremely formal system of pleading and procedure, who is not familiar with a whole scheme of actions with repulsive names. There are large and fertile tracts of history which the historian as a rule has to avoid because they are too legal.[12]

Or again, returning to the same theme shortly after his inaugural lecture:

The history of law thus appears as means to an end, but at the same time we come to think of it as interesting in itself, it is the history of one great stream of human thought and endeavour, of a stream which can be traced through centuries, whose flow can be watched decade by decade and even year by year. It may indeed be possible for us, in our estimates of the sum total of national life, to exaggerate the importance of law; we may say, if we will, that it is only the skeleton of the body politic; but students of the body natural cannot afford to be scornful of bones, nor even of dry bones; they must know their anatomy. Have we then any cause to speak despondently when every writer on constitutional history finds himself compelled to plunge more deeply into law than his predecessors have gone, when every effort after economic history is demonstrating the absolute necessity for a preliminary solution of legal problems . . .[13].

Maitland was pre-eminently the specialist in an age which had come to see the specialisation of historical study as a prerequisite of the augmentation of knowledge: 'The old common fields must be enclosed that two blades may grow where one grew before.'[14] But he was no less aware that the cross-fertilisation of the different intellectual disciplines – 'the study of interactions and interdependencies'[15] – was essential for healthy growth. He was the specialist legal historian, sensitive to the interdependence of human affairs and therefore responsive to the interdependence of legal with political, social, economic and religious history. It is time to watch this particular type of historian actually at work in some specific contexts, for example is a better teacher than precept.

We have Maitland's own word for his preference for the practical demonstration of the historian's craft over any abstract discussion about methodology. The context is the memoir he wrote of William Stubbs in 1901. What he admired most in the distinguished constitutional historian we may safely apply *a fortiori* to Maitland himself:

> No other Englishman has so completely displayed to the world the whole business of the historian from the winning of the raw material to the narrating and generalising. We are taken behind the scenes and shown the ropes and pulleys; we are taken into the laboratory and shown the unanalysed stuff, the retorts and test tubes; or rather we are allowed to see the organic growth of history in an historian's mind and are encouraged to use the microscope. This 'practical demonstration', if we may so call it, of the historian's art and science from the preliminary hunt for manuscripts, through the work of collation and filiation and minute criticism, onward to the perfected tale, the eloquence and the reflexions, has been of incalculable benefit to the cause of history in England and far more effective than any abstract discourse on methodology could be.[16]

It would be possible to choose many illustrations from Maitland's books and articles of this whole range of activity from processing manuscript material to the 'perfected tale'. Two such must suffice.

The County Court
In his inaugural lecture, Maitland had spoken eloquently of the unique quality and quantity of the source material for the writing of English legal history and of its ready accessibility in the Public Record Office in London: 'for continuity, catholicity, minute detail and authoritative value [having] . . . no equal, no rival in the world . . . the most glorious store of material for legal history that has ever been collected in one place, and it is free to all, like the air and the sunlight'.[17] His first book, the edition of the Gloucester plea roll for 1221, was the result of his first foray into this treasure-house. The roll itself was not unknown to readers of the thirteenth century's most important legal writer, Henry Bracton, among whom Maitland was shortly to emerge, as will be seen, as the most diligent and perceptive. It had been used a little by several writers of the early nineteenth century. Its full potential for the historian, however, had still to be realised. This Maitland proceeded to do in his introduction to the edition of the text. This little masterpiece shows how apparently unpromising legal material can make its own contribution to general history and reveals

many of the characteristic features of Maitland's work.

A prime function of any introduction is to tell the reader what the author hopes to achieve. Maitland defined his objectives quite amply. He saw his plea roll, primarily a record of court proceedings in serious criminal charges, as contributing to different specialist areas. For the legal historian it provided a stock of actual case histories, invaluable as constituting 'a body of flesh and blood for the ancient rules which, whether in the pages of Bracton or in those of modern historians, are apt to seem abstract, unreal, impracticable'.[18] The social historian in any age has crime as a fact of which he must take note. To watch, through the record of the county court, the practical operation of those local institutions by which law and order were to be enforced, brought the material into the domain of constitutional history. The whole was 'enlivened' by more than a touch of national politics of significance, for *Magna Carta* itself was relevant at more than one point for the proper understanding of what was happening in the courtroom at this time. And conversely, court actions illuminated the significance of *Magna Carta* after 1215.

Maitland set his scene with great care. His 'ropes and pulleys' were chronology, people, the region and ideas: men and ideas in time and place.

First as to time: the year 1221, in the context, had its significance from different points of view. In the literature of the law it stood about midway between two classic books, those of Glanvill and Bracton. Hence a plea roll for that year was strategically placed for the judicious reading of history backwards and forwards to clarify development and continuity. Further, this was the first eyre in Gloucester since *Magna Carta* and also the first since Pope Innocent III had forbidden the clergy any longer to take part in ordeals. Plea rolls allowed a check to be made on consequent change in legal practice and how men's lives were affected by decisions of those in high places.

The introduction teems with people: politicians; the seven judges of the eyre seen both as individuals and as part of the nascent professional judiciary to whose emergence Maitland attached so much importance; the 'hated foreign sheriffs . . . instruments of John's misrule named for condemnation in *c*.50 of *Magna Carta*'; officers of the Crown; and a 'crowd of men neither rich nor famous' who came to the assembly of the county court in a whole variety of capacities. Maitland reminds us that regional variation still counted for something in the thirteenth century. If there is 'less need to speak of place than of time' nevertheless the historical imagination should localise itself and Gloucestershire becomes something more than just a place-name.[19]

Through his narrative and discussion of the technicalities of the text being edited, Maitland threads suggestions, reflections and observations of a generalising kind, some of which have significance well beyond the purely legal sphere. In one context, he concluded that the mass of crime that went absolutely unpunished in the age of John was 'enormous'.[20] Elsewhere he could not be so clear-cut and presents judgements that are rather food for reflection than definite conclusions for immediate assimilation. A good example concerned the humble and anonymous, summoned to give suit of court:

> Every township again was in theory present before the judges by its representatives. A township could confess that it had failed in its duties, that it had not presented crimes, or pursued malefactors or the like, and it could be amerced accordingly. Its half corporate character is well illustrated by some strange grammar, for the word *villata* governs now a singular and now a plural verb. Some very deep roots of representative government are laid bare by those eyre rolls.[21]

To the clarification of the notion of corporate personality, particularly in relation to boroughs, Maitland was to give some of his hardest thought. To link representation in local communities with national representation in Parliament was no new idea in 1884. Maitland is simply drawing the attention of constitutional historians to a class of material they should explore.

Of the specifically legal issues discussed by Maitland in the context of the county court, there is one of major general interest. It has been noticed earlier how Maitland, with O. Wendell Holmes, saw law as registering the 'painful steps' by which men progressed from savagery to civilisation. One such step was being taken in these years. The method which determined whether a person on a criminal charge was innocent or guilty was in process of radical improvement. The ordeal was giving way to the jury; superstition was yielding to reason.

The ordeal was in theory an appeal to the judgement of God; in fact it was an irrational procedure. Its commonest form for freemen in post-Conquest England was the ordeal by hot iron according to which the accused was deemed innocent if after three days the hand that had grasped and carried a hot iron proved clean on removal of the bandage. Since the procedure took place in church in the course of a religious service, Innocent III's withdrawal of the clergy from it meant some new method of proving guilt had to be substituted. Already by 1219, as Maitland was here one of the first to point out, the English government had begun to devise a new procedure and it was to be a rational one. Ultimately the new procedure was an extension and adaptation of the jury system. Maitland used his 1221 plea roll to conduct a meticulous examination of the state of the law in this matter at this critical time of change.[22] His findings, in the nature of the source and the time, were tentative but it was a theme which was often to engage his attention.

Many of Maitland's virtues are to be seen in this short but dense introduction: his knowledge of mediaeval law so sure that it is almost as if he were himself one of its professionals, the vivid style, from which the flick of humour and the touch of irony is never far distant, breathing life into even the most technically complex of sources, the never-failing awareness that ideas and institutions only come alive when the historian's imagination sees them at the service of living people and that it is the life of society itself that is mirrored in the law.

Parliament

In 1889 a writer in the *English Historical Review* made a derogatory comparison between the historians of law in Germany and America and those in England. It seemed to him unlikely that anyone in this country would have the 'patience and the learning' to attempt to write the history of English law. Maitland, though always the most modest of men, was nettled – and with good reason. He had followed up his edition of the Gloucester plea roll with *Select Pleas of the Crown (1200–1225)* (1888); the three volumes of his *Bracton's Notebook* had appeared the year before; *Select Pleas in Manorial and Other Seignorial Courts (Reigns of Henry III and Edward I)* was published in 1889. It had been due very largely to his efforts that the Selden Society, founded specifically 'to encourage the study and advance the knowledge of the history of English law', had been well and truly launched in 1887 and had produced three important volumes in two years, two of them written by Maitland himself. With no little personal confidence he could assure the critic that it was unnecessary to speak in any 'hopeless tone' about what Englishmen might accomplish in this field. Much had already been done and 'the times are becoming favourable for yet greater achievements'.[23] To drive his point home, Maitland compiled a long survey, *The Materials for English Legal History*, demonstrating in his easy mastery of the sources that here was learning enough to build strong foundations on which the legal history of England would be written.

At the very time of writing this article he was already preparing a 'big work' of synthesis, which he had planned initially with Frederick Pollock.[24] He was also actively discussing plans with Henry Maxwell Lyte, Deputy Keeper of the Public Records, for an edition of some of those parliamentary materials whose importance for the history of law he was currently signalising in the *Political Science Quarterly*.[25] His sunny optimism about his own personal contribution to future achievement in legal history was undimmed by the dark cloud of deteriorating health under which he now worked. It was at this time that he confided in Vinogradoff about the precarious state of his health: 'Many things are telling me that I have not got unlimited time at my command.'[26]

Some of that time yielded the *Memoranda de Parliamento* (*1305*) published in the Rolls Series in 1893. He had at first intended to edit parliamentary petitions, several thousand of them. But he soon found that, however glorious the store of material in the Public Record Office, it was arranged and itemised in such a way as to make it barely accessible for this purpose. With an unerring eye for the proper matching of sources to the historian's objectives, Maitland made an important modification to the original plan. Instead of compiling a mere collection of petitions, he embarked on an edition of one of the earliest Parliament rolls. Publishing it in full for the first time, Maitland bonded it with both the petitions presented in the Parliament and with the writs and other documentation relevant to the government's responses to the petitions. In this way Maitland was to provide another photograph of a different section of English life. This time it was 'the whole governmental force of England which is brought into a focus'[27] in a picture of Edward I's Parliament of 1305. It was, of course, a historian of law who was selecting the angle of the camera and we will not be surprised that it was Parliament's judicial component that received particular highlighting.

This was certainly needed. Much had been written recently about Edward I's Parliaments and little enough of it concerned Parliament's function as a dispenser of justice. Indeed, William Stubbs, the master of English mediaeval constitutional history, seemed to come perilously close to dismissing it totally as a parliamentary function.[28] Maitland was able to point out that the Parliament roll was at least in part a plea roll. Offenders were summoned by the king to answer, 'before us and our council in our forthcoming parliament'.[29] He further drew attention to the fact that by far the greater part of the parliamentary roll was occupied by entries concerning the audience of petitions and that the line dividing the hearing of petitions and judicial business was a very thin one.[30] The destruction of current orthodoxy was beginning.

A comment made by Maitland when the *Memoranda* was going through the press – 'I am trailing my coat through many fairs'[31] – leaves no doubt that he was aware of the challenging nature of his work. His manner of making the challenge was totally unpolemical and no individual historian was directly assailed. But one can hardly doubt that he had Stubbs in mind when he argued that there was still much to be discovered about the Parliaments of Edward I, a subject on which Stubbs had written at his most magisterial. 'Those who have done most for the constitutional history of the middle ages', wrote Maitland, 'would probably be the first to admit that much more remains to be done.'[32] He was reopening the whole question, partly because he appreciated how small a portion of the relevant evidence had been systematically analysed and partly because he had detected that a prejudice had been at work in the minds of those who had read such thirteenth-century evidence as had been printed. The Parliament rolls of Edward I's time had been read anachronistically; the later history of Parliament had been read into its earliest records.

> It is hard to think away out of our minds a history which has long lain in a remote past but which once lay in the future; it is hard to be ever remembering that . . . ancient terms . . . were once new terms; it is hard to look at the thirteenth century save by looking at it through the distorting medium of the fourteenth.[33]

Maitland was giving a simple lesson in historical methodology: the rolls of Edward I's reign should be judged on their own merits.

When Maitland had done this, it being granted that the 1305 Parliament was a typical Edwardian Parliament, there emerged a view of that institution quite different from the one currently in vogue. It is virtually impossible to measure the distance that separated Maitland from the orthodoxy of his day without a direct confrontation with the interpretation of Stubbs. We should share Maitland's admiration for Stubbs and his recognition that controversy tends to make for misrepresentation.[34] But the two positions must be put against each other in order to understand the important methodological principles Maitland was demonstrating. He once wrote that 'some statement about the thirteenth century does not become truer because it has been constantly repeated, that a "chain of testimony" is never stronger than its first link'.[35] He was to show in the parliamentary context how contemporary evidence, read, so far as possible, with the contemporary mind, made necessary the forging of a new first link.

In 1876, the year after he had published Volume II of his *Constitutional History* in which he had dealt at length with the Parliaments of Edward I, Stubbs published a short book which included an epitome of his interpretation. He presented Edward I as a 'constitutional reformer' whose Parliaments showed the 'clearest, most distinct steps of growth, which led to the complete organisation of the three estates of the realm in one central assembly'. Of especial importance in this growth were the classes which 'Simon de Montfort had called up from both shires and boroughs, representatives to aid him in the new work of government'. Simon's initiative, however, was not lasting.

> The task was left for Edward I to be advanced by gradual, safe steps but to be thoroughly completed, as a part of a definite and orderly arrangement, according to which the English Parliament was to be the perfect representation of the Three Estates of the

Realm, assembled for purposes of taxation, legislation, and unified political action.[36]

Maitland's Edward I had nothing of the parliamentary constitutionalist. The Parliament roll showed an Edward exercising power very differently:

> The king has a very tight and immediate control not only over all purely government affairs but also over 'administrative justice'. This control is exercised for him in his 'parliaments' by his council or by committees of the council, the greater cases and those which have most of 'grace' in them being reserved for his own hearing. The exchequer, the financial department, is controlled by the chancery, the secretarial department, and the chancery is controlled by king and council.[37]

Stubbs saw the estates of the realm as the essence of Parliament. Maitland showed that Parliament was still called 'full' and 'general' when the bulk of the prelates, barons, knights and burgesses had been sent home. Those who remained were members of the council.[38] It was the council, not the estates, which constituted the core and essence of the Parliament. The very nature of the Parliament roll itself made the point. It is not a record of the business done by the estates of the realm but by the council, 'sometimes with, but much more often without, the concurrence of the estates of the realm'.[39] Nor could Parliament be considered to have achieved anything like a complete or definite organisation: 'A parliament is rather an act than a body of persons',[40] a colloquy rather than a formal institution. As to the three functions which Stubbs saw as pertaining to Parliament as an assembly of the estates, there was no request for taxation in the 1305 Parliament and such legislation and political action as came up tended to do so after all save the council had been dismissed.[41] Finally, on the role of the representatives of counties and towns ('the commoners'), far from helping in the work of government, their part in the Parliament was so obscure as to reduce the historian to 'guess-work'. Maitland gave his view of the part they had been cast to play in very low key: 'After all we have to fall back upon the words of the writ of summons: the commoners have been told to come in order that they may do what shall be ordained.'[42] In other words they had not been summoned to represent an estate of the realm, to share with the king in the work of government, to help to ratify with their consent, taxation or legislation. They came to be told what was wanted of them. Once there, they were permitted to petition for redress of grievance or grant of favour.

Maitland's introduction to the *Memoranda*, no less than his introduc-

tion to the *Gloucester Plea Roll*, showed all his qualities of imagination and style in re-creating, before our eyes, the interplay of men,
officials, political ideas and institutional action in a living scene. It was
no mean achievement to do this while laying new and enduring
foundations, textual and interpretative, for a properly historical
appraisal of the crucial formative period of our most important political
institution.

The History of English Law Before the Time of Edward I (1895) was
the 'big work' of which Maitland had spoken in 1889. Big it certainly
is – in size, two volumes, each of nearly 700 pages; in quality, un-
questionably a major classic of historical writing. 'Twice in the history
of England has an Englishman had the motive, the courage, the power
to write a great, readable, reasonable book about English law as a
whole.' So wrote Maitland about Bracton and Blackstone.[43] Both these
men wrote commentaries on the law of England as it stood in their
own day. Maitland wrote one on the law of a past age. But despite this
difference, his book deserves to rank with those he so admired, a comparison which would most probably have shocked the over-modest
Maitland.

The focal period of the *History of English Law* was defined by
Maitland as the one that lay between the accessions of Henry II and
Edward I, 1154–1272: 'the critical moment in English legal history
and therefore in the innermost history of our land and our race'.[44]
There is, however, many a reference to earlier and later times as
interpretative circumstances demanded. In the course of writing, however, Maitland decided to hive off into a separate book the bulk of
what he had to say on Anglo-Saxon England and the immediate post-
Conquest period. *Domesday Book and Beyond* (1897) is, in effect, a
third volume of the *History of English Law*.

Within his major period, it was the totality of the English legal
system that Maitland set out to elucidate. In the chronology of legal
history it was the period which lay between the treatises of Glanvill
and Bracton. Bracton's book was of special importance in the construction of Maitland's great synthesis. For *On the Laws and Customs
of England* (1250–58) was his central point of reference, the basis on
which the *History* ultimately rests, the beacon of his researches. However distant in time Maitland might be at any given point in the study
of the evolution of a legal doctrine, Bracton was still not far from
his mind. He is generally to be discovered investigating the long-term
origins and development of something he had found in Bracton. It is
perhaps not too much to say that Maitland's *History of English Law*
may be read as a general and wide-ranging commentary on the treatise
he considered to be 'the crown and flower of English medieval jurisprudence'.[45]

Bracton's was a learned book, drawing on the work of Christendom's leading juridical academics. But Bracton was himself a very experienced royal judge and much the most substantial part of his treatise had been quarried from the plea rolls of the king's courts. Early in his career he had compiled in a 'note-book' some 2,000 cases heard before two distinguished judges of the early thirteenth century, Martin Pateshull and William Raleigh, whose plea rolls were at his disposal. Some 500 of their decisions were expressly cited in his treatise. It was of cardinal importance to Maitland's work that Bracton was no mere theorist. His book was a fair representation of what actually happened in the royal courts, as Maitland, with his voracious appetite for plea rolls, was continually testing: 'enough has been published [much by Maitland himself] to prove that he is a guide who will not mislead us'.[46]

Maitland's earliest articles show that he had been reading Bracton in depth since the early 1880s. He had published the 5,000 cases of Bracton's compilation that made the three volumes of *Bracton's Note-book* (1887); and his Selden Society volume *Bracton and Azo*, an analysis of Bracton's indebtedness to Roman law, appeared in 1895. He had published two collections of early thirteenth-century plea roll material. The preparation of his two Selden Society volumes, *Select Pleas in Manorial Courts* (1888) and *The Court Baron* (1890), had taken him deep into the wide range of sources available for the study of seignorial jurisdiction. Here he reaped the harvest of seed sown in the publications of local societies whose proliferation is one of the glories of nineteenth-century antiquarianism. Professional scholarship provided him with much material, especially that of the Record Commissions, active between 1800 and 1837, which had edited government records, and the Rolls Series,[47] which had started to appear in 1858. Though not an unqualified admirer of this government-sponsored work – 'Chequered indeed were the books in which public money was invested; the scandalously bad elbowed the admirably good'[48] – Maitland pressed them all into service. His use of chronicles now readily available in the Rolls Series, with their reports of lengthy and acrimonious litigation, was especially imaginative, enlivening many a dreary tract of legal technicality. Maitland read his English sources with a European mind. He was exceptionally well versed in the continental literature, ancient and modern.

The *History* is divided into two books of very unequal length. Book I is a relatively brief introductory sketch of the general outlines of English legal history down to the age of Bracton. The last four chapters of the section are also a contribution to constitutional history in their emphasis on the legal dimension of the growth of the power of the Crown, especially in the reign of Henry II.[49] The sketch reaches a climax with a typical reflection on the long-term significance of the period in the history of this country:

In the middle of the thirteenth century, the high courts that do justice in the king's name are rapidly taking what will long be their final form. When in 1875 a Supreme Court of Judicature once more absorbs them, the Court of King's Bench, the Court of Common Pleas, the Court of Exchequer and the Court of Chancery will be able to claim some six centuries of existence as distinct and separate courts.[50]

Book II puts under the microscope the process whereby the common law was 'converted from a rude mass of customs into an articulate system'.[51] Bracton supplies an accurate and comprehensive guide to the system. Maitland sets himself to trace its evolution in all the detail of its principles and procedures, but it is with the system as a whole that he is concerned. His setting is no narrowly legal one. Legal doctrines are skilfully related at need to their political and economic causes and effects. Relatively few individual people figure in the story but the whole is suffused with the presence of humanity. The history of law is a key to the history of society itself.

The tracing of the articulation of the system proceeded according to a carefully constructed logic. Its premiss, inevitably in a feudal society, was that law of land tenure which provided the framework of that society and its government. The ways in which land was owned, possessed, transferred were the first concern. The second was a matter intimately linked with tenure. The way men held land did much to determine their legal status. Hence 'the sorts and conditions of men', from king to serf, followed as the next step in the logic. This led, in turn, to a third, entwined with tenure and status: jurisdiction. Men were subjected to authority in terms of their holding of land and of their status. Jurisdiction in its mediaeval form was enmeshed with fiscal and administrative as well as judicial concerns. Further, the different sorts of court reflected communities: the shire, the hundred, the manor, the borough. Tenure, personal condition, jurisdiction, community were the terms of the logic on which Maitland constructed the first part of Book II.

Villeinage, the condition in which a substantial proportion of the population of thirteenth-century England found itself, affords an excellent example of the interconnection. Bracton comprehended both unfree tenure and unfree status under the one term *villenagium*. Villeins were subject to the jurisdiction of the manorial court and, as Maitland was at pains to point out, 'the village community was also a villein community'.[52] Thus the villein class can be photographed, to use one of Maitland's favourite metaphors, from four different angles. So with other institutions, the Crown itself, the church especially.[53] Sometimes, however, one angle will suffice: for the borough, for example, the treatment of which constitutes one of the more enduring sections of the *History*.

In the second part of Book II (which forms all of Volume II), Maitland could not construct any comparably tight logic; but his arrangement of the subjects to be analysed was coherent enough. Property returned for consideration from a different point of view under Ownership and Possession, Contract, Inheritance. He completed his scheme with Family, Crime and Tort, Procedure. Mediaeval historians, with their differing specialisms, will disagree among themselves which they consider to be the most important of these themes in Maitland's hands. The ecclesiastical historian will certainly value his delineation of the influence of religious ideas in many areas – the making of contracts and wills, the action after intestacy, the vast and fundamental matter of marriage and related questions and of the operation of the ecclesiastical courts in relation to some of the commonest of human acts which the common law did not punish as crime. There is much here that Maitland had discussed in a more restricted way in his earlier work, now given its mature formulation: the evolution of the jury system is an outstanding example. His misgivings about the adequacy of the king's criminal courts, expressed in a local way in relation to Gloucestershire in 1221, are now generalised: 'We must not end this chapter without recording our belief that crimes of violence were common and that the criminal law was exceedingly inefficient.'[54]

The *History* is a unique book in English historiography for at least two reasons. Its nature is to be something between a practical handbook of thirteenth-century law and the analysis of the structure of a feudal society at a specific point in time. Its author possessed a combination of unique qualities of which unparalleled expertise in mediaeval law, the historical imagination to match it with a vivid sense of the realities of life in a particular society, and a stylistic elegance to communicate his personal vision, were perhaps the primary ones.

No English historian has been more lavishly praised from his own day to ours than Maitland. Of his mediaevalist contemporaries it was A. L. Smith who supplied the aptest succinct compliment: 'If all his theories could be overthrown, all his positive results peptonized into textbooks, he would still live as a model of critical method, a model of style and a model of intellectual temper.'[55] This chapter has been an attempt to demonstrate and illustrate that proposition. Maitland continues to pass muster with the most hard-headed historians of our own time. Professor Geoffrey Elton has called him the 'patron saint' of professional historians, having regard no doubt to Maitland's patent exhilaration in the use of first-hand evidence and his sober recognition[56] that 'it is easier to make theories of sociology than to ascertain facts'.[57] Sir Richard Southern, referring to Maitland's 'extreme virtuosity as a craftsman', considers that his 'virtues are the virtues we should all like to possess; his way of doing things is the way of all modern research'.[58] Maitland is manifestly the historians' historian; and not least when in one simple sentence he both defined what the historian should be doing and suggested what was the intellectual challenge of his discipline: 'It is a hard task to see old times just as they were.'[59]

NOTES: CHAPTER 7

1 *Pleas of the Crown for the county of Gloucester before the abbot of Reading and his fellows, justices itinerant, in the fifth year of the reign of King Henry the Third and the year of grace 1221* (1884), p. vii.
2 'Why the history of English law is not written' (inaugural lecture, 1888), *The Collected Papers of F. W. Maitland*, ed. H. A. L. Fisher (1911), Vol. I, p. 490. Subsequently referred to as *CP*.
3 'A survey of the century: law', *CP*, Vol. III, pp. 437–8.
4 'The making of the German civil code', *CP*, Vol. III, p. 487. Maitland amplified this comment with a generalisation: 'Nowadays we may see the office of historical research as that of explaining, and therefore lightening, the pressure that the past must exercise upon the present and the present upon the future. Today we study the day before yesterday, in order that yesterday may not paralyse today, and today may not paralyse tomorrow.' *CP*, Vol. III, p. 439.
5 Inaugural lecture, *CP*, Vol. I, pp. 490–1.
6 Maitland was referring to William Blackstone, 'History of English law', reprinted in *Selected Historical Essays of F. W. Maitland Chosen and Introduced by H. M. Cam* (1957), p. 116.
7 'The body politic', *CP*, Vol. III, p. 294.
8 Shown to best advantage in his introduction to *Political Theories of the Middle Ages* (1900).
9 *The Letters of F. W. Maitland*, ed. C. H. S. Fifoot (1965), no. 332.
10 *Year Books 1 and 2 Edward II (1307–9)*, ed. F. W. Maitland (Selden Society, Vol. 17, 1903), title page and p. xx.
11 'Survey of the century', *CP*, Vol. III, p. 433.
12 Inaugural lecture, *CP*, Vol. I, pp. 485–6.
13 'The materials for English legal history', *CP*, Vol. II, p. 3.
14 *The Life and Letters of Leslie Stephen* (1906), p. 442.
15 *Essays on the Teaching of History* (1906), introduction by F. W. Maitland, p. xx.
16 'William Stubbs, Bishop of Oxford', *CP*, Vol. III, p. 498.
17 Inaugural lecture, *CP*, Vol. I, pp. 482, 496.
18 *Pleas of the Crown, Gloucester*, p. vii.
19 ibid., pp. xvi, xxiv, xix.
20 ibid., p. xxiii.
21 ibid., p. xxv. Maitland became increasingly fascinated by the concept of corporateness, not least in connection with the borough. He made this the theme of one of his books. '. . . his discussion of corporate personality in

relation to the history of Cambridge, in which the general and the particular are made each to illuminate the other with a marvellous delicacy of touch, made *Township and Borough* (1897) the most subtly engaging study in the whole literature of English town history': G. H. Martin and S. McIntyre, *A Bibliography of British and Irish Municipal History*, Vol. 1 (1972), p. xxix.

22 *Pleas of the Crown, Gloucester*, pp. xxxviii–xliv.
23 'Materials', *CP*, Vol. II, p. 1.
24 *Letters*, no. 73.
25 ibid., nos 55 (6 January 1889) 70, 71, 73 (1 October 1889; this letter details the revised plan).
26 ibid., no. 62.
27 *Records of the Parliament holden at Westminster on the twenty-eighth day of February, in the thirty-third year of the reign of King Edward the First (AD 1305)*, Rolls Series, 98 (1893), pp. lxxi–lxxii. *Memoranda de Parliamento* is the short title which appears on the spine of the book.
28 'Of the four normal powers of a national assembly, the judicial has never been exercised by the parliament as a parliament'; *Select Charters*, 9th edn, p. 50.
29 *Memoranda*, p. lxxix.
30 ibid., p. lxxvi.
31 *Letters*, no. 127.
32 *Memoranda*, p. lxxxviii.
33 ibid., pp. lxxxiii–lxxxiv.
34 *Letters*, nos 87, 276.
35 ibid., no. 98. Maitland was referring to the method he admired in the historical writing of his grandfather, S. R. Maitland.
36 W. Stubbs, *The Early Plantagenets (Epochs of Modern History)* (1876) pp. 221–2.
37 *Memoranda*, p. lxx.
38 ibid., pp. xxxvi, lxxxvii.
39 ibid., p. lxxxviii.
40 ibid., p. lxvii.
41 ibid., pp. liii, 1, xlix.
42 ibid., pp. lxxv–lxxvi.
43 *Bracton's Notebook* (1887), Vol. I, p. 8.
44 *The History of English Law before the Time of Edward I*, 2 vols (2nd edn 1898; repr. 1968), Vol. II, p. 673. Referred to subsequently as *HEL*. cf. '. . . that history of morals which is the innermost history of mankind'; *Year Books . . .* , Selden Society, Vol. 17, p. xix.
45 *HEL*, Vol. I, p. 206.
46 *HEL*, Vol. I, p. 210.
47 M. D. Knowles on the Rolls Series: 'Without all these texts it is difficult to see how the great revolution in academic history, which has sprung primarily from medieval constitutional and institutional history, could ever have taken place'; *Great Historical Enterprises* (1964), p. 134.
48 'The laws of the Anglo-Saxons', *CP*, Vol. III, p. 456. But at least the state had done better than the universities: 'We cannot say that any organized academic opinion demanded the work that was done by the Record Commission, by the Rolls Series, or by the Historical Manuscripts Commission, or that the universities cried aloud for the publication of State Papers and the opening of the national archives'; 'The teaching of history', *CP*, Vol. III, p. 413.
49 *HEL*, Vol. I, ch. vi.

50 ibid., Vol. I, p. 190.
51 ibid., Vol. I, p. 133.
52 ibid., Vol. I, p. 624.
53 The careful division of the book into clearly headed sections and the itemised Table of Contents provide excellent guidance.
54 *HEL*, Vol. II, p. 557.
55 A. L. Smith, *F. W. Maitland: Two Lectures and a Bibliography* (1908), p. 57.
56 cf. Professor Elton's words as general editor of the series 'The Sources of History. Studies in the Uses of Historical Evidence': 'a proper acquaintance with [historical evidence] tends to prove both exhilarating and sobering – exhilarating because it opens the road to unending enquiry, and sobering because it reduces the inspiring theory and the new method to their proper subordinate place in the scheme of things'.
57 *Pleas of the Crown, Gloucester*, p. xxxv.
58 'The letters of F. W. Maitland', *History and Theory*, 6 (1967), pp. 105–11 at pp. 108, 110.
59 *HEL*, Vol. I, p. 687.

NOTE ON FURTHER READING

The essential biography of Maitland is that of C. H. S. Fifoot, *F. W. Maitland: A Life* (1971). *The Letters of F. W. Maitland*, ed. C. H. S. Fifoot (1965) are a mine of information about Maitland's working life. Two memoirs written by men who were very close to him are important: H. A. L. Fisher, *F. W. Maitland. A Biographical Sketch* (1910), and P. Vinogradoff, 'Frederic William Maitland', *English Historical Review*, vol. 22 (1907), pp. 280–9, reprinted in *Collected Papers of P. Vinogradoff*, Vol. 1 (1928), pp. 253–64. Several selections of his work have been published: *Maitland: Selected Essays*, ed. H. D. Hazeltine *et al.* (1937); *Selected Historical Essays of F. W. Maitland Chosen and Introduced by H. M. Cam* (1957); V. T. H. Delany, *F. W. Maitland Reader* (1957); R. L. Schuyler, *F. W. Maitland, Historian* (1960). There are two useful introductory analyses: J. R. Cameron, *F. W. Maitland and the History of English Law* (1961); H. E. Bell, *Maitland. A Critical Examination and Assessment* (1965). Two useful shorter analyses are: T. F. T. Plucknett, 'Maitland's view of law and history', *Law Quarterly Review* (1951), pp. 179–94; R. L. Schuyler, 'The historical spirit incarnate: F. W. Maitland', *American Historical Review*, vol. 57 (1952), pp. 303–22. Maitland gained early the appreciation of the *Annales* school: G. Le Bras, 'Le sens de la vie dans l'histoire du droit – l'oeuvre de F. W. Maitland', *Annales d'histoire économique et sociale* (1930), pp. 279–301.

8 Marc Bloch

Marc Bloch was born in 1886 into a scholarly Jewish family at Lyons, France; son of Gustave Bloch, professor of ancient history and author of *La Gaule romaine*. Graduated in history and geography from the École normale supérieure at Paris in 1908, studied at Leipzig and Berlin 1908–9, and then at the Fondation Thiers in Paris 1909–12. Taught for two years at Montpellier and Amiens, but was called to the colours in 1914, serving first as an NCO during the Battle of the Marne and then as a commissioned officer. In 1919 was appointed to the chair of mediaeval history at Strasbourg, and in 1928 became one of the founding editors of the very influential periodical *Annales d'histoire économique et sociale*. Moved to a chair of economic history at the Sorbonne in 1936 but rejoined the army in 1939, serving as 'the oldest captain in the French army'. Witnessed at first hand the defeat of 1940 and the capitulation. Taught in Vichy France at Clermont-Ferrand and Montpellier and in March 1943 joined the Resistance. Captured in the spring of 1944 and, after suffering interrogation, brutality and torture at the hands of the Gestapo, was executed by firing squad 16 June 1944. Principal publications include *L'Ile de France* (1913), *Roi et serfs* (1920), *Les Rois thaumaturges* (1924), *Les Caractères originaux de l'histoire rurale française* (1931) and *La Société féodale* (two vols, 1939–40). Among his works published posthumously, two little books have a special importance: *Apologie pour l'histoire, ou Métier d'historien* (1949) and *L'Etrange défaite* (1957).

The bare bones of Bloch's career speak for themselves and help to explain why he became so powerful a symbol to the immediate postwar generation. Frenchman and Jew, scholar and soldier, staff officer and Resistance worker, there was much to respect in his career for a wide spectrum of opinion among the broad majority in the new liberal humanistic West after 1945. Bloch, the man of action, was articulate on the present as well as on the past: indeed one of the tenets of his faith was the folly of separating past from present. In the precarious central years of the war he produced (though did not and could not publish), in prose that was sometimes vivid and angry, a brilliant account of the incongruities of the defeat of 1940. During the same years he also wrote a calm and temperate (and unfinished) analysis of the nature of the historical discipline to which he had devoted so much of his intellectual life. The final outrage of his execution, his bravery in the face of death, bore the flavour of martyrdom; and to many Bloch appeared a true martyr for liberal humanist virtue at the hands of tyranny, brutality and oppression.

Two features of his career call for special mention: the straight-forward course of his personal life and academic position, and the intrusion of wars into what would otherwise have been read as a rather humdrum, though distinguished, path. George Altman, in his moving introduction to L'Etrange défaite,[1] talks of Bloch's devotion to his wife and children, his wife 'si vaillante et si douce', who died when Bloch was in prison at Lyons, his four sons and two daughters. Academically he was early recognised as one of the outstanding figures of his generation. Trained in the best professional schools in France and Germany, his promise was evident even before the First World War. After that war he operated as one of a distinguished group at the Faculty of Letters in Strasbourg from a powerful teaching base in the provinces but was also quickly known by publication and presence in Paris. His move to the Paris chair in 1936 centralised his activities to some extent, and there are several teachers in universities in Britain today who still remember the force and intellectual tone of his seminars. Contrary to what some of his English pupils believed, he was not an orthodox Jew. His Jewish background was important because of the political state of the times and for no other reason. In a France where repercussions of the Dreyfus affair still echoed (he once referred to his age-group as 'the last of the generation of the Dreyfus affair') and in a Europe where Hitler's virulent anti-semitism emerged as a dominant political issue, to be a Jew carried inevitable consequences. Bloch was clear in his own mind on the issue. He stated solemnly that it was only anti-semitism that made him want to affirm his Jewishness. In his testament, written at Clermont-Ferrand on 18 March 1941, he asked that no orthodox Jewish prayers should be offered over his grave, that no appeal should be made in his name to an orthodoxy whose credo he recognised not at all. Yet he avowed – and proved his word later by his deed – that he was willing in the face of death to testify that he had been born a Jew. His allegiance, in spite of all the difficulties and treacheries of 1941, still went with a simple patriotic nobility direct to France and all things French.

Attached to my country by a family tradition that is already long, brought up in her spiritual heritage and in her history, incapable in truth of conceiving another land where I could breathe at ease, I have loved her and served her with all my strength. I have never found that my Jewishness put the slightest object in the way of these sentiments. In the course of two world wars it was not given to me to die for France. At least may I in all sincerity offer this witness. I die as I have lived, a good Frenchman.

'Je meurs comme j'ai vécu un bon Français.'[2] Bloch asked no better epitaph.

The secret of this Roman simplicity may be found in large part in his experiences in the two wars. He was a good soldier and a brave man, hating muddle, negligence and lack of foresight, accepting the courage, the squalor and the cruelty of the experience with a curiosity that he described almost in the terms of a saving grace. He attributed his calmness in action to 'the spirit of curiosity which never left me'.[3] He was interested in the anatomy of courage. Bravery was an attribute that could be acquired by example. It was the duty of the NCO and the officer to give that example; and he showed considerable contempt for the coward. Fear was the ugly thing he resented almost more than death. 'I have always noted', he remarked reflectively on the Battle of the Marne, 'that by a happy reaction death ceases to be terrifying from the moment it seems close: there is the basic explanation of courage.'[4] There is a delightful consistency in the man. The same irritations shine through his accounts of both wars. Lack of communication was one of the bugbears that affronted him. In a revealing sentence he expressed sentiments applicable directly to his experiences in August 1914 but applicable generally to his career as a soldier, scholar and historian: 'Rien ne m'énerve comme le sentiment que l'on me cache la vérité.'[5] One feels that nothing upset him more than such concealment, whether it was stupidity of superior officers or incompetence of mediaeval scribes that hid the truth from him. Divine curiosity and intense irritation at the concealment of truth were the two driving forces behind so many of Bloch's actions. They drove him to write, with events fresh in mind, his splendid analysis of the reasons for the French defeat in 1940: the incapacity of the high command, inadequate communications between the staff and the fighting men, an intellectual failure to recognise the difference in tempo between the war of 1914–18 and the 1940s, deeper questions of provision of material or education or morale. *L'Etrange défaite* gives many insights into Bloch's personality. 'A historian does not easily become bored', he writes,[6] but 1939 to May 1940 was boring enough. A note of tetchy efficiency creeps into his prose and his sentiments. He had indeed had his two wars and looking back could see a long story of family involvement in the defence of

France, his father in 1870, his great-grandfather in 1793. There are parallels on this side of the Channel, both among those who fought, especially in the First World War with its savage casualty lists, and among those who did not but who saw so many of their contemporaries die. Bloch was during his most creative period in the full sense a survivor; and the accompanying awareness of his responsibility as a survivor (as with R. G. Collingwood in Britain) helps to explain his industry and the intensity of the controlled emotion in his writing. He bore the responsibility for communicating serious ideas on serious matters for the greater part of his whole generation.

In a perceptive note on Bloch's work, prompted by the appearance of some of his main works in translation in the 1960s, R. R. Davies made the shrewd point that in one respect Bloch's promise was never quite fulfilled. He never wrote 'the detailed monograph that might have evoked his genius at its fullest'.[7] Indeed, Davies went on to suggest that as a meticulous historian who left a definitive work he will probably wear less well than not only Maitland or Stubbs but even less able historians. If the standard of 'definitive' is put high enough this is true, and one recognises Davies's explanation as just. So much of Bloch's energies were directed towards teaching his own brilliant constellation of pupils, notably research students, and towards reshaping academic history to a view of general synthesis which involved a true totality of approach. On a more modest definition of 'definitive', Bloch still wears very well. A generation after his death students find ideas and material in his work that guide their own inquiries on kingship, serfdom, slavery, coinage, feudal and rural society, topics vital to an understanding of the Western mediaeval world. Bloch himself chose the right problems to examine. We applaud, even when we differ in our conclusions, the sagacity that directed the choice.

    The cult of Marc Bloch, a development which would surely have given Bloch himself both amazement and amusement, flourished in the postwar years. There is an Association Marc Bloch, and its publication, *Mélanges historiques*, as Davies reminds us, lists a bibliography of his writings which stretches over seventy-four pages. We are sufficiently detached now, half a lifetime after his death, to be able to evaluate the direct contribution of his written work to mediaeval studies. One achievement stands alone. His founding with Lucien Febvre of a new journal, the *Annales d'Histoire Économique et Sociale* (1929), stands out as a triumph of imaginative insight and organisation. It is salutary and useful even now for a mediaevalist to read carefully through these prewar numbers of the *Annales*. There is no better way of savouring the mastery of Bloch's vigorous and active intelligence. The weight of his personal production, articles, reviews, learned notes, is astonishing, both in quantity and quality. His confident and cool mind, sometimes praising, sometimes criticising, made itself aware of what was going on in mediaeval or feudal studies in Japan, Finland, Norway, Corsica and Wales as well as in the heartlands of feudal Europe. New techniques in historical and archaeological method were carefully appraised, air photography, ecological study, pollen analysis, the application of economic theory and the statistical approach. In advance of many of his British colleagues, for example, he noted the value of William Rees's extraordinary achievement in producing his map of mediaeval *South Wales and the March*.[8] Later periodicals, the *Annales* in postwar guise, *Past and Present* at Oxford, have made a formidable impact on the scholarly world. There have been good editors since Bloch. Few men, if any, however, have succeeded in stamping their own personality (on the mediaeval side at least) quite so firmly on a periodical that set out so deliberately to reform scholarly attitudes to history. Without some awareness of the achievement of Bloch's sharp, probing intelligence in the creation of the *Annales,* an appreciation of the force of his work of synthesis in *La Société féodale* is diminished: in this sense Bloch's work for and in the first nine or ten numbers of the *Annales* may be read as work 'Preparatory to *La Société féodale*'.

Four of Bloch's major publications provide convenient halting points for analysis and natural moments in his career when we can reflect on his direct contribution to historical scholarship: *L'Ile de France* (1913, English translation under the same title 1971), *Les Rois thaumaturges* (1924, English translation *The Royal Touch* 1973), *Les Caractères originaux de l'histoire rurale française* (1931, English translation *French Rural History* 1966) and *La Société Féodale* (1939–40, English translation *Feudal Society* 1961). We shall refer in the rest of this section to the English titles and editions, and where necessary to the translations of his collected essays under the title *Land and Work in Mediaeval Europe* (1967).

The little book on the Ile-de-France appeared before the First World War when the author was 27 years old. It is light, readable, general and far from trivial. For its date it is a remarkable production, reminiscent of the work of human geographers such as Fleure in England, wide-ranging, concerned with the soil, the language, the archaeological remains and the architecture. One chapter gives the historiographical dimension up to the nineteenth century; another deals with contemporary history and the Ile-de-France. Bloch's scholarly apparatus is splendid but his concern was often with the general questions that interest the informed citizen as much as the professional historian. How good is the spoken French of the Ile-de-France? Is there evidence for the existence of a school of Romanesque architecture there? Are not the origins of Gothic architecture shrouded in mystery? His conclusions have an important bearing on his later attitudes to historical method. He recognises that the term *Ile-de-France,* even in its limited geographical range, means different things to different men and to different historians. The linguist's Ile-de-France differs from the bounds set by the feudal lawyer. Human history is not patient of arbitrary divisions made by administrators; scholars carve out their own regions according to the nature of their disciplines. In a sense, after the years of action and of brooding of the First World War, this carving is precisely what Marc Bloch initiated.

When *L'Ile de France* appeared, Bloch was a teacher with the experience of five or six years of intense research behind him. In 1924 he was a mature scholar, battle-hardened in a cruel war, and a professor at Strasbourg. He had already indicated in 1920, as the first product of his new academic status, in a rather curious loose-knit monograph, his own selected regions for study. *Roi et serfs* (1920) is a programme rather than a book. Later criticism that he was better at serfs than kings, or that his authoritative work on the transition from classical slavery to mediaeval serfdom was never completed, should not mask the good sense of his basic choice. Kings and serfs, authority and freedom, were proper matters for reflection in the between-war period. Yet the first large-scale onslaught, *Les Rois thaumaturges, The Royal Touch,* proved a shade incongruous. The approach seemed a little old-fashioned for its day. Kern had produced his magisterial work on kingship and the right of resistance in 1914. Bloch's own review of it[9] had been a shade niggling, taking the German scholar to task for being so German! But Kern had laid down massively the lines for con-structive analysis of mediaeval kingship and it was not immediately apparent why Bloch should need well over 500 pages (including appendixes, learned notes and bibliography) to treat a topic with a flavour of the antiquarian. This is, indeed, as the subtitle states in the original French version, a study in the supernatural character attributed to royal power, particularly in France and in England. Bloch's treat-ment saves it from the charge of mere antiquarianism. There is abundant interest in medical details, the nature of the 'king's evil', the rational explanation of miraculous cures, the origins of this special royal power that touched on anthropological material proper to Frazer's *The Golden Bough.* Bloch investigates deep into the eighteenth and even into the nineteenth century the practice of touching for the king's evil. The central core of the book is nevertheless a serious study of the belief in the divinity that hedges a king and of the social implica-tions of such beliefs. He draws attention judiciously to questions that have been too much neglected. The diversity of evidence drawn on suits his mind and pen. He makes mistakes, especially in the handling of material relating to Edward the Confessor and over the question of priority, England or France, in the adoption of the custom. Much more important, he brings into serious discussion a body of problems and related evidence that breaks down artificial chronological barriers and that opens the way to a better understanding of the evolution of Western society in one of its significant attributes, its attitude to royalty. The 'curious by-way', as an English friend referred to it, turns in the hands of a first-class craftsman into a powerful contribution to the political and social history of Europe.

If kings were at the centre of Bloch's scholarly activities in the early 1920s, peasants and serfs took their place later in the decade. Politically this was a time when much of Bloch's energies went into support of the new venture that was bringing into being the International Congresses of Historical Sciences, and the first meeting of that body in Oslo in 1928 was an important event in his own development and in the development of historical studies in Europe. From the welter of activity that led among other things to the creation of two permanent institutions, the *Annales* and the congresses, Bloch drew inspiration that prompted the creation of what many would regard as his work of most long-lasting value, *Les Caractères originaux, French Rural History*. It was published in Oslo in 1931, the ultimate product of an invitation to lecture on the themes in Norway the preceding year. The result, 'mon petit livre', as Bloch calls it, proved to be one of the most helpful and thought-provoking books of the generation, as fruitful, though with a wider range and more general approach, as Tawney's great work on agrarian problems in the late mediaeval and early modern periods in England.

A splendid clarity in analysis is the dominant characteristic. Bloch locates problems in time, giving a realistic and intelligible picture of the flow of agrarian life in France from the beginnings to the time of the revolution. All the new apparatus that can be brought in is used to make a successful synthesis. Bloch is strong on the new techniques of field study, examination of regional variations in methods of agriculture, advances in knowledge concerning the shape of the fields, the nature of the plough, the harnessing of plough-beasts, the evolution of the watermill and the windmill, the use of water-power and wind-power, the methods of maintaining fertility in the soil, two-field systems, three-field systems, the provision of adequate manuring. Clarity does not lead to oversimplification, merely to an honest and open simplification necessary for the communication of general ideas on matters utterly complex in detail. His grasp of legal history and of the history of institutions is great, and his exposition at its best is worthy of Maitland. He is not so good at describing individual human beings. He is no Eileen Power, and his peasants do not come to life as hers do in *Mediaeval People*. His special strength comes in giving an accurate impression of types of men and of development in time. He is quite honest about his methods and about what is to be expected from the results. 'In the development of a discipline, there are moments when a synthesis, even if apparently premature, is of greater use than a work of analysis. In other words it is more important to state the questions than to try to answer them.'[10] The questions that he asks concern the sociological tensions of rural life quite as much as the technical triumphs. He recognises the agrarian achievements involved in providing regular food supplies for a developing population in the hazardous climate of Europe and in very subtle fashion counterpoints a vigorous analysis of the village community with a brilliant and authoritative account of seignorial lordship. By common sense and historical insight he is able at times to redress the balance of the records which were tilted solidly on the seignorial side. A village without a lord tended indeed to be a village without history. Bloch carries the story forward to the agrarian changes of the modern period, through even the French Revolution itself to the contemporary scene. He discusses in depth, with reasonable explanations, the origin of differences in the agrarian scene evident in modern France. He uses with full critical force the types of evidence available in modern estate maps, place-names, and archaeological finds to establish a proper framework for discussion of rural France. Social strands intertwine with the economic and agrarian. Some of the shrewdest pages deal with the disappearance of slavery and modifications in serfdom. Not only the agrarian structure of mediaeval France but that of the *ancien régime* is illuminated by this admirable piece of historical exposition.

Bloch himself realised that *Rural France* was an interim judgement, informed and thoughtful to be sure but in no way the last word. Throughout the 1930s, in the pages of the *Annales* and elsewhere, he added to it, prodding away at his favourite problems of currency, coinage, freedom and servitude. The influence of Henri Pirenne, *cher maître* as he used to call him, strong in the 1920s, grew stronger in the early 1930s. The *Annales* became an instrument for carrying forward the debate of the scholarly world over the shape of mediaeval economic development suggested by the great Belgian scholar. Logically and sensibly, Bloch's final substantial work, *La Société féodale* (1939–40), *Feudal Society* (1961), brought to a fine point his thinking over such development.

Postan points out that *Feudal Society* should not be read in isolation, that it concentrates and thereby complements Bloch's other studies, that it is essentially a *traité fleuve,* not the consummation and climax of the historian's career.[11] Very acutely Postan adds that among the volumes to come might well have been a major work on the history of ideas in the Middle Ages. This may well be true but must not detract from the value of the work as it is. *Feudal Society* does two essential things. It places the feudal age, or rather, as Bloch would have it, the two feudal ages AD *c.*800 to AD *c.*1050 and AD *c.*1050 to AD 1250, fair and square in the mainstream of European economic revival after the disasters of the later Roman Empire and early mediaeval period. It also gives full attention to sociological problems of great moment and urgency to the mid-twentieth-century mediaeval historian. Bloch establishes his chronological location firmly with a powerful political account of the last invasions, that is to say, the ninth- and tenth-century onslaught of Vikings, Magyars and Moslems against the Romano-German Carolingian world. Discussion of his more general themes, the conditions of life, the classes and types of men, the social bonds, the intellectual and emotional climate, fit them into proper sequence. His division of the central Middle Ages into two feudal ages did not meet universal approval but it fits well with general modern awareness of the importance of the change that came over Europe in the mid-eleventh century. The reform of the papacy, the break with the Eastern Church, the Norman Conquest of England and of Apulia, the Hilde-brandine Revolution, even the First Crusade: all these have been interpreted as massive external manifestations linked with changes that came over the inner life of Europe, its attitudes to architecture, philosophy and theology. Anselm's views of the atonement have been interpreted as a necessary product of the change from the first to the second feudal age, the movement from Epic to Romance. Other elements in Bloch's synthesis have proved fruitful and helpful to the succeeding generation. In rugged but effective fashion the mind of the reader is drawn back again and again to his main theme of social change in time. The static analysis relating the ties that bound man to man (kinship, vassalage and fiefs, the ties of dependence among the lower classes) is strengthened and made more real by the picture given, for example, of the transformation of a nobility through social custom and action into a legal class. He lays a good solid basis for understanding the growth of the traditional political organisations with their judicial attributes, the monarchies, the territorial principalities, the peace-keeping movements, the great fiefs. A shrewd summing-up of the term 'feudal', avoiding mere semantic pedantry, and comments on the fundamental characteristics of Western feudalism, round off his massive work. Disagreement in detail, some disappointment at apparent blindness to other detail, is to be expected, but there has been little but admiration for the sweep and control of the whole picture. Bloch's distinctions, sometimes crude but always useful, between feudalism and manorialism, between the ties of kindred and the ties of lordship, have been used, tested and found most valuable. He draws ideas from many communities, and indeed from many disciplines, to give us an intelligible general account of Western European development, rustic-based with mud on boots! Italy, the Mediterranean world, aspects of urban life, fit uneasily in the picture, as uneasily as they fitted in the feudal world proper. The agrarian heart of feudal Europe, France north of the Loire, much of Germany and the empire, are well under-stood and well described.

Feudal Society was published in the opening years of the war. For the remaining four years of his life Bloch was busy adjusting to his new life in Vichy France and then to perilous activity in the Resistance. His pen was still far from idle. The impressive, at times testy, *L'Etrange défaite* was written in 1940–1, though not published until long after the war. He also left behind him the unfinished manuscript, *Apologie pour l'histoire, ou Métier d'historien,* published in 1949 thanks to the efforts of Bloch's friend and colleague Lucien Febvre. This proved to be the first work to be translated and published in English – in 1954 with an introduction by Joseph Strayer. Bloch was 58 when he was shot; and close on nine of his mature years had been spent in one way or another under active war conditions. In volume and integrity, his written memorial bears favourable comparison with all his con-temporary scholars.

From his earliest days Bloch was conscious of his role as historian, and conscious also of the need to justify it and to explain his methods. Much of his early book on the Ile-de-France is taken up with comment on the material available and on the use and limitations of the evidence that can be brought to bear on the problems. He is aware of a degree of high moral purpose behind the craft. As editor of *Annales* he was self-conscious almost to a fault over questions of technique and method. His reviewing had a mixture of confidence in what was to be looked for, courtesy, and yet sharpness if standards were not perceived and maintained. Clarity of analysis was one of his consistent criteria. Asking the right questions was perhaps the principal and most significant. An inexperienced young researcher received the courteous but devastating comment that 'better questioned, the documents would probably have yielded more'.[12]

Bloch was interested in new techniques, such as air photography, but cautious in his appraisal of conclusions drawn from them. Undue con-centration on the meaning of terms (an obsession of the 1930s) alarmed him: to be useful terminology had to be used systematically but not to the point where system gave way to distortion. Much of the con-temporary debate on feudalism worried him for that reason. He was prepared to recognise the fief as an essential constituent of the feudal world; but there was more to feudalism than the fief. As a form of society he placed it as an intermediary stage between tribalism and the state, but not an essential stage; and he ranged far outside Europe, particularly to Japan, to sustain and test that basic thesis. His abstrac-tions were related to hard historical evidence and not allowed to become unreal. A study of institutions that neglected the study of society was to him a dead discipline; and the study of society involved the study of men, their status, their attitudes, their modes of life and thought. Class structure and the problem of serfdom occupied much of his attention.

Obsession with terminology was one thing, clarification quite another. He aimed at precision in the use of phrases such as 'natural economy' or 'closed economy'. The questions 'how can we know?' and 'how can we communicate knowledge?' were on his lips as often as the question 'what do we know?'. Conclusions that were to all appearances predetermined received his harshest strictures. He was modest in confessing ignorance, whether on the big things such as the truth of Pirenne's great thesis, or on the relatively small such as the precise meaning of the term *mansus*. Much of his groping towards a justification and explanation of an historian's job appears as he reflects on other people's work. Fittingly, it was in a note of appraisal of Pirenne's *Histoire de Belgique* that Bloch hit out his early definition that above all else history was a science of movement.[13] Human settlement and human thought were pre-eminently the true concern of the historian. For problems such as that of settlement, Bloch called for co-operation among the various disciplines in full awareness of the methodological complications involved, for example, in place-name study or in matters concerning currency, the use of gold, the establishment of a working gold-to-silver ratio. Technological advances in the harnessing of plough-beasts in the Middle Ages, in the introduction of watermills and windmills, in the handling of the agrarian routine, were commented on by Bloch in the pages of the *Annales* and steadily absorbed into his own body of ideas. Bloch's knowledge grew and his ideas developed visibly in the *Annales* of the 1930s, but his attitude towards method remained consistent throughout. Institutions were to be studied because our records deal with institutions but in the last resort society itself found means of creating institutions to satisfy its needs. Soaked in relevant material, Bloch, the conscientious editor, prepared himself for the writing of *Feudal Society*. He also fitted himself for important reflection on historical method.

The first of his wartime productions, *Strange Defeat,* will be read by all serious historians of the campaigns of 1940. Bloch gives full weight to faults in morale and education in French society as well as in the army. Something of a poet emerges in him and he proves able to convey the taste of the defeat he has lived through: he knew at first hand the contrast with the hard-earned success of 1918. He was self-conscious, a shade diffident about this attempt at contemporary history. In his own defence he invokes Pirenne, who had declared that it was the first duty of an historian to interest himself in life. Bloch also justifies himself by stating that his training as an historian has taught him from the study of many documents how to differentiate truth from falsehood. In those two *apologia* are embodied the essentials of

Bloch's straightforward philosophy of history: always to be interested in life and to seek the truth. It is in his posthumous little book, unfinished yet revealing, *The Historian's Craft,* however, that we get our clearest insight into Bloch's beliefs on method and approach.

Historians are not always effective when they try to philosophise about their discipline. They are so used to walking the perilous tight-rope between abstraction and reflection of past reality that they condition themselves to reject the essential abstract and general element needed to sustain the philosopher's balance. Few historians (Collingwood is a conspicuous British exception) are professional philosophers. Bloch therefore planned his little book, as he called it himself, as a simple 'memorandum of a craftsman'. As it stands (Lefebvre in his introduction gives some insight into the original plan) it contains four reasonably substantial chapters on History, Men and Time; Historical Observation; Historical Criticism; and Historical Analysis; together with a fragment of a fifth chapter on Historical Causation. The old problems of the use of history and the position of history in the galaxy of contemporary sciences are dealt with in a short but powerful introduction. Bloch's approach is that of the thoughtful humanist. He acknowledges the will to understand rather than the will merely to know as the motive force behind all serious science. He resembles Croce and Collingwood in recognising the relative novelty of history as we now understand it, a science in movement but 'like all those which have the human spirit for their object . . . a science in its infancy'.[14] The rejection in the scientific world generally of the old Comtian certainties had brought history to a new point of importance. Twentieth-century science was becoming more flexible, truth more relative; and Bloch argues stoutly that the uncertainties of our own historical science should not be concealed from the world. A shade mystically he finds in the uncertainties themselves the historian's *raison d'être.* When it comes to direct exposition of his themes, however, the uncertainties disappear. There is an engaging direct honesty about Bloch which is the principal source of strength of all his work. An intelligent man talks to you directly and frankly. His basic view of history was ostensibly simple. To Bloch, history was 'the science of men in time'.[15] His handling of the theme, however, was far from simple. He disliked the need to split up history into periods and centuries, convenient, to be sure, but often misleading. In a sense he went further along the idealist path than even his contemporary, Collingwood. The idea of one, and just one, serious science of men in time, requires us to join the study of the dead and the living. We understand the present by the past and the past by the present. Sometimes imperfectly, even rawly formulated, Bloch's humanist passion, miraculously preserved in the grim days of 1942–4, shines through his analysis. History is the intellectual force which can over-ride the specious distinctions which men make between the past and the present. Bloch is exceptionally powerful on two aberrations, as he sees them, of his contemporary colleagues: the 'demon of origins'[16] and an obsessive desire to make judgements, usually with political or religious objectives in view. It is good to look for origins but something vital is lost when the present, and awareness of the present, are divorced from the past. Origins do not explain; and explanation and understanding, not judgement, were Bloch's objectives.

The involvement of the present in the past is one of the strong strands running through Bloch's discussion of the nature of history. He recognises fully the difficulties. Men resemble their times rather than their fathers', and hard training is needed to effect sensible observation of the past. The past is unchanging, but knowledge of the past changes from day to day, from thought to thought. Mere passive observation, even assuming that were possible, is not enough. Some technical competence is essential, and it is the need to acquire such competence that has helped to make history so difficult a science. Method as well as knowledge is required. To Bloch himself, a mediaeval cartulary made splendid reading because he knew what questions to bring to it. Modern critical method, as Bloch himself says, can be traced back to Mabillon and his contemporaries, men born in the 1620s and 1630s who, if not themselves Cartesian, were trained in the Cartesian spirit of inquiry. Bloch shows some of the passion of the serious-minded survivor from war and disaster when he arraigns those to whom the critical method has become an end in itself. It is good to show one's tracks, to provide insight into one's own evidence, to write an accurate and helpful footnote. We have no right to make any assertion which cannot be verified. Against that, writes Bloch in a fine purple passage, 'there is no waste more criminal than that of erudition running, as it were, in neutral gear, nor any pride more vainly misplaced than that in a tool valued as an end in itself'.[17] Yet it is that same critical method that gives the historian his standing as a scientist, that enables him to make serious investigations of fraud and error. From the past there is no reliable witness in the absolute sense, only reliable testimony. Awareness of the difficulties of the critical method did not lead to despair. Bloch never wavered in his belief that the truth would out. In his testament he asked that there should be inscribed over his tomb (echoes of Hildebrand but with a vital difference) the words *dilexi veritatem*: I have loved truth. Great truths, within the historical framework of question and answer and evidence, can be revealed. It is often only the most immediate antecedent causes that are rendered uncertain by 'the psychology of evidence'.[18] The logic of the critical method does not lead to a denial of truth, but to the establishment of a plausible range from the infinitely probable to the barely credible. Historical criticism resembles other scientific probes in providing means for estimating the probable and improbable, though the gradations of degree of truth are subtler and more difficult to disentangle because historians are dealing with human situations.[19] In the last resort Bloch comes back to his 'men of flesh and bone' who rest at the centre of serious historical inquiry: he comes close to Collingwood in positing human consciousness as the proper subject-matter of history.

In a phrase of outstanding nobility (when all circumstances, including his own fate, are borne in mind), Bloch describes understanding as 'the beacon light of our studies'.[20] The historian's duty is not to judge but to understand. Bloch comments drily that the habit of passing judgements 'leads to a loss of taste for explanations'.[21] There is nothing passive about understanding (as there could be among those who attempt to follow Ranke's advice to describe things as they were). The involvement of the historian is wholehearted. He has to find an adequate terminology to express himself clearly and to make his thoughts intelligible to others. He has to be courageous in his search for causes and in his recognition that such causes can be complicated and multiple. With man himself the greatest variable in nature, serious explanation and serious investigation of historical causation cannot be simple. And yet there is a simple integrity to the argument in *The Historian's Craft* that appeals and holds. The value of the critical method is recognised. The novelty of the historical discipline, the science of men in time, is acknowledged. The difficulties are appreciated, but so is the purpose, the better understanding of men in time. In the light of his career, his achievements, and his fate, the passion of Bloch's search for truth and his calm certainty that it can be achieved emerge in all their simplicity as qualities of supreme inspiration to the succeeding generation.

NOTES: CHAPTER 8

1 Paris (1957), pp. 17–18.
2 *L'Etrange défaite*, p. 224.
3 *Souvenirs de Guerre, 1914–15* (1969), p. 16.
4 ibid., pp. 49–50.
5 ibid., p. 12. 'Nothing unnerves me as much as the feeling that they are concealing the truth from me.'
6 *L'Etrange défaite*, p. 28.
7 *History* (1968), p. 269.
8 *Annales*, vol. VI (1934), pp. 582–4.
9 *Revue Historique* (1921), p. 247.
10 *French Rural History*, p. vii.
11 Introduction to the English translation, *Feudal Society*, p. xii.
12 *Annales*, vol. III (1931), p. 259.
13 *Annales*, vol. IV (1932), p. 480: 'l'histoire est, avant tout, science de mouvement'.

14   *The Historian's Craft*, p. 13.
15   ibid., p. 27.
16   ibid., p. 31.
17   ibid., p. 86.
18   ibid., p. 103.
19   ibid., p. 151 .
20   ibid., p. 143.
21   ibid., p. 140.

NOTE ON FURTHER READING

The essay 'Marc Bloch' by R. R. Davies, *History*, vol. 52 (1967), pp. 265–86, provides a convenient and important introduction to Bloch's career and writings for English readers. Full references are given in it to earlier tributes, and the author pays special attention to the translations which had recently appeared when he wrote of Bloch's key works of agrarian history, *French Rural History* (trans. Janet Sondheimer, 1966) and *Land and Work in Mediaeval Europe* (trans. J. E. Anderson, 1967). Both translations were published by Routledge & Kegan Paul, who have more recently still produced English renderings by J. E. Anderson of *The Ile-de-France* (1970) and *The Royal Touch* (1973). Bloch's fragmentary but significant memoirs of the First World War have been published as *Souvenirs de Guerre, 1914–15* (1969). Bloch's skill as an historian is most readily appreciated by reading *Feudal Society*, and as a thinker about the nature of history by reading *The Historian's Craft*. Both works are discussed in the text. Among secondary works on Marc Bloch, the following essays are valuable: J. A. Raftis, 'Marc Bloch's comparative method and the rural history of Mediaeval England', *Mediaeval Studies*, vol. XXIV (1962), pp. 349–68, and W. H. Sewell, 'Marc Bloch and the logic of comparative history', *History and Theory*, vol. VI (1967), pp. 208–18.

9 *Lewis Bernstein Namier*

Lewis Bernstein Namier was born in 1888, in Polish Russia, of Jewish parents named Niemirowski; educated privately, at the London School of Economics, and at Balliol College, Oxford. Took British nationality in 1913 and changed his name; spent the war years at the Foreign Office and devoted most of the 1920s to research into eighteenth-century parliamentary history. Published in 1929 *The Structure of Politics at the Accession of George III*, followed in 1930 by *England in the Age of the American Revolution*. The following year was appointed professor of modern history in the University of Manchester, holding the chair until retirement in 1951. In the 1930s became increasingly involved in political activity and published numerous reviews and essays on diplomatic history, many of them subsequently reprinted in book form. Knighted in 1952, spent the last nine years of his life editing *The House of Commons, 1754–90* for the History of Parliament Trust. Died in August 1960.

There are not many historians whose names have been used to describe a school or an historical method: we do not often talk of Stubbsites or Gibbonists, of Actonism or Maitlandism. Yet for many years, historians have been applauded or censured as Namierites and, as an approach to history, Namierism continues to conjure up strong responses.[1] The two books on which Namier's reputation was based came out in quick succession in 1929 and 1930.[2] In the following year he was appointed to the chair of modern history in the University of Manchester. Recognition then came speedily. Professor Richard Cobb has written how, as a schoolboy at Shrewsbury in 1934, he fell under the spell of the Namier approach.[3] In 1953, when the *Times Literary Supplement* surveyed the outstanding books of the half-century 1900–50, it reprinted the original review of the *Structure*. E. H. Carr referred to him in 1961 as 'the greatest British historian to emerge since the First World War', and nine years later Professor Arthur Marwick wrote that 'there is agreement that the great man of the twentieth century is L. B. Namier'.[4] In the 1950s and 1960s, the influence of

Sir Lewis Namier was so great that almost every historian writing on eighteenth-century England felt under an obligation to establish in his preface where he stood in relation to the master's work – whether as a disciple or a revisionist. At times his influence seemed to reach almost the point of parody. An article in an American journal entitled 'Sir Lewis Namier considered' was followed by another entitled ' "Sir Lewis Namier considered" considered'. It looked as though the authors had stumbled on the ideal self-perpetuating academic controversy.[5]

In many ways it is surprising that such a man should have had so marked an influence upon British historiography. First, he was born and brought up in Galicia and, though he lived in England from the age of 19 onwards, he retained a pronounced foreign accent.[6] Namier was all his life something of an outsider: he was a double exile, a foreigner and a Jew. He had nothing of the casualness and little of the *bonhomie* cultivated by many English academics: in consequence he was frequently obsessive and occasionally tedious. Secondly, the period to which he devoted most of his energy – the eighteenth century – has never been a particularly fashionable area of study. Schools tended then, as they do now, to concentrate on the Tudors and Stuarts or jump to the nineteenth century. Yet Namier's work on the 1750s and 1760s produced effects which were felt in many other periods of English history, as well as in other disciplines.

The avowed intention of his two great books was to prepare the ground for an examination of the political life of the early decades of George III's reign. But, as Namier himself confessed, his sense of time was faulty, other occupations supervened and his love of detail took over. In the end, only the foundations were laid: the building was left for others to erect. In assessing Namier's work, therefore, we must bear in mind that it was incomplete.

Namier's approach to his task was almost clinically Cartesian – to divest himself of all previous assumptions about the period. Commentators have remarked that his foreign origins may have helped in this – he escaped soaking in the liberal and Whiggish traditions so prevalent in early twentieth-century England. Together with his close friend, Romney Sedgwick,[7] Namier dismantled, piece by piece, the traditional interpretation of the 1760s as the period in which the young George III, assisted by his mother and his tutor Lord Bute, strove to restore royal absolutism, aided by massive corruption and by a clique of subservient politicians known as the King's Friends. This was, in itself, enough to cause substantial rewriting, but the wider implications were even more controversial. The old explanation had provided a framework for understanding and interpreting the American Revolution: the Rockingham Whigs and American rebels had been seen in common opposition to tyranny and despotism. But if George III was guiltless, how had this interpretation arisen? Namier was forced to challenge and discredit Horace Walpole and, above all, Edmund Burke, on whose writings the original case rested.[8] He dismissed with contempt the claim to a unique political contribution on behalf of the Rockingham Whigs, whose spokesman Burke had been: Namier, in reaction, was excessively hard on the Rockinghams, regarding them as a self-important faction. This sent shock-waves through the Whig-liberal tradition. The Rockinghams had been described by Macaulay as 'men worthy to have charged by the side of Hampden at Chalgrove, or to have exchanged the last embrace with Russell in Lincoln's Inn Fields': Macaulay's nephew, G. M. Trevelyan, three years before Namier's *Structure* appeared, had described the conflict between Whigs and Tories as 'the most lasting element in our public life from the days of Clarendon and Shaftesbury to the days of Salisbury and Gladstone'.[9] Namier swept it all aside. The history of the period could well be written, he maintained, without reference to party or party names at all. As for Burke's *Thoughts on the Cause of the Present Discontents*, Namier dismissed it as a 'polemical pamphlet . . . which has often been treated as if it were an impartial verdict on George III'.[10]

The reception of the *Structure* was not unanimous. It received a somewhat disdainful notice from Richard Lodge, who remarked that the Newcastle papers had long been known as a dust-heap and that Namier had 'rescued from the dust-heap an immense number of details with regard to parliamentary representation'.[11] But, by and large, Namier's new interpretation carried all before it. One reviewer wrote that the author of the *Structure* had 'destroyed more legends and modified more preconceived ideas than any historian of this generation . . . the whole picture of the political structure of England at this time is altered profoundly'.[12] If, as Namier subsequently wrote, the test of a great historian was that, after he had done his work, 'others should not be able to practise within its sphere in the terms of the preceding era', he had, at one stroke, established his own claim to that distinction.[13]

Yet even with a triumph on this scale there remained difficulties and not all the pieces of the new interpretation fell into place. Some objected that Namier was better at demolishing old legends than at suggesting what should replace them. As the 1930s and 1940s proceeded, with no sign of the further work Namier had promised, this view gained weight.[14] Eighteenth-century historiography began to resemble a battlefield: it was clear that furious and bloody encounters had taken place, whiffs of exploded legends and interpretations swirled like gun-smoke, the corpses of vanquished historians lay thick upon the ground, yet it was not easy to see in full perspective what the outcome had been.

In detail, too, there were criticisms. It was argued that, in acquitting George III of the melodramatic charge of attempting to subvert the constitution, Namier had gone to the other extreme and denied that there was anything questionable about the king's conduct. But the decision to promote Lord Bute to the Treasury, however understandable, was at the very least an error of judgement, and might be regarded as a breach of the conventions of the constitution.[15] Namier's description of the King's Friends as embryonic civil servants was felt by some critics to be positively misleading and anachronistic.[16] Most persistently questioned were Namier's views on party. Though he had asserted that the political life of the period could be fully described 'without ever using a party denomination', it was notable that he never attempted to do so himself. On the contrary, his account of Shropshire politics, which formed the fifth section of the *Structure*, opened with the observation that the county was something of an oddity in that 'situated in what then was the Tory belt' it returned at least eight Whig MPs.[17] In his later years, Namier was persuaded to accept that his conclusions on party held true for the whole eighteenth century, but a vast amount of work in recent years has testified that party remained an important ingredient in the political life of the nation.[18]

This reinterpretation of the central years of the eighteenth century, which was Namier's greatest historiographical achievement, does not suffice to explain why he became so important and contentious a figure. To understand that, we must look at his advocacy of an historical technique which could be applied to other fields, and at the challenging nature of Namier's general views on man and his history.

The technique came to be known as structural analysis. It was an attempt to get away from the purely narrative approach to history, to stop the machine in order to examine its component parts and its functioning. The main feature of the *Structure* was therefore a detailed investigation of the composition of the House of Commons, together with a further investigation of the electoral process by which men entered Parliament. Namier warned his readers not to begrudge time spent on details, which were often revealing and instructive. Interested in the cogs as well as the machine, Namier devoted loving care to the reconstitution of the lives of hitherto obscure Members of Parliament: a final chapter, fascinating if inconsequential, traced the careers of 'parliamentary beggars' – men who needed to be in Parliament as an insurance against arrest for debt.

Namier's impatience with accepted myths and his zeal for exactness led him to quantify his findings more than his predecessors had done. When Horace Walpole asserted that, at the general election of 1761, 'West Indians, conquerors, nabobs and admirals' attacked every borough, Namier set himself to enumerate how many in each category had, in fact, been returned. When Sir Nathaniel Wraxall in his *Memoirs* repeated the old story that the ratification of the Peace of

Paris had been secured by bribery on the grand scale, Namier turned to examine the secret service accounts.

Much of this information could be obtained only by collective endeavour. Only a systematic and organised search of archives could ferret out the detailed evidence required; only the pooling of information could prevent historians from wasting their time by repeating what others had done; only the sharing of resources and facilities could provide scholars with the assistance they needed. The proposal for a national History of Parliament, supported by public funds, therefore arose naturally out of Namier's research approach, and he advocated it with enthusiasm. This, too, had its critics. Some saw it as a sinister attempt at academic empire-building, whereby Namier would preside over a vast patronage machine, much as the Duke of Newcastle had done; others suspected that Namier would steal the credit for their contributions. Nor was Namier's zeal for collective undertakings in principle shared by all: it was objected that such enterprises might undermine the individual responsibility for findings which is essential to true scholarship.[19]

Somewhat surprisingly, a major historiographical conflict developed over the technique of structural analysis. Enthusiastic exponents hailed it as an innovation which would revolutionise the writing of history, freeing the historian from reliance upon previous work and enabling him to investigate problems in a more direct, precise and impartial manner. Distinguished work making use of the technique was certainly produced.[20] Critics argued, sometimes with passion, that it was a technique that might corrupt historical study. It could easily deteriorate into detail for the sake of detail and, in the hands of historians less gifted than Namier, become the instrument for the cultivation of minute cabbage-patches. Indeed, with the general public, Namierism acquired something of a reputation as myopic peering at the ever smaller. Sir Herbert Butterfield, in *George III and the Historians*, devoted a whole chapter to 'the disease of the structural historian', arguing that it might produce atomised and splintered history, devoid alike of meaning and charm.

In retrospect, it is clear that structural analysis was neither so novel nor so baneful as was maintained. As a technique it can be traced back at least as far as Edmund Burke, who incorporated into his *Reflections on the French Revolution* a celebrated analysis of the membership of the National Assembly in 1789. In the period immediately before Namier began his researches, Edward and Annie Porritt and W. T. Laprade had published work involving similar techniques and drawing upon the categories of evidence which Namier was to exploit so successfully. A list of theses in progress, printed in *History* in January 1928, shows two on the personnel of Elizabethan Parliaments, under the direction of Professor J. E. Neale.[21]

The root cause of the misunderstanding seems to have been the assumption that Namier intended structural analysis to be the alternative to narrative history. We have seen that it was meant rather as a preliminary and as an adjunct. In his essay on 'History', which contains some of his most considered reflections, Namier made his position clear:

> As history deals with concrete events, fixed in time and space, narrative is its basic medium − but guided by analytic selection of what to narrate . . . what matters in history is the great outline and the significant detail; what must be avoided is the deadly morass of irrelevant narrative.[22]

As advice, this could hardly be bettered, yet the fact remains that Namier never succeeded in completing 'the great outline'. There must be some suspicion that this was not merely the result of his personal problems − the 'defective sense of time' to which he referred − but the inescapable outcome of a method of inquiry which made too heavy demands on the historian and which, by fragmenting the past, rendered it very difficult to construct any overall synthesis.

An historian's views on human nature and conduct can never be a matter for his private life alone. It may be that an engineer, a chemist or an astronomer can operate while keeping his professional and private views quite separate. The historian never can. He deals with the human mind, and his assumptions about its working are bound to affect the quality of his explanations and, indeed, the value which he attaches to historical study.

With most historians, these assumptions are neither identified nor made explicit, though they exist just the same. With Namier, they were not merely avowed, but brandished and flaunted. Deep within him was the desire to provoke and he could rarely resist the temptation to expound his opinions. Much of the controversy surrounding him stems from this source.

Namier grew up in the early 1900s at precisely the time that Freud's views on the importance of the subconscious were winning wide acceptance. In the 1920s he consulted psychoanalysts in an attempt to ease some of his emotional difficulties. Though the sessions were of no great benefit to him, Namier retained confidence in the theories and he incorporated Freudian explanations into his writing. A very explicit avowal of them is to be found in his essay on 'Human nature in politics':

> We have learnt about fixations in both individuals and groups, about psychological displacements and projections, and the externalization

of unresolved inner conflicts. A man's relation, for instance, to his
father or to his nurse may determine the pattern of his later
political conduct without his being in the least conscious of the con-
nexion; and self-deception concerning the origin and character of
his seemingly intellectual tenets enables him to deceive others . . .[23]

Much of what was often regarded as Namier's cynicism stemmed
from this basic assumption. It followed, for example, that historians
should be peculiarly on their guard against the rationalisations which
men employ to cloak their motives – hence Namier's deep mistrust of
ideologies and the zest with which he pursued and destroyed the legends
fostered by politicians and their supporters; hence his emphasis on
what politicians did rather than on what they said, and his comparative
lack of interest in the debates of the House of Commons – the last
place where the real springs of human conduct would be revealed, save
by accident. This suspicion of ideologies encouraged his distaste for
radicals, progressives, revolutionaries and 'do-gooders', and imparted a
distinctively 'Tory' bias to much of his writing. Men, in his view, convinced themselves that they were thinking when all they were doing
was to 'wobble with the brain', and on another occasion he wrote that
'the correlation of human activities to their avowed purposes is in
most spheres so dim and uncertain that one wonders how anything
is ever achieved'.[24]
    To many of Namier's readers these opinions seemed refreshingly
honest. If man's powers of reason were more limited than had been
supposed, if his motives were even more self-oriented than most had
thought, it was better to face the fact than to live in a fool's paradise.
And, in Namier's hands, psychoanalysis often became a tool for
delicate and revealing insights into character. On the other hand, a
large and probably increasing number of readers were irritated by
these reiterated and rather shrill assertions. First, as the star of Freud
began to wane, Namier's total acceptance seemed hasty and some of
his judgements crude. Secondly, there were critics who argued that
the logical outcome of Namier's views must be to render all history
meaningless. The historian, occupied as he is with his attempt to
explain the meaning of the past, is peculiarly likely to be haunted by
the fear that perhaps it has no meaning at all. I am sure that John
Brooke is right in suspecting that Namier had his own misgivings.[25]
His public utterances were almost deliberately casual:

Possibly there is no more sense in human history than in the changes
of the season or the movement of the stars; or if sense there be, it
escapes our perception. But the historian, when watching strands
interlace and entwine and their patterns intersect, seeks for the

logic of situations and the rhythm of events which invest them at least with a determinist meaning.[26]

This nonchalance, real or assumed, seems to have touched a raw nerve in others. Sir Herbert Butterfield, speaking from a Christian standpoint, protested against Namier's dismissal of ideologies in tones of genuine anguish:

> The reaction against ideas . . . is a thing that may be carried too far . . . It should not leave us desolate and bewildered in a land entirely without shapes and contours – leave us with a feeling that in fact there is no larger course of history.[27]

There were other objections to Namier's views, less lofty, but no less effective. Namier's arguments, his antagonists observed, must apply to Namier himself. Supposing one postulated a rootless intellectual from Eastern Europe, disinherited by his father, who settled in England and made himself the intellectual master of the most stable society in modern English history – the Hanoverian regime – would it be surprising if he should manifest a marked indifference to those forces that were undermining that society; indeed, that in the course of his lifetime, he should appear almost incapable of contemplating reform, radicalism, American rebels or the growth of party? Namier would not be the first historian to have succumbed to the charm of eighteenth-century England, to be captivated by Capability Brown.

Against some of these strictures Namier defended himself staunchly. He had been accused, he wrote, of 'taking the mind out of history':

> It certainly seems impossible to attach to conscious political thought the importance which was ascribed to it a hundred, or even fifty, years ago. History is primarily, and to a growing extent, made by man's mind and nature; but his mind does not work with the rationality that was once deemed its noblest attribute – which does not, however, mean that it necessarily works any worse . . .[28]

I am not certain that Namier realised the full significance of what he was asserting in this passage. If the world is *essentially* an irrational or non-rational one, it is difficult to see any sensible role for lecturers and historians, or indeed for discussion of any kind. Infantile experiences merely confront each other in blank incomprehension. Fortunately Namier, as an historian, did not push his logic to the extreme:

> Although we know that man's actions are mostly conditioned by factors other than reason, in practice we have to assume their

rational character until the contrary has been specifically established.[29]

An example of Namier's work in which his theory of motivation is
of more than common importance is the lecture delivered to the
British Academy in 1944 on 'The revolution of the intellectuals in
1848'.[30] The choice both of subject and title was highly significant.
Namier went back deliberately to an episode in German history which
had traditionally been interpreted as a humiliation for liberal intellectuals, revealed in the moment of crisis as empty rhetoricians,
deficient in experience and common sense. In many ways, the lecture
was one of Namier's most powerful and impressive performances.
Focusing in the main on that disturbed region of Eastern Europe where
the old Prussian, Russian and Austrian Empires met over the corpse
of partitioned Poland, Namier was revisiting the Europe of his youth
and showed the easy mastery of one ruminating on his own local and
family history. He seemed always to possess the critical fact or the
telling illustration. His range of sources was vast, his command of
languages – French, German and Polish – imposing. The conclusion
was, of course, predictable: 'the revolution of the intellectuals
exhausted itself without achieving concrete results'.
    Despite the undoubted brilliance of the lecture, it revealed something
of Namier's deficiencies. The construction was idiosyncratic, not to say
rambling: the inability to control his material, which critics had
noticed in his two great books on English history, was still apparent.
The revolutionaries themselves were given short shrift. In the opening
paragraph of the preface to the *Structure* in 1929, Namier had
deplored the triteness of constitutional discussions – 'which usually
happens when masses act but are supposed to reason'. Fifteen years
later, the German masses came in for the same dismissive treatment:

> The mob had come out in revolt, moved by passions and distress
> rather than by ideas: they had no articulate aims, and no one will
> ever be able to supply a rational explanation of what it was they
> fought for, or what made them fight.

One does not feel that Namier had made a very determined attempt
to find out. And, indeed, the extract draws attention to an oddity in
his own thinking – that despite his mistrust of political theory and his
contempt for intellectuals, his own definition of what constitutes a
'political idea' remains an unreasonably cerebral one. Of course the
masses rarely express their grievances in articulate statements of intent,
but the ideas that help to change society are often comparatively simple
ones – why should peasants be forced to work other people's land, why

should Austrians rule Italians, why should women not have equal rights with men?

Namier's attack upon the German intellectuals also involved him in certain difficulties. Writing under the immediate influence of the Second World War, he was anxious to demonstrate, not merely that German intellectuals had been ineffective, but that they had cherished unpleasantly brutal sentiments of national domination. First Namier argued that nations are made by force, not by ideas. This was a false antithesis, derived from an over-mechanistic approach: if ideas are of no real importance, why should nations wish to be united at all? Namier was confusing means with ends. Secondly, he poured scorn on liberals who wished to see Germany united 'sword in hand'. In particular, he castigated Jordan's crude and chauvinistic speech calling for a healthy German national egoism, based upon 'the right of the stronger, the right of conquest'. These, remarked Namier severely, were principles in which the German intellectuals revelled, 'but which other nations . . . would hesitate to proclaim'. But Namier himself, in an earlier passage which the reader was unlikely to have forgotten, had declared that 'nations are freed, united or broken by blood and iron, and not by a generous application of liberty and tomato-sauce'. This was no great eminence from which to rebuke the German liberals for practising *realpolitik* and smacked too much of Satan reproving sin to be wholly convincing.

Namier's theory of human conduct seems too rigid. If it is true, as A. J. P. Taylor and others asserted,[31] that he took a cynical view of human behaviour, this did not necessarily derive from Freudian psychoanalysis, which would admit the possibility of self-sacrificing actions, even if the deeper motivation was a subconscious desire to win favour with a dead mother or appease an angry father. Most historians are content to work on the general principle that in every individual there is a mixture of altruism and self-interest, that since it varies from man to man and from circumstance to circumstance no general formula for the proportions can be suggested, and that it is this very mixture of motivation that helps to make history so fascinating a subject. In an Oliver Cromwell, a Chatham or a Gladstone, we see in grand terms that clash of interests to be found in all of us. As for Namier's refusal to credit that ideals or principles could sway actions, it was strangely at odds with his own devotion to the cause of Zionism.

Namier left evidence that his own interest in the study of history was aroused when, as a boy, he read a letter addressed to a relative and was intrigued at the difference between the writer's assessment of the situation and his own.[32] The profession of historian gives one a splendid excuse for reading other people's letters with a clear conscience, indeed in the call of duty; and it is certainly true that Namier was at his best in close commentary on letters, whether he was dealing with Napoleon's correspondence with Marie-Louise, or inferring from George Grenville's letters to Bute the secret wish to replace him.[33]

A second motive was the need to work out some of the tensions of his family and personal life. The two changes of name are significant. Arriving in England as Ludwik Bernstein, an obvious Jew, he changed it in 1910 to Naymier, derived from his Polish grandfather's name of Niemirowski, but retaining an unmistakably foreign flavour. Three years later, it was further Anglicised to Namier – surely an attempt to bridge the gap between Galicia and Balliol College, Oxford, his own past and present.

There is a passage in *England* in which Namier expounds the basic content of political history.[34] In view of his interest in psychoanalysis, one might have expected him to point to conflict or the struggle for power between individuals. Instead, he insisted that it was 'the relationship of groups of men to plots of land' – and then, as though perceiving that this was not a totally convincing definition, he added, defensively, that even in modern urban society land was of greater importance than was often supposed. He ended with a declaration that there was 'some well-nigh mystic power' in land ownership – a place in the world in which a man is rooted, 'the superiority of a tree to a log'. Namier was the log who wished to be a tree. He felt acutely his father's action in disinheriting him from the Polish estate that was his birthright. Hence the attraction for him, as a man, of the landed gentry and, as an historian, of the great houses of Hanoverian England.

As a young man, Namier may have felt contempt for the anxiety of his parents to pass themselves off as Polish gentry, but he absorbed a good deal of their aspirations. In an early essay, he developed an almost lyrical description of the landed estates of Eastern Europe – 'centres of high culture and mainstays of economic life . . . They resembled Roman villas in semi-barbaric lands. Their inhabitants read the works and thought the thoughts of the most advanced civilisation in the midst of an illiterate peasantry.' It is impossible, as one reads this, not to be reminded of Chatsworth and Blenheim, of Stowe and Wentworth Woodhouse. In a later passage, Namier revealed a streak of sentimentality when paying tribute to the tenacity of the peasantry: 'they can make and unmake governments . . . The peasant has conquered.' Here Namier was led astray by his own liberal decency: it did not occur to him that totalitarian governments would shoot the peasants and drive off their cattle.[35]

Since his death in 1960, Namier has fallen into some disfavour. In part this is the natural reaction which most writers and artists must expect. But there are more particular reasons in Namier's case. His 'Tory' sentiments fit uneasily into an increasingly democratic and egalitarian world. Interest has shifted from the aristocrats and gentry who fascinated him to other groups with which he was little concerned. His technique of historical investigation has been so completely absorbed into the general methodology of historians that they rarely feel under an obligation to salute the man who helped to pioneer it.

In many respects, this reassessment is welcome and salutary. Namier, like most of us, was capable of pushing his arguments to unreasonable lengths, and he rode his prejudices hard. It is right that his excesses be pointed out and his conclusions modified. At times, however, there are indications that the reaction is unbalanced and the prefatory renunciations of Namier and all his wicked ways are in danger of becoming routine and tedious. Can Namier be blamed if his influence became disproportionate? It is asking a lot of a man to be both expounder and critic, architect and demolition expert.

Namier is said, for example, to have taken an absurdly limited view of the political nation of eighteenth-century England, restricting himself to Westminster politicians and country-house correspondents. His well-known remark that the political life of the period could be explored through 'that marvellous microcosm, the British House of Commons' is regarded as a quaint demonstration of class prejudice and élitism. It is worth noting, however, that in this passage Namier put the term 'political nation' into inverted commas – a device we all use for drawing attention to difficulties of definition which we do not wish to discuss at the moment.[36]

Many of the charges advanced against him are really aimed at the period to which he belonged. When Namier was born, Bismarck was still in office and Mr Gladstone had another term as prime minister ahead of him. Elitism is a charge that can be levelled against most historians of that generation – if it is thought worth doing. It did not occur to many of them that rioters, smugglers, frame-breakers, pirates, strikers and gin-drinkers were of much historical interest or importance – nor, before the proliferation of record offices, was information about their multifarious activities easy to come by. Richard Cobb noted the distaste with which Namier once greeted the suggestion that a post-graduate might work on the *sans-culottes*.[37]

In the context of his own day, however, Namier's approach broke fresh ground. In 1928 he published what was, in effect, a prospectus for a Dictionary of Parliamentary Biography, to be undertaken as a great national co-operative enterprise.[38] He began by criticising the undue attention still paid by historians to kings, statesmen and wars: 'biographies of famous men still hold the field, though hero-worship is no longer the creed of the writers'. He went on to suggest the need for studies of humbler politicians, businessmen, administrators and the like. The article was entitled 'The biography of ordinary men'. Today it may seem laughable to regard the gentlemen who made up an eighteenth-century House of Commons as ordinary men, but it is a reminder how quickly historical assumptions change. It also suggests that more recent investigations into ever more obscure and humble individuals may represent an extension of 'Namierite' methods rather than a repudiation of them.

It is surprisingly hard to reach a balanced assessment of Namier as an historian. In part this is because there is some danger of over-reacting to the adulation he received towards the end of his life. 'He combines nearly all – if not all – the virtues of the writing of history', wrote one admirer in 1952.[39] That is hyperbole. Namier had little interest in or knowledge of the art, music or literature of Hanoverian England.[40] He did not have, and did not claim to have, wide historical learning. Indeed, it would have run counter to his approach to his subject, which was, above all, to concentrate the gaze. He had little confidence in world history or grand historical designs. One can hardly quantify civilisations. 'You try to see the tree as a whole,' he told Arnold Toynbee, chief practitioner of the world view: 'I try to examine it leaf by leaf.'[41] Despite his own contribution, I doubt whether he was much interested in historical methodology: he merely used whatever methods were necessary to answer the questions he had set himself.

Though the total list of his publications is formidable, there is hardly one work which was wholly successful. The two books on English history that made his name are episodic and undisciplined: Namier scarcely begins to engage on the theme he is ostensibly pursuing.[42] *Diplomatic Prelude, 1938-39* remains of value to those studying the Munich period and the many volumes of essays on European history are full of delightful and subtle comments, yet they do not add up, as Namier himself confessed, to the History of Modern Europe he had always wanted to write – yet another unfinished enterprise.[43] The one full-length biography he attempted remained incomplete at the time of his death.[44] Of course, one can understand and explain this. Considering his severe physical infirmities – the sleeplessness which tormented him all his life, the crippled hand that made note-taking so difficult – it was a triumph that he achieved so much. He was not helped by the painstaking and laborious way he revised every draft again and again which, though it made for superb writing, made for slow progress as well. Namier is not the only historian described in this volume who took on more than he could accomplish: though this suggests grand ambition and an admirable intellectual zest, yet, in the final analysis, Namier's lack of constructive powers remains a serious weakness.

Perhaps his most striking characteristic was that 'sheer intellect' which A. F. Pollard had mentioned when supporting Namier's unsuccessful candidature for an All Souls fellowship at the age of 23.[45]

Namier had stature and commanded attention, even when he was being perverse and obstinate. This did not always work to his advantage in that even his casual opinions were felt to require solemn refutation. Chief among his virtues were clarity of mind and directness of diction. He had a Johnsonian dislike of cant. His command of English – not his native language – was imposing: 'constant, diligent care of language and style is a mental discipline', he wrote,[46] and though it is easy to disagree with Namier, it is hard to misunderstand him. He had an eye for the comic and a quirky sense of humour. H. A. L. Fisher, in a foreword to Namier's first and forgotten book on *Germany and Eastern Europe* in 1915, identified a lasting characteristic: 'in a world of many echoes, here at least is an independent voice'.

Coupled with this direct approach was a most rigorous and demanding scholarship. Not content with consulting manuscripts, Namier spent much time tracking them down, and his forays and beats on behalf of the History of Parliament in his later years have passed into legend. He practised what he preached, and soaked himself so completely in the period he studied that it was extremely rare to catch him out in an error or oversight. He expected from others the same standards of punctilious accuracy and his reviews were detailed and often disparaging. It is scarcely an exaggeration to say that, through his work, he succeeded in jacking up the whole level of English historical scholarship. He was the scourge of slovenly editors. Among his most influential books was one hardly known to the general public – a volume in 1937 entitled *Additions and Corrections to Sir John Fortescue's Edition of the Correspondence of King George the Third, Volume One*. Eighty-six pages were devoted to the edition's shortcomings. 'Terrifying', wrote a reviewer, 'is his relentless pursuit and devastating exposure of what he believes to be evil.'[47]

Such a man was greatly feared and made many enemies. At times he was aware of this and would become almost paranoically suspicious. He saw slights and plots where none was intended, as well as some that were. It is frequently said that Namier was arrogant and opinionated, particularly as a young man. 'His ego-centrism', wrote a not unfriendly commentator, 'was proverbial' and he was capable of 'the most implacable hatred'.[48] His long involvement with Zionism and his forthright denunciation of the men responsible for the Munich settlement added to the number of his foes. But this was not the whole story. Arnold Toynbee, who had himself suffered from Namier's touchiness, wrote that he was 'invincibly lovable, from first to last',[49] and, indeed, he had a kind of blundering innocence which was quite disarming.

The combative side of his nature was less prominent in his historical writings. In the essay on 'History', he remarked that the historical approach was intellectually humble: 'a consciousness of his own limitations' was the mark of a real historian.[50] He could write about historical characters with compassion and understanding.

Of the Duke of Newcastle – his favourite subject – Namier commented:

> Like so many sufferers from obsessionist neurosis, great, middling, or insignificant, Newcastle wasted his life on trifles, pursuing them with an intensity which was to hide their inanity . . . With an abundant substratum of intelligence and common sense, he looked a fool, and with an inexhaustible fund of warm, human kindness and sincere goodwill, he acquired a reputation for dishonesty.[51]

Of George III's change from youthful indolence to mature meticulousness, Namier wrote: 'There is a legend about a homunculus whose maker not knowing what to do with him, bid him count poppy-seed in a bag. That George III was doing . . .'[52] It is revealing that Namier should write so well about the vulnerable and the obsessive.

Namier's commitment to the study of history was total and lifelong. The years after his retirement from Manchester were spent, day after day, writing biographies for the History of Parliament, hunched over his typewriter in the dismal basement room in the Institute of Historical Research which he called his Black Hole of Calcutta. It was a pity, wrote one reviewer after his death, that the master-builder should have spent so long in the brick-field.[53] Namier did not know it was a brick-field. To his very last day, he found uncommon difficulty in pulling his material into shape, and for months he worried about the organisation of the preliminary survey he was to write for the first volume of the *History*. He went straight from his desk to hospital where he died the following day: waiting for the ambulance, he confided to his wife that he at last saw how the survey should be tackled. We shall never know whether he was afforded a genuine insight or whether it was the mirage of a dying man.

NOTES: CHAPTER 9

1 Quite by chance, as I write, I have in front of me a review article, dated 22 October 1976, entitled 'Namierism of the Left' (J. D. Clark, *Cambridge Review*). Karl Marx, who gave rise to Marxism and Marxists, is commemorated more as a political thinker than as an historian.
2 *The Structure of Politics at the Accession of George III* and *England in the Age of the American Revolution*, subsequently referred to as *Structure* and *England*. A short early volume called *Germany and Eastern Europe* was published in 1915 but attracted little attention.
3 *A Sense of Place*, p. 43.
4 *Times Literary Supplement*, 28 August 1953; E. H. Carr, *What Is History?*, (Pelican ed., 1961), p. 37; A Marwick, *The Nature of History* (1970), p. 90.

5 H. C. Mansfield and R. Walcott, *Journal of British Studies*, vol. II, pp. 28–55, and vol. III pp. 85–108.

6 He was born at Wola Okrzejska in Russian Poland and moved at the age of 2 into Austrian Poland. His father, Joseph Bernstein (formerly Niemirowski), was a Polonised, but not practising, Jew.

7 Sedgwick's most important works were the edition of the memoirs of Lord Hervey (published 1931) and of the *Letters from George III to Lord Bute* (published 1939). He was subsequently editor of the History of Parliament volume covering 1715–54.

8 'No doubt can be entertained but a plan had been early formed of carrying the prerogative to very unusual heights. The Princess was ardently fond of power': H. Walpole, *Memoirs of the Reign of George III* (1894), ed. G. F. Russell Barker, Vol. I, p. 14. 'To secure to the court the unlimited and uncontrolled use of its own vast influence, under the sole direction of its own private favour, has for some years past been the great object of policy': Edmund Burke, *Thoughts on the Cause of the Present Discontents* (1770).

9 Macaulay, *Essay on the Earl of Chatham*; G. M. Trevelyan, 'The two-party system in English political history', Romanes lecture, 1926.

10 *England* (2nd edn, 1961), p. 161.

11 *History*, Vol. XIV, p. 269.

12 *Oxford Magazine*, 14 February 1929, review of *Structure*. For review of *England*, see 20 November 1930.

13 'History', in *Avenues of History*, pp. 8–9.

14 In the preface to *Structure*, Namier had written: 'In a future book, I propose to deal in detail with the four Parliaments of 1761–84'; in the conclusion to *England*, he remarked 'my next book, if ever written, will be on "The rise of Party"'.

15 These objections were developed in R. Pares, *King George III and the Politicians* (1953); H. Butterfield, *George III and the Historians* (1957); W. R. Fryer, 'King George III, his political character and conduct, 1760–84: a new Whig interpretation', *Renaissance and Modern Studies*, vol. VI, pp. 68–101.

16 See particularly Butterfield, op. cit., pp. 294–5.

17 *Structure* (2nd edn, 1967), p. 235.

18 A convenient summary up to 1969 may be found in John Cannon, *The Fox-North Coalition* (1969), pp. 238–43. Since then the main contributions have been W. Speck, *Tory and Whig: The Struggle in the Constituencies* (1970); F. O'Gorman, *The Rise of Party in England: The Rockingham Whigs, 1760–82* (1975); B. W. Hill, *The Growth of Parliamentary Parties, 1689–1742* (1976). Something of a restoration of the Rockinghams is suggested by I. R. Christie, *Myth and Reality in Late-Eighteenth-Century British Politics* (1970). An excellent review article on the problem is H. T. Dickinson, 'Party, principle and public opinion in eighteenth century politics', *History*, vol. 61, no. 202, pp. 231–7.

19 See Butterfield, op. cit. Revealing is Butterfield's admission, in an exchange with Namier in the *Times Literary Supplement*, 1957, p. 721, that he felt he was 'braving a giant and a system'.

20 Examples of work on other centuries include J. E. Neale, *The Elizabethan House of Commons* (1949); D. Brunton and D. H. Pennington, *Members of the Long Parliament* (1954); F. Eyck, *The Frankfurt Parliament of 1848–1849* (1968). For further discussion of the technique, see A. J. Toynbee, *Acquaintances* (1967), pp. 76–85, and P. B. M. Blaas, *Continuity and*

Anachronism: Parliamentary and Constitutional Development in Whig Historiography (1978), pp. 4–9.

21 E. and A. Porritt, *The Unreformed House of Commons*, to which Namier paid tribute in *Structure*, p. 75, appeared in 1903. In 1916, W. T. Laprade published an article on 'Public opinion and the election of 1784' in *English Historical Review*, and six years later edited for the Camden Society *The Parliamentary Papers of John Robinson, 1774–84*.

22 *Avenues of History*, p. 8.

23 *Personalities and Powers*, p. 2. In an amusing reminiscence, Sir Isaiah Berlin relates how, at their first meeting, Namier urged him to study not Marx but Freud. 'A personal impression', *Encounter*, November 1966.

24 *Conflicts*, p. 72; *Structure*, p. 134. In the first edition of *Structure*, Namier added 'e.g. in education'. This offended the teachers and in the 1957 revised edition the phrase was removed: even Namier learned prudence. Namier's aphorism has been so much admired that it may be worth remarking that it is really rather silly: in fact buses frequently arrive at their destinations and books get written.

25 'Namier and his critics', *Encounter*, 24 February 1965.

26 'Basic factors in nineteenth-century European History', *Vanished Supremacies*, p. 165.

27 *George III and the Historians*, p. 298.

28 *Personalities and Powers*, p. 5.

29 ibid., p. 3.

30 Published in considerably expanded form in *Proceedings of the British Academy*, vol. XXX (1944), pp. 161–282.

31 A. J. P. Taylor in *The Trouble Makers: Dissent over Foreign Policy, 1792–1939*, ch. 1, commented on the *Structure* that its central doctrine was that 'jobbery not ideas, places not principles, were the motive force of politics'. Namier seems to have suffered a strangely sudden conversion on the subject, since in 1919 he had written in a private letter that 'men matter little in politics, systems and ideas are everything . . . In the realm of politics a man cannot act efficiently except through one faith – in a leading idea'; quoted in Julia Namier, *Lewis Namier: A Biography* (1971), p. 138. At the risk of appearing captious, it seems to me that he went from one extreme to the other without ever touching firm ground.

32 *Times Literary Supplement*, 25 May 1967, p. 429.

33 'The end of Napoleon', *Vanished Supremacies; The House of Commons, 1754–90*, Vol. II, pp. 538–9.

34 *England*, p. 18.

35 'The Agrarian Revolution', first published in August 1922, and reprinted in *Skyscrapers*, pp. 145–55.

36 *Structure*, p. x. That Namier was aware that his views were contentious may be inferred from the fact that in *Skyscrapers*, pp. 45 and 51, he twice more used the phrase in inverted commas.

37 *Times Literary Supplement*, 21 May 1971, p. 578.

38 *The Nation and Athenaeum*, 14 July 1928, reprinted in *Skyscrapers*, pp. 44–53.

39 Review of *In the Nazi Era* and *Monarchy and the Party System*, *Times Literary Supplement*, 1952, p. 741.

40 See John Brooke's contribution to *Dictionary of National Biography* (1951–60), pp. 763–6.

41 Toynbee, op. cit., p. 76.

42 Richard Lodge, reviewing the *Structure*, had complained that its title was 'too ambitious' for its contents; *History*, vol. XIV, p. 269.

43 Preface to *Vanished Supremacies*.
44 *Charles Townshend* was completed by John Brooke and published in 1964.
45 Julia Namier, op. cit., p. 101.
46 'English prose', first published in the *Spectator*, 10 April 1942, and reprinted in *Conflicts*, pp. 217–23.
47 *Times Literary Supplement*, 1952, p. 741.
48 J. L. Talmon, 'Lewis Namier', in *The Unique and the Universal: Some Historical Reflections* (1965), pp. 296–7.
49 Toynbee, op. cit., p. 68.
50 *Avenues of History*, pp. 4 and 8.
51 *England*, pp. 72 and 68–9.
52 'King George III: a study of personality', reprinted in *Personalities and Powers*, pp. 39–58.
53 Review of Julia Namier's biography, *Times Literary Supplement*, 21 May 1971.

NOTE ON FURTHER READING

A systematic assessment of Namier's work must begin with the two major books on English history, *The Structure of Politics at the Accession of George III* (1929) and *England in the Age of the American Revolution* (1930). In addition, important articles on eighteenth-century England are included in *Personalities and Powers* (1955) and in *Crossroads of Power* (1962). Namier's only full-length biography was the life of *Charles Townshend*, finished by John Brooke and published posthumously in 1964, but he contributed many shorter biographies to *The House of Commons, 1754–90*: among the most interesting are those of George Grenville, Chase Price and Lord Shelburne. Namier's work on modern European history is scattered through many volumes, of which the most important are *Diplomatic Prelude* (1948), *Europe in Decay* (1950), *Avenues of History* (1952) and *Vanished Supremacies* (1958). General reflections on the study of history are contained in *Personalities and Powers* and *Avenues of History*.

The biography by his second wife, Julia Namier, is indispensable for an understanding of the man and is very full for his early years: it makes no attempt at an historical appreciation, however, and is inclined to melodrama. Namier's most persistent critic in his lifetime was Sir Herbert Butterfield, whose misgivings were expressed in *George III and the Historians*, published 1957. The article on Namier in the *Dictionary of National Biography* is by John Brooke, his closest collaborator, who also contributed valuable comments in 'Namier and Namierism', *History and Theory*, 1964, and in 'Namier and his critics', *Encounter*, 24 February 1965. Other personal sketches are by Dame Lucy Sutherland, *Proceedings of the British Academy*, 1962; Sir Isaiah Berlin, *Journal of Historical Studies*, 1968; J. L. Talmon, *The Unique and the Universal: Some Historical Reflections* (1965); A. Toynbee, *Acquaintances* (1967). The account by Ved Mehta in *Fly and the Fly-Bottle: Encounters with British Intellectuals* is second-hand, gossipy and lurid, but includes some interesting comments.

10 *Mortimer Wheeler*

Robert Eric Mortimer Wheeler was born in 1890 in Edinburgh; pupil of Bradford Grammar School, 1899–1904; scholarship in classics, University College, London, 1907; awarded Franks studentship in archaeology 1913; became Assistant Editor for Royal Commission on Historical Monuments for England 1914. On the outbreak of war, was commissioned in the Royal Artillery and subsequently awarded the Military Cross and mentioned in dispatches. In 1919 appointed Junior Investigator to Royal Commission on Historical Monuments, but moved in 1920 to become lecturer in archaeology at Cardiff and Keeper of Archaeology in the National Museum of Wales; Director of the National Museum 1924–6. Moved to the London Museum in 1926 and was keeper and secretary until 1944; honorary director of the London Institute of Archaeology, 1934–44. Joined Territorial Army in 1939 and served with the Eighth Army in Africa, reaching rank of brigadier-general. Director general of archaeology in India 1944–8 and adviser in archaeology to the government of Pakistan 1949–50. In 1948 was elected professor of the archaeology of the Roman provinces, University of London, holding the chair until 1955; secretary of the British Academy 1949–68. Knighted 1952; in the 1950s became a well-known broadcaster and television star. Died in July 1976.

Mortimer Wheeler was born in Edinburgh in 1890, but five years later his father's work took the family to Bradford, where the boy attended the excellent local grammar school. Wheeler found some of his teachers inspiring. Of one, he wrote later:

The Latin which I learned from Barton was of no great consequence, and indeed in the aggregate I may not have learned much from him of anything. But he had the faculty of stimulating our callow minds and of indicating rather than illuminating new horizons.[1]

However, the main influence in these formative years was that of his father, a classics graduate from Edinburgh, who retained a love of scholarship. In his father's library, Wheeler found ample materials to stimulate his own intellectual development, but the relationship affected more than reading.

Save when school was inescapable, the afternoons were devoted to our walks together, my father and I, in unfailingly successful search of adventure and new scraps of knowledge. On one memorable day in the woods beyond Saltaire we might find an unrecorded cup-marked stone . . . on yet another afternoon, when the mist lay heavily on the hills and concealed our guilt, we hewed most scandalously into the flank of an ancient barrow on Baildon Moor, happily without result . . . in these impressionable years the insidious poisons of archaeology were already entering into my system.

These archaeological excursions provided a significant pointer, but Wheeler's early ambitions leaned more towards an artistic career. In 1904 his father's work again removed the family, this time to London. Entrance to London University was now the immediate objective, but at 14 Wheeler was still too young. He had no formal education for the next two years; instead, his father instructed him to educate himself, providing him with a map of London and fourpence a day for food. Many years later, Wheeler wrote:

I can still recapture the almost tremulous excitement of those years. Unharassed by sex, my eager mind fluttered freely in an objective world, entirely friendless but never lonely. Except for the brief train journey from West Dulwich or Herne Hill to Blackfriars, I walked everywhere, map in hand, from the City to Kensington and as far afield as Hampstead Heath, whence I could gaze across the pit of London to the Crystal Palace on the horizon behind my home.

The experience provided a novel introduction to fieldwork. Art galleries and museums played their part in the process of self-education, but in other ways so did a Brompton Road pub and a boxing match in the East End.

In 1907, a scholarship in classics safely secured, he entered University College, London, a close-knit academic community about a thousand strong, with considerable resources of talent among both staff and students. In his undergraduate career, Wheeler displayed originality in the way in which he managed to vary the classics degree course to enable him to pursue his artistic inclinations at the Slade School. At the same time, though he worked hard, a certain liveliness of temperament involved him in a number of brushes with the college authorities.

On his graduation in 1910, it was with surprise as well as gratitude that he welcomed the offer of a post as private secretary to the college provost, a formidable personality whose previous dealings with his new secretary had sometimes been of a distinctly disciplinary character.

Scholarship, however, proved a more powerful magnet, and in 1913 Wheeler emerged as the successful candidate for a newly founded studentship in archaeology. The new opening, though poorly paid, gave him his first taste of practical archaeology and, in the event, served as a step to better things, for later in 1913 he was given a junior post on the staff of the Royal Commission on Historical Monuments, an exchange which involved a crash course on architecture. His apprenticeship there lasted less than a year, for the coming of war in 1914 brought an abrupt change.

Wheeler became an artillery officer. Until 1917 he was employed in Britain, but thereafter he saw active service both on the Western Front and in Italy. The award of the Military Cross, and three mentions in dispatches, demonstrated that as a soldier he proved more than competent. Army experience in two world wars exerted a powerful influence on him. Military analogies are scattered throughout his writings, and the leadership role thrust upon him played a part in moulding him for his civilian career. In another way, too, the Great War left a considerable mark. Many of his friends and contemporaries were killed: Wheeler was the only survivor from a group of five young men who had worked together at Wroxeter in 1913. He was profoundly conscious that he was one of the fortunate survivors of a generation which had been decimated. This did not lead him into any strenuously pacifist beliefs, but imbued him instead with an acute sense of personal responsibility, as if in some sort a representative of the many who had not come back from the war.

In 1919 Wheeler returned home to pick up the threads of his chosen career. Before following this, however, it is necessary to give some account of the state of archaeology in Britain at that time.

In his later writings, Wheeler often used caustic language on this topic, though always with a vein of understanding within his criticisms:

> Every generation is liable to belittle the achievement of its predecessors. This attitude is often enough unjust . . . It is unprofitable to blame Xerxes for omitting to deploy torpedo-boats at Salamis, or Napoleon for attacking the British squares with cavalry instead of machine-guns.[2]

Even with this salutary caution, however, there was much to criticise in British archaeology in the early twentieth century. There was certainly a great deal of public interest. Schliemann, of Troy and Mycenae, had died in 1890. Sir Arthur Evans began his work at Knossos in 1900. Egyptology was a matter of wide interest, to be markedly enhanced by the discovery of the tomb of Tutankhamun in 1922. The general level of archaeological skills was, however, extremely low. There could scarcely be said to be a competent body of archae- ologists, no facilities for formal training existed, and there was no central body capable of effecting significant improvement. The leading archaeologists of the day commonly drifted into this field from adjacent disciplines such as classics or history, and rarely displayed any very sophisticated appreciation of the opportunities which archaeology offered. For example, one of the leading authorities on Roman Britain was Professor Haverfield. He planned to take a holiday in northern England in 1907 and decided to combine this with the initiation of a series of large-scale excavations on the key Roman site at Corbridge. To direct the excavations he chose the young Leonard Woolley, who had never so much as seen an excavation before. Haverfield dropped in about once a week to see how things were going. Such an approach was by no means uncommon. There was little understanding of what could be learned from a careful study of stratification in trenches, and the systematic study of many categories of excavated objects was still in its infancy.

This low level of attainment was more remarkable in that the way forward had been pointed out a generation earlier by one of the most notable of British archaeologists. In his masterly work during the 1880s General Pitt-Rivers had shown how even in the difficult prehistoric field major results could be achieved by carefully planned and executed excavations, with meticulous attention to the sections cut and the recording of the objects recovered.[3] This brilliant achievement, how- ever, had found very few imitators. Wheeler was among those who fully appreciated its significance.

When Wheeler returned to the Historical Monuments Commission in 1919 he intended to propagate and apply the kind of standards which Pitt-Rivers had pioneered. Knowing what ought to be done was one thing, achieving it was much more difficult. He found little under- standing or sympathy among his colleagues and so, in 1920, he applied for a post in Cardiff, a joint appointment as university lecturer in archaeology and keeper of archaeology in the infant National Museum of Wales. In 1924, at the age of 33, he became director of the National Museum at a time when that project faced serious problems. He was able to inject new life into the institution, and eventually saw the project materialise as one of Britain's major museums, with a strong archaeological content.

Wheeler was not the only scholar concerned to improve the standard of British archaeology at that time, but his Cardiff base enabled him to inculcate his views and demonstrate their value in practice. In 1921 he set about his first major excavation, at the Roman fort of Segontium, near Caernarvon. Long afterwards he reconsidered the standard of work involved there: 'The section displays a certain crudity but, with the privilege of advancing age, I can say that it has all the right stuff in it . . . The whole bones of the matter are there.' This verdict can be contrasted with the experience of a younger archaeologist, A. L. F. Rivet, whose introduction to digging some years later reflected the survival of an older tradition:

The first excavation in which I was ever involved took place in a field beside a river. When we arrived, we were conducted to a sort of clearing in the four-foot high grass and told to dig *here*. This we did, undisturbed by any further information or advice . . . And when evening came, we mounted our bicycles and rode away. I am still not sure what it was all about (though I suspect that it had something to do with the Bronze Age).[4]

From the outset Wheeler's students had a very different experience, for he knew that the success of his reforming crusade must depend upon the training given to the emerging generation of British archaeologists. His success in this crucial aspect was demonstrated by the significant number of eminent archaeologists who learned much of their practical trade during Wheeler's early excavations.

Another result of Wheeler's thinking on the future of archaeology was already apparent. He was well aware of the existing public interest in archaeology, and determined to build upon it. When he set about work at the Roman legionary fortress at Caerleon, he put this unorthodox concept into practice. His immediate target was the amphitheatre outside the fortress, and he deliberately organised widespread press coverage for the project, aided by the structure's local name of 'King Arthur's Round Table'. An agreement with the *Daily Mail* produced heavy financial support in return for priority publication rights as the work progressed. Wheeler had no contempt for the general public. It was plain to him that only by arousing and retaining wide interest, and by erecting possible claims on public funds, would it be possible to support the expansion and reform of British archaeology which he had in mind. Years later, he wrote:

A present-day excavation must provide for the General Public as a routine activity . . . The popes and princes of the Renaissance have in fact been replaced by the British taxpayer. However embarrassing its attentions may be on occasion, the public is now in one way and another our patron, and must be cultivated and suitably rewarded.[5]

In his deliberate attention to popularisation, Wheeler made a substantial contribution to the extension of public patronage, which was to become of crucial importance in future years.

During his Cardiff years Wheeler was also planning his next step, and by 1926 his next objective was clear. He envisaged the creation of a national institute for archaeology, which could serve as a centre for systematic training and for the exploitation of the new techniques which a more advanced scientific world could now offer to supplement the excavator's trowel and spade. His work in Wales had reached a point at which he could reasonably leave. London would be a better base for his plans, and a timely opportunity arose at the London Museum, an institution very much in need of reform: 'The London Museum had to be cleaned, expurgated, and catalogued; in general, turned from a junkshop into a tolerably rational institution.' Wheeler set about this task efficiently, while at the same time he applied himself to the archaeology of London and campaigned on behalf of his proposed national project. In London he was faced with the archaeological problem of a Roman city smothered under many centuries of later development, and with little guidance from earlier work. His teenage lessons in London topography were now a useful asset. After only two years Wheeler produced an important introduction to a major work on the remains of Roman London. Half a century later another historian of Roman London had this to say:

> Wheeler's Introduction was a brilliant survey which dealt with all aspects of the matter on the basis of the evidence then available. Hypotheses were boldly formulated, and though some details of these are no longer acceptable, much of the overall picture, drawn with imagination and scholarship, has never been superseded.[6]

Meanwhile, the campaign to launch the institute was being fought with determination and considerable skill in an economic context in which money for such creations was scarce. The Institute of Archaeology of London University began its life in 1934, and its permanence was signalled by a prestigious formal ceremony in April 1937, with Wheeler's careful coaching evident in the importance which the dignitaries involved attributed to systematic training and the exploitation of new scientific techniques.

This campaign had been aided by the prestige accumulated by a series of major excavations carried out elsewhere. In 1928–9 Wheeler excavated at the important Romano-British and post-Roman site at Lydney in the Welsh border country. After Lydney came St Albans, where four long seasons were devoted to the Roman city and its Iron Age predecessor. In each case the choice of site was a careful one, directed to places where important questions might be answered. After

St Albans, he moved away from the Roman world to some extent, and 'once again the new objective was one on which I had secretly meditated for several years before the moment came for action'.

The excavations on the great Iron Age hill fort at Maiden Castle in Dorset (1934–7) were the best known of all Wheeler's excavations in Britain. The site is grand enough in its formidable physical dimensions, the excitement heightened by dramatic discoveries about the siege and capture of the native fortress by the conquering Roman armies. Public interest was again deliberately fostered, with diggers told off in turn to escort parties of visitors – and a useful added revenue in the shape of donations and the sale of many thousands of postcards and interim reports. When A. L. F. Rivet came to Maiden Castle he found his second experience of excavation very different from his first:

> Here the contrast was complete. No question here of not knowing what we were about: from the first we were *told* – indeed we were given (or more probably sold) the interim reports for the preceding years, which had, of course, been promptly produced; and thereafter we were compelled to keep abreast of developments. The most serious crime – and the only one which produced those spectacular rages – was to appear at a loss when asked the question: 'Now what are you doing *here*?' . . . Anyone who was consistently late for work was politely but firmly asked to leave.[7]

The reference to rages illuminates one aspect of Wheeler's personality. He could be an immensely charming and witty companion, but he also had a temper. He was well aware of the value of the work he was engaged upon, and did not always take kindly to criticisms. Such characteristics are not rare in the world of scholarship.

The shift of interest from the Roman world of St Albans to Maiden Castle had been a purposeful one, and the next step was already planned. The Iron Age precursors of Maiden Castle were to be sought in the Gallic world from which its inhabitants had removed. The hill forts of northern France had barely been touched by modern archaeology, and it was to this scene that Wheeler turned in the summer of 1938. He returned in the following summer to continue the pioneer fieldwork, but by now his mind was increasingly on considerations other than archaeology. In mid-August 1939 Wheeler relinquished the command of his team in France to a competent deputy and returned home.

At the outbreak of war, Wheeler was once more in uniform as an artillery officer. In the hectic days of September he created first a battery and then a four-battery artillery regiment. In 1941 he was sent to North Africa as a lieutenant colonel commanding a regiment of anti-aircraft artillery, and by 1943 he was a brigadier-general commanding the anti-aircraft formations of the Eighth Army. Wheeler was among the first troops to enter the capital of Mussolini's African empire:

> Just before midday we struck the road, our goal the harbour of Tripoli. At 12.45 hours we entered the city, and at 13.00 hours the guns were in action on the quays – the first AA guns in Tripoli. We surveyed the wreck-filled harbour and ate a contented meal.

Wheeler's last active service was in Operation Avalanche, the allied landings at Salerno during the Italian campaign:

> It was a long, fidgety but interesting battle. It had one rather particularly uneasy moment on the seventh day (15th. September) I remember, when an expected infantry brigade failed to arrive from Tripoli and left our line very thin on the ground. The right flank of 10th Corps was in fact penetrated by the enemy and an ugly situation was in the making. At midnight I was called up by the corps commander and ordered to collect an emergency force of all available gunners to fill the gap as infantry. In the course of half an hour some four hundred of my artillery-men, armed with an assortment of Bren-guns, Tommy-guns and rifles, were assembled from all quarters in the vivid moonlight, formed into a hollow square for a rapid appreciation of the situation from their brigadier, and marched off in groups to the broken front line. One group, under Major Sir Basil McFarland, redoubtable ex-Mayor of Londonderry, came quickly into action; the gap was sealed, and next day 'Gunnerforce' was creditably relieved for its proper duties by reinforcements brought in by air and sea.

Wheeler's participation in this operation had been at his own insistence, for a few weeks earlier his career had taken another turn, and a return to archaeology was imminent.

Indeed, archaeology had resurfaced earlier when, as the victorious allied forces swept through Tripolitania, Wheeler had been able to improvise caretaker custody of the region's magnificent ancient monuments after the collapse of Italian authority. Then, early in August 1943, an incident occurred which Wheeler relished on more than one count:

> In the sunset the end of the day's planning operations of the forthcoming British and American invasion of Italy had drawn to its just close, when the Corps Commander, General Sir Brian Horrocks,

dashed across towards my doorway with a signal in his hand and the remark, 'I say, have you seen this – they want you as – (reading) "Director General of Archaeology in India!" – Why, you must be rather a king-pin at this sort of thing! You know, I thought you were a regular soldier!' If the general ever paid an extravagant compliment, he did so then, although there was, I thought, a hint of pain and disillusionment in his voice. For my part the proposition was a complete bombshell.[8]

With the Salerno operation safe, Wheeler agreed to go to India, a country he had never before visited. In the four years after his arrival there in 1944, he carried out one of the most remarkable campaigns in the history of archaeology. He had no illusions about the difficulties involved. Apart from the administrative and archaeological problems, these years were not likely to be easy for a newly imported British official taking up a very senior post during the last years of imperial rule. It was not surprising that an aggrieved nationalist asked in the Legislative Assembly what Roman Britain could possibly have to do with India.

The official Archaeological Survey of India, one of India's intellectual imports from the West, had been founded in 1871 and reorganised under Curzon's viceroyalty in 1902. By 1944 it had experienced severe decay, and Wheeler's appointment represented a race against time to produce reformation before independence was effected. Wheeler brought to the task considerable personal advantages. He had ample recent experience of large-scale organisations engaged in urgent tasks. Few people could have brought to bear superior qualifications in archaeology. He enjoyed a high prestige, valuable contacts and a justified self-confidence. Meekness would have been a fatal weakness in the task that confronted him, but this had never been among his characteristics.

From his first acceptance of the mission he had devised a firm plan of action. First, the Indian government's archaeological service must be reorganised, with emphasis placed upon the recruitment of competent Indian archaeologists and administrators. The second task was to carry out practical work in the field, based upon modern techniques. Both tasks went hand in hand, the results in the field directed to demonstrate that reforms were both necessary and fruitful. The task of administrative reform was briskly undertaken, and if the attainment of efficiency meant a number of premature departures from the service and consequent political criticism, this was something which Wheeler was prepared to face with equanimity.

Even before his arrival in India, Wheeler had selected two areas for practical work, one in north-west India and the other in the south. In the north-west lay a series of major archaeological sites which had been in part excavated but inadequately interpreted in previous years. A few months after his arrival in India, Wheeler took himself off to one of these, Taxila, with sixty students obtained by scouring Indian universities. For six months Wheeler combined excavations with an intensive training course in modern archaeological methods, emerging with new understanding of a major ancient city, but more important with a core of trained Indian archaeologists.

Even before then he had prepared the ground for a major achievement in south India. Earlier work there had demonstrated the existence of successive cultures which had left behind substantial monuments. These existed, however, in a kind of chronological no-man's-land with virtually no fixed dating for it. To someone of Wheeler's experience it was immediately obvious that a key to this problem might well be readily available. The products of the classical Graeco-Roman world of the Mediterranean could certainly be dated with reasonable certainty. Classical authors had recorded a considerable body of trade with south India, and indeed scattered finds of Mediterranean objects in India were already known. If datable objects from the classical world could be found in meaningful association with native Indian cultures, then a fixed historical datum could be established.

In search of this key Wheeler made a flying visit to Madras and Pondicherry early in his Indian sojourn. In a cupboard in the Madras Museum, he unearthed a large fragment of a typical Mediterranean amphora or wine-jar. This had come from a site near Pondicherry, and the next clue came from cases in the public library there:

> I strode hopefully forward, and, removing the dust with an excessively sweaty arm, peered into them. For the second time within the month, my eyes started in their sockets. Crowded together were fragments of a dozen more Roman amphorae, part of a Roman lamp, a Roman intaglio, a mass of Indian material – potsherds, beads, terracottas – and several fragments of a red-glazed ware which no one trained in the school of classical archaeology could mistake. After much searching, the keys were discovered and I found myself handling the fragments of cups and dishes of the time of Augustus and Tiberius from the famous potteries of Roman Arezzo. My search was nearly over.

In the spring of 1945 this detective work was followed up in the excavation of the site from which this material had come, in order to tie in the Roman material with a recognisable Indian context. After twelve days of digging,

> an Indian student of mine emerged excitedly from a deep trench beside the Bay of Bengal waving a large slice of a red dish in his

hand. Removal of the slimy sea-mud revealed the dish as the signed work of a potter whose kilns flourished nearly 2,000 years ago and 5,000 miles away. Were drama admissible to the archaeological scene, I should have been tempted to describe the moment as dramatic.[9]

From these discoveries at Arikamedu, near Pondicherry, a fixed point in time for the associated Indian remains could now be established, and these in their turn related to other Indian cultures with which they were found in association. The episode may fairly be seen as a distinguished example of the successful application by an expert of careful planning and specialist knowledge, and Wheeler might well reflect that after all Roman Britain *did* have something to do with India.

Further work in the north-west added significantly to an understanding of the extensive Indus civilisation – one of the great societies of the ancient world – which had flourished between about 2500 and 1500 BC. Here again, the combination of a trained and experienced eye, a flair for interpretation and a gift for organisation were the qualities which Wheeler brought to bear in ways which Indian archaeology needed.

His years in India coincided with the final moves to independence and partition, with the disputes and bloodshed which attended the birth-pangs of the states of India and Pakistan. Wheeler relinquished the direction of a reformed Indian Archaeological Survey, but went on to spend part of the two years 1949–50 helping the infant archaeological service of Pakistan to establish itself, work which included a major excavation at Mohenjo-Dara, one of the twin centres of the Indus civilisation. For the most part, however, Wheeler's career now returned to the British scene.

Wheeler returned home with his personal prestige heightened, as well it might be, by his Indian achievements. To some extent he returned to practical work in British archaeology, notably in his work on the great Iron Age fortifications at Stanwick in 1951–2. From 1948 to 1955 he held a part-time professorship in London University. His writing and lecturing did much to spread his concepts of archaeology to wider audiences. In another way his continued policy of maintaining wide public interest in archaeology achieved an unexpected success. In the mid-1950s the young television service introduced a quiz, entitled *Animal, Vegetable, Mineral* and based upon archaeology, in which eminent scholars were invited to identify a series of objects. Wheeler, who years before had invited the newsreel cameras to his excavations at St Albans, was an enthusiastic participant: although he shared the honours with Glyn Daniel and others, he was very much the star of the show. He displayed his wide learning with a confidence and wit which attracted to matters archaeological a much wider audience than it had ever known, and earned him the viewers' accolade as Television Personality of the Year.

However, Wheeler's main achievement in his sixties and seventies came in a very different field. He was not devoted to university life, and another important theatre for his energies absorbed much of his attention in these years. In the old-established and prestigious Royal Society, the sciences possessed a highly influential central body to champion their interests. In 1901 the British Academy had been created to serve as a similar focus for the humanities, but had not succeeded in fully measuring up to the task. Wheeler had been elected a fellow of the Academy in 1941, but at that time he had more urgent business on hand. On his return from India he became the Academy's secretary and in the following years spearheaded a campaign to rejuvenate the institution and equip it to play a much larger role in British scholarship. As in India, rapid reform could not be accomplished painlessly, but it was accomplished none the less. The Academy's governing body saw considerable change and a much more dynamic leadership emerged, in which Wheeler took a prominent place.

New resources were necessary if the Academy was to play its designed role. Intensive lobbying produced in 1952 an agreement with the Treasury, whereby a substantial annual grant was made to enable the British Academy to sponsor research by British scholars. Other negotiations established the Academy as the body through which government grants to British schools and institutes abroad were channelled. At the same time, Wheeler was much involved in the negotiations which created the Council for British Archaeology as a focus for his own subject. It comes as no surprise to learn that the CBA receives an annual government grant administered by the British Academy. The overall effect of this work was to produce a distinctly healthy increase in the support and organisation available to help research over a wide area of scholarship. This was particularly important in a context in which patronage in older forms had become limited.

Wheeler died on 27 July 1976 in his eighty-sixth year. In his autobiography, published in 1955, he had offered a personal testament which, if somewhat bleak, was not ignoble: 'I do not believe in much except hard work, which serves as an antidote to disillusion and a substitute for faith.'

His career provides an opportunity to consider the relationship between archaeology and history. Are archaeologists working in a different subject or are they a specialised variety of historian? Wheeler had often addressed himself to the question of the nature of archaeology, but if we were to rely upon his explicit answers, we could be disappointed: [10] 'What in fact is Archaeology? I do not myself really know . . . I do not even know whether Archaeology is to be described as an art or as a science.' He was clearer on the subject of what archaeology was not:

> It has indeed been stated by an American writer that . . . the archaeologist, as archaeologist, is really nothing but a technician. I have no hesitation in denouncing that extreme view as nonsense. A lepidopterist is a great deal more than a butterfly-catcher. [11]

He reflected upon the possible limitations of archaeology's findings:

> In a classic sentence it has been observed that a great nation may leave behind it a very poor rubbish-heap. And are we, as practising archaeologists, to award the palm to the unknown Sumerian who was buried at Ur with sixty-three helmeted soldiers, grooms, and gold-garlanded damsels, two chariots and six bullocks, or to the Nazarene in a loin-cloth who was nailed up on Golgotha between two thieves? I merely ask the question, but cannot help feeling that, were archaeology alone the arbiter, the answer would not be in doubt. Give us helmets and gold garlands every time . . . But let us at least, in our gratitude for these things, remember the missing values that cannot be appraised in inches or soil-samples or smudges in the earth. [12]

As an archaeologist, Wheeler was concerned to employ techniques which could extract the fullest and most precise evidence which could be derived from excavations and the study of excavated objects. From the beginning of his career he stressed the need for the most meticulous observation of the stratified structural evidence revealed by digging, and the need for the most careful recording of the objects found in association with such structures. He was happy to embrace any new analytical aid which might be proffered as a by-product of progress in the physical or biological sciences, and to advocate the application of refined statistical techniques to various archaeological contexts. This might suggest that we are dealing with a development very different from the main forms of historical work, but this would be a misleading impression, for Wheeler was in fact a considerable historian. He did not only employ archaeological materials in his work. His approach to the archaeology of north-west India was based in part upon the narrative, by the Greek historian Arrian, of Alexander the Great's irruption into that area in 327–6 BC. At Maiden Castle, in northern France, at Stanwick and at St Albans, he was concerned to fit the archaeological evidence into a historical framework already in part established by surviving written sources. Indeed, at St Albans his high regard for the documentary sources was partly responsible for his erroneous conclusions about the nature of that community in the fifth century. His achievements in south India owed much to his knowledge of classical descriptions of ancient commerce, and his subsequent evaluation of the trade involved the use of much non-archaeological evidence. In considering the importance of pepper he noted that the exaction of 3,000 lb of pepper formed part of Alaric's demands on Rome in AD 408, and added in an aside that the pepper in a Spanish carrack captured by Frobisher off the Azores in 1592 was alone valued at £102,000. For India's trading links in mediaeval times he drew upon contemporary written sources from China.[13]

Much of Wheeler's work lay in areas for which at least some documentary evidence was available, and often he was in reality correlating specifically archaeological evidence with other forms of historical evidence. If he seemed reluctant to accept archaeology as a part of history explicitly, the relationship is often implicit in his work. The way in which he naturally turns to historians when discussing the nature of archaeology is a case in point. Discussing the need for archaeology to make a wide appeal he noted that 'Years before Tutankhamun came to the rescue, G. M. Trevelyan had been protesting that "if historians neglect to educate the public, if they fail to interest it intelligently in the past, then all their historical learning is valueless except in so far as it educates themselves"'. Analysing the nature of archaeology in a textbook he observed:

as the Oxford historian, Sir Llewellyn Woodward, remarks, 'Historical understanding is more than a series of detective tricks. It requires a mind already attuned to the scale of human action and practised in the subtlest use of language to express the depths and heights'. That is well said. The historian, and with him I group the archaeologist, must have a spark of the intuitive comprehension which inspires the painter or the poet.[14]

Clearer still is Wheeler's repeated emphasis on the objectives which ought to inspire the archaeologist. Time and again in his lectures and his writings he stressed that the archaeologist is not primarily interested in digging up *things,* but as it were in digging up *people.* The tools and the techniques of archaeology are not objectives in themselves, but rather the means to be employed in helping to enhance our understanding of people in the past. It is difficult to make a meaningful distinction between this and the nature of history. Wheeler made this point repeatedly. The province of the archaeologist, he wrote, is 'to view the past and the present as a single, continuous and not always unsuccessful battle between Man and his environment and, above all, between Man and himself'.[15]

Yet perhaps the best demonstration of the relationship between history and archaeology to be derived from Wheeler's work comes from the end-product. Some of his books, notably *Rome beyond the Imperial Frontiers,* are very much history books in which archaeological evidence is much employed. Even when he was describing the results of specific excavations, the same spirit is plainly at work. Two British examples illustrate this admirably. At Lydney,

> the site owes its major distinction to the fact that about AD 370 it became a popular centre of religious pilgrimage. A remarkable basilical temple, a guest-house, a 'long building' of disputed function, and a sumptuous bath-building attracted worshippers and their humble offerings – several thousands of coins, and all manner of trinkets and tokens – to the mysterious god Nodens and the pantheon of pantheistic properties which he had encompassed. He was amongst other things a healer; those troubled with their eyes, with unhealed sores, with the ills of child-bearing, might come to him for the relief of their ailments. He had power over the sun and the sea; fishermen from the Severn must have toiled up the narrow rocky path to this shrine. No doubt he catered for all the miscellaneous physical and metaphysical needs of the countryside with the universality of a village store. He flourished in a time of confused and groping thought, and in a remote countryside to which the dust of the old temples was more apt and homely than the specious furnishings of the new church. Anyway, at the end of the fourth century, and in the fifth, when Nodens held court at Lydney, Ravenna and Byzantium and Jerusalem were an uncommon long way off if you had the toothache or a broken arm or had lost your nets in the Severn tide which comes upon you like a moving cliff at Newnham.

An even more compelling instance of historical reconstruction occurred in the interpretation of Maiden Castle. Again note the basis on which Wheeler approached the site:

> Up to a point Suetonius had prepared us for it in his 'life' of the Emperor Vespasian, who, as a divisional commander, led the Second Royal Legion into south-western England in AD 43–4. Vespasian, he tells us, reduced 'two very formidable tribes and over twenty fortified native towns (*oppida*), together with the Isle of Wight'.

However, the new archaeological evidence serves to fill out the historical account:

It was now easy enough to reconstruct the sequence of events. Before the close fighting began, the regiment of catapults or *ballistae,* which habitually accompanied a legion on campaign, put down a barrage across the gateway, causing casualties at the outset. Following the barrage, the Roman infantry advanced up the slope, cutting its way from rampart to rampart, tower to tower. In the innermost bay of the entrance, a number of huts had recently been built; these were now set alight, and under the rising clouds of smoke the gates were stormed. But resistance had been obstinate and the attack was pushed home with every sort of savagery. The scene became that of a massacre in which the wounded were not spared. Finally the gates were demolished and the stone walls which flanked them reduced to the lowly and ruinous condition in which we found them, nineteen centuries later.

The sequel was no less apparent. That night, when the fires of the legion shone out (as we may fairly imagine) in orderly lines across the valley, the survivors crept forth from their broken stronghold and, in the darkness, buried their dead as nearly as might be outside their tumbled gates, in that place where the ashes of their burnt huts lay warm and thick upon the ground. The task was carried out anxiously and hastily, and without order; many of the dead were still in rigor mortis, contorted as they had fallen in the struggle; in any event, the living were in no condition for the niceties of ritual. Yet from few of the graves were omitted those tributes of food and drink which were the proper perquisites of the dead. The whole war-cemetery as it lay exposed before us was eloquent of mingled piety and distraction, of weariness, dread and darkness but yet not of complete forgetfulness. Surely no poor relic in the soil of Britain was ever more fraught with high tragedy.

We are not concerned here with the technical question of whether or not Wheeler had all the details right, but rather the point that it is difficult to see in this account anything other than history. For Wheeler, this kind of imaginative historical reconstruction was the centre of the proper objectives of the archaeologist. Just as there is no history, so there is no archaeology, of wood or iron, clay or stone, except in so far as these dead objects enshrine evidence which can tell us something about past human activity. The distinction between the archaeologist and other kinds of historian is not a fundamental one, but merely a matter of specialised methods and materials which different kinds of historians may employ to a common basic end.

NOTES: CHAPTER 10

1 Here, and at other points where quotations appear without specific references, the passage is taken from Wheeler's autobiography, *Still Digging* (1955).
2 Wheeler, *Archaeology from the Earth* (1954), p. 1.
3 Pitt-Rivers's career, an interesting and varied one. is summarised in the *Dictionary of National Biography*, Vol. XXII.
4 D. Hill and M. Jesson (eds), *The Iron Age and its Hill-Forts* (1971), p. 1. This volume is a tribute presented to Wheeler in his eightieth year.
5 *Archaeology from the Earth*, p. 192.
6 R. Merrifield, *The Roman City of London* (1965), p. 11.
7 *The Iron Age and its Hill-Forts*, p. 1.
8 Wheeler, *My Archaeological Mission to India and Pakistan* (1976), p. 9.
9 Wheeler, *Rome beyond the Imperial Frontiers* (1954), p. v.
10 *Archaeology from the Earth*, pp. 1–2.
11 ibid., p. 200.
12 ibid., p. 214.
13 *Rome beyond the Imperial Frontiers*, pp. 122 and 162.
14 *Archaeology from the Earth*, p. 202.
15 ibid., p. 217.

NOTE ON FURTHER READING

Wheeler's autobiography, *Still Digging*, published in 1955 provides the best account of his life. Among his more important books and papers are *Archaeology from the Earth* (1954), *Rome beyond the Imperial Frontiers* (1954), *The Indus Civilisation* (1953, supplementary volume to the *Cambridge History of India*), and *Early India and Pakistan* (1959, rev. edn 1968). For a fuller discussion of the relationship between history and archaeology, see D. P. Dymond, *Archaeology and History* (1974). In Chapter 5 of *The Use and Abuse of History* (1975), M. I. Finley also discusses the relationship between the two subjects and, in particular, considers some of the arguments for seeing archaeology as a separate subject.

11 Herbert Butterfield

Herbert Butterfield was born in October 1900; educated at the Trade and Grammar School, Keighley, and Peterhouse, Cambridge, where he was a scholar. Fellow of Peterhouse from 1923 to 1955, master from 1955 to 1968. In 1944 elected professor of modern history at Cambridge, and in 1963 became Regius Professor of Modern History; knighted in 1968. President of the Historical Association from 1955 to 1958. His main publications were: *The Historical Novel* (1924); *The Peace Tactics of Napoleon* (1929); *The Whig Interpretation of History* (1931); *Select Documents of European History, 1715–1920* (1931); *Napoleon* (1939); *The Statecraft of Machiavelli* (1940); *The Englishman and his History* (1944); *George III, Lord North and the People* (1949); *The Origins of Modern Science* (1949); *Christianity and History* (1949); *History and Human Relations* (1951); *Christianity in European History* (1951); *Christianity, Diplomacy and War* (1953); *Man on his Past* (1955); *George III and the Historians* (1957). He died on 20 July 1979 at Cambridge.

The work of Sir Herbert Butterfield was one of the major influences upon the evolution of English historiography in the years immediately before and after the Second World War. Few historians were so highly regarded both within and beyond the narrow confines of the academic world. Butterfield's influence was largely, though not exclusively, the result of his willingness to tackle great issues, to roam the centuries with a freedom usually associated with an earlier generation of historians. He wrote about Machiavelli as well as Napoleon; he lectured on the origins of modern science as well as on the history of Europe since the Renaissance; he was constantly preoccupied with the meaning of history as a humane discipline. For some this wide range of interests made him suspect, and he was sometimes accused of showing a greater interest in the books of others than in advancing the techniques of research. But his fame demonstrated that there was still a thirst for historical writing on the broad scale, and that many who were in no sense professional historians sought a meaning and a purpose in history.

Butterfield's career was dominated by three major concerns. First there was his work on the history of the late eighteenth and early nineteenth centuries, which embraced studies of Napoleon's career and diplomacy as well as English politics in the reign of George III. Second, there was his interest in historiography, which was given expression in books such as *The Whig Interpretation of History, Man on his Past,* and his controversial *George III and the Historians.* Third, there was his readiness as a Christian to reflect on the meaning of his faith for the study of history: this was most popularly displayed in his published lectures, *Christianity and History.*

He began his career as a diplomatic historian, very much in the tradition of his great teacher at Peterhouse, H. W. V. Temperley, the author of the finest study of the foreign policy of Canning. Butterfield's *The Peace Tactics of Napoleon* reflected a similar combination of the meticulous analysis of the details of diplomatic negotiation with an imaginative sympathy for the personalities of the period. Parts of the book showed affinities with the literary historian's fondness for the thrilling setpiece or the memorable character-sketch. The book opened with a vivid evocation of the confusions which followed the battles of Jena and Auerstadt:

> The fine show of armies arrayed and kings in proud postures had collapsed into medley and muddle in the twin battles . . . It littered the countryside and strove painfully to sort itself out afresh, as the din subsided and the smoke cleared away. Napoleon, sprawling upon the ground to study his maps, fell into an undignified sleep, and his guard took silent stand around him. Murat, writing to his master, apologised; 'Your Majesty will pardon my scribble, but I am alone and dropping from fatigue', and he who was no weakling blundered the strokes of his pen, as if he had been drunk. The release from the tension of battle liberated the worst elements in an army. The forces of the very victors seemed endangered by indiscipline.[1]

Butterfield's imaginative sympathy was extended to all the protagonists in the drama. He contrasted the personalities of Napoleon and Talleyrand in a series of vivid phrases:

> Napoleon was essentially a man of visions and impulses, every conjecture, every trick of circumstance only prompting him to more grand designs, only luring his eye to more untrodden hills. But Talleyrand could not go with him all the way, and, aristocrat at heart, would not consent to be a mute unreasoning tool. Talleyrand's thought was of that withering kind that was so fashionable and attractive in the gilded world of his youth. He talked with a wink and a smile, his sarcasm would charm a salon, and, in repartee, he would cover a

sword-thrust with velvet; but always his was the talk of a sceptic rather than the enthusiast, the critic rather than the dreamer; he could be delightfully oblique, he was never daringly grand. He thought best when on the defensive. This was where he differed from his master. This was why he was able to play a sort of second critical self to Napoleon, checking his flights of ambition, softening his intemperate expressions, and moderating his indiscreet outbursts – and, on the positive side, furnishing him expedients rather than grand designs. Hence he was perhaps the man to know Napoleon, and realise the true situation of affairs, better than Napoleon himself.[2]

Writing of this quality – pungent, individual, perceptive – demonstrated that Butterfield, who was to gain fame as a critic of the literary school of historians, could match them in those arts in which they had excelled – the lively delineation of character, the sense of historical conflict heightened by a poignant phrase, the intensification of historical analysis by a feeling of dramatic involvement. Butterfield was conscious of the link between history and literature; as a young man he had written a prize essay on the historical novel. Although he believed that the era of literary history had gone for good, he was prepared to admit that, in their own time, literary historians such as Carlyle and Macaulay had greatly advanced the understanding of history, and that a novelist such as Sir Walter Scott had contributed much to historical awareness.

But it was with the publication of *The Whig Interpretation of History* in 1931 that Butterfield became known to a wider public, and this book revealed the second of his main interests, the study of the manner and significance of historical writing itself.

The Whig Interpretation must be placed in context of its own day. The modern student might feel at times that much of what is being said is obvious, and that the generalised use of the term 'Whig historian' confuses the argument. The strength of the reaction against Whig history, and the way in which many of Butterfield's ideas passed (sometimes unconsciously) into historical thought and practice, make it all the more necessary for the modern reader to recall the dominance of the Whig – or more accurately, the Liberal – view of history in the years up to the First World War. What Butterfield described, partly misleadingly, as the Whig interpretation of history, may now be seen as chiefly a Victorian and Edwardian phenomenon. But there is no doubt that particularly among historians writing in English there was a strong tendency to write history in terms of the triumph of enlightenment and progress. Historians such as Edward Augustus Freeman, Bishop Stubbs, and J. R. Green had been confident in their conviction that English history was primarily the story of civil and religious liberty, and that the friends and foes of liberty could be clearly identified in the past. The conventional picture of the Reformation or the English Civil War or the Glorious Revolution showed little sympathy with the Catholic or Royalist side of these questions, while the work of Sir George Otto Trevelyan, for example, had depicted the reign of George III in terms of a stupidly reactionary king seeking to restore personal government by means of corruption and losing the American colonies in consequence.

Butterfield argued that the Whig historian studied the past in a fashion that was crude and unimaginative, and he singled out for special condemnation 'the study of the past with direct and perpetual reference to the present'.[3] The historian ought rather to focus upon unlikenesses. If all he did was to seek anticipations of the present in the past he would draw misleading analogies. Such a method would make history converge on the present, with an obvious principle of progress being seen at work, Protestants and Whigs being its perennial allies and Catholics and Tories its perpetual opponents. By viewing history from the standpoint of his own time the historian fell into the trap of suggesting that only in relation to the twentieth century could historical events be said to have any significance. Against such an assumption Butterfield affirmed, with considerable vigour and much repetition, that real historical understanding was achieved only by making the past our present and by seeing life with the eyes of centuries other than our own. The past deserved to be understood for its own sake. For the men of the past the issues that divided them and which drove them to conflict or catastrophe were as valid as the issues of modern times.

Butterfield urged that the 'Whig' approach transcended mere party bias. Men who were staunch reactionaries in their own time had written history that was in all essentials Whig. It was all too easy for any historian, whatever his bias, to go to the past with the present in mind and to produce an oversimplified abridgement primarily geared to the demands of his own age. Butterfield's warnings were just as applicable to Marxist or New Left or Romantic Royalist or Old Catholic versions of the past as to 'Whigs', although his title, and his repeated denunciations of Whig historians, too few of whom were precisely identified, blurred this implication. Butterfield's attack was directed against all who ransacked the past in order to justify a contemporary viewpoint: 'The study of the past with one eye, so to speak, upon the present is the source of all sins and sophistries in history, starting with the simplest of them, the anachronism.'[4]

This was the essence of Butterfield's argument. He expounded it with too limited a range of illustration, however. Too much of what he wrote referred to the Reformation of the sixteenth century, and somewhat surprisingly, given his interest in the Napoleonic period, his references to the impact of the French Revolution or the rivalry between Pitt and Fox were few and brief. Again and again, in what was a short essay, he returned to the struggles between Luther, Calvin and the popes, reiterating that the Protestants and Catholics of the sixteenth century had had more in common with each other than either party had with the twentieth century. To suggest that one side was fighting for the modern world while only the other was seeking to delay its emergence was false. Historical development was the product, not of the victory of one side over the other, but of the interplay between the two. History was not the study of origins; it was 'the analysis of all the mediations by which the past was turned into our present'.[5]

Butterfield stressed the limited competence of the historian. He was not concerned with discovering general truths of universal validity. His real role, and the secret of his art, lay in the intense study of actual events. By temperament and experience he was bound to have a healthy distrust of disembodied reasoning: 'the value of history lies in the richness of its recovery of the concrete life of the past'.[6] The historian sought to reveal the complications underlying seeming certainties. Behind every generalisation lay a series of complexities. Judgements were relative to time and circumstance, but above everything else the historian should be conscious of the uncertain and tragic element of human conflict.

Despite his anxiety to denounce history written by the friends of progress, Butterfield recognised that history without bias might be seen as merely dull. Here the contribution of disciplined historical imagination was decisive. Butterfield was scathing about those who thought that the writing of history amounted to little more than the transcription of card-indexes. He criticised Whig historians not because they showed imagination and sympathy but because they extended imaginative understanding only to those of whom they approved. The historian was an observer of the past but he was no passive spectator. Only the historian could make the past intelligible to the present: 'It is in this sense that history must always be written from the point of view of the present. It is in this sense that every age will have to write its history over again.'[7] The historian was involved in more than the collection of facts, for men went to the past to discover not merely facts but 'significances'. It was therefore necessary for the historian to approach his task with a sensibility that was similar in some ways to that of a poet.

Butterfield conceded that Whig historians had been moved by enthusiasm, often for some aspect of the present which they sought to trace in the past, but true historical fervour was the love of the past for the sake of the past, the fervour that had been roused in Gibbon by the sight of the ruins of ancient Rome. The exercise of historical imagination brought its own satisfaction – 'those glimpses of a new interpretative truth, which are the historian's achievement and his aesthetic delight'.[8] This threw the problem of abridgement into greater relief: it coarsened and cheapened historical insight, yet every work of history was an exercise in abridgement. Every abridgement ought, therefore, to suggest complexity. And much more serious than conscious bias was the undemonstrative bias that nevertheless warped the pattern of interpretation.

Though the title of Butterfield's book called to mind Macaulay, his most serious shafts were directed not so much against Macaulay, Green, Freeman or Stubbs, as against Lord Acton, the great representative of the historian as a judge: in the sense, not of the impartial presenter of evidence, but of the defender of moral values. Acton was averse to anything which smacked of extenuation, and Butterfield singled out for special condemnation the statement: 'Suffer no man and no cause to escape the undying penalty which history has the power to inflict on wrong.' Too often, in Butterfield's view, Acton's advice amounted to denying historical sympathy to selected people or causes in the past. Acton had been right in protesting against the shoddier sort of historical whitewash, but Butterfield believed that by urging the historian to err on the side of severity he was evading the moral problem rather than maintaining a lofty standard of historical rectitude. To say that it was better to be unjust to the dead than 'to give currency to loose ideas on questions of morals' was the *reductio ad absurdum* of moral judgements in history. Acton had come very close to arguing that it was better to be unhistorical than to lower the moral dignity of history.

Butterfield preferred to depict the historian as a reconciler rather than a moral arbiter. The historian was neither judge nor jury. He was more like an expert witness, and he therefore required the closest cross-examination. History was all things to all men. She was a hireling, a harlot, a reprobate, liable to lie to the end of the last cross-examination:

> If we must confuse counsel by personifying history at all, it is best to treat her as an old reprobate, whose tricks and juggleries are things to be guarded against. In other words the truth of history is no simple matter, all packed and parcelled ready for handling in the market-place. And the understanding of the past is not so easy as it is sometimes made to appear.[9]

Such were the main themes of Butterfield's essay. Some critics felt that it misrepresented the primary tradition of English historical writing, others that it was repetitive and laboured. D. C. Somervell described the essay as interesting because its author was grappling with an insoluble problem: 'but he hardly seems to be master of his thesis. Consequently he worries round and round, repeats himself again and again.'[10] One of the wittiest retorts came from another Cambridge historian, who was also, like Butterfield, a nonconformist: Bernard Lord Manning. Manning conceded the value in Butterfield's warnings against seeking the wrong sort of witness from history but sharply rebuked the book's one-sidedness:

Why Mr Butterfield has chosen to flog this particularly dead horse at this particular moment in the *post-mortem* I do not know. For if there has been, and is, a Whig and Protestant view of history, there has been, and is, a not less vicious Tory and Communist and Popish and Atheistic twisting of history; and I refuse, as a Protestant Whig, to have this particular vice attributed solely or chiefly to me.[11]

But Butterfield was not insensitive to the positive elements in the English Whig tradition, or to the complexity which marked the evolution of English historiography. In *The Englishman and his History* he dealt more charitably with the Whigs, though he preferred Whig politicians to Whig historians, arguing that they had an attitude to history which amounted to a means of 'co-operating with the forces of history, an alliance with Providence, which the Whig historians were much slower to achieve – which they were even perhaps too partisan to discern'.[12] Possibly with some of the criticisms of his earlier book in mind he suggested that the Whig interpretation of history was really the English interpretation of history. There had been no viable alternative in England until the twentieth century. There was no truly Tory tradition, for the Tories had not rejected the Whig interpretation. They simply retold the story of liberty in such a way as to suggest that they and not the Whigs were the true authors of constitutional government and civil liberty. Englishmen of all parties appealed to the past, seeking to place themselves within an evolving historical tradition, rooting change in continuity. Macaulay himself had contrasted the relationship with history common among most English statesmen and the rejection of the *ancien régime* by most French politicians in the nineteenth century. But while Englishmen clung to their past it was a highly edited version of events which passed for history. 'The good terms', Butterfield wrote, 'that Englishmen have managed to keep with their bygone centuries have been the counterpart of their ability to make the past move with them, so to speak.'[13] The worship of Magna Carta, a concern for historical rights (both real and imagined), and the Whig interpretation of history itself were 'joint producers of one live piece of history'. They had prevented any sharp breach with the past and they had ensured the continuity and richness of institutional development. He remained fully aware of the defects of the Whig tradition in so far as it claimed to offer an accurate picture of the past, but he recognised that it had been part of history itself, and that it had contributed to the harmony of national development, however partisan its interpretation of events had been.

Butterfield has sometimes been accused of creating a new 'Tory' school of history, and even those who shrink from this terminology have taken refuge in talk of a Peterhouse or Butterfield 'connection'. This seems unnecessarily conspiratorial. Butterfield never saw himself as presiding over a school of historians: one of his criticisms of the Namierites was that they always hunted in packs, though the charge was hotly refuted by those against whom it was made. Butterfield was consistently hostile to the imposition of any single orthodoxy upon events. During the 1950s he became particularly unhappy at the way in which one school of historians appeared to dominate the study of the English eighteenth century. Here his concern for historiography and his love of one particular period combined to make his response intense, passionate and committed.

He had long been devoted to the eighteenth century. For many years he had worked on the career of Charles James Fox, and he was preoccupied with the history of politics in the reign of George III. He had become convinced of the unique importance of the crisis of 1779–80, when the nation faced severe challenges abroad and the outburst of agitation at home. His book *George III, Lord North and the People* sought to redress the balance, not only against those who had portrayed George III as an enemy of the constitution, but also against those whom Butterfield thought too limited and too mechanical in their understanding of the workings of the eighteenth-century political system. As well as doing justice to George III, Butterfield was eager to analyse the newer developments which were, in his view, beginning to reshape English politics. Here he turned his attention not only to the Rockinghamites and the other opposition Whigs but also to the radical movement in the country, which he saw as the precursor of modern parties.

Some historians have argued that Butterfield exaggerated the significance of the Yorkshire Association and the scale of the crisis of 1779–80. Richard Pares believed that he had mistaken 'a portent for a crisis' and complained of what he called 'the excessive profusion of strident metaphors'.[14] But Butterfield's work can now be seen as possessing something of a pioneering character. He tried to relate the conflicts and confrontations of high politics to the broader currents of opinion in the country and thereby to escape from too obsessive a concern with high politics. This aspect of late eighteenth-century politics is still being investigated by a number of younger historians, and while few of them would claim to be consciously following Butterfield's example, his work remains an indication of the line later historical inquiries were to take.

Butterfield's anxieties about prevalent methods of approaching the problems posed by the reign of George III were given full expression in *George III and the Historians* published in 1957. It was coolly, even disparagingly, received in some quarters on its first appearance. One reviewer claimed that it would have been better if the manuscript had remained in a drawer of the Master of Peterhouse's desk. Like so much of Butterfield's work it had a strong historiographical element. It outlined a variety of interpretations of the early years of George III's reign from the work of men such as Horace Walpole, John Adolphus and Robert Huish, through the nineteenth century, to the work of Sir Lewis Namier and his disciples in the twentieth century.

The book began with a chapter on the historian and his evidence, which was a plea for critical reading, and for a sober realisation that historians, and particularly research students, may show an exaggerated reverence for primary as distinct from secondary sources. Butterfield believed that a thorough knowledge of the secondary literature was essential for any historian: if he ignored the work of others he would lose sight of what a long tradition of scholarship had established. Butterfield repeated his warnings against regarding the writing of history as mere transcription; the student was urged to treat his evidence in the manner in which a detective treats his clues. Each piece of evidence had to be confirmed, supplemented, qualified by others:

> At the last stage of the enquiry, the real clue may lie in the more personal communications; and some scrap of paper not in the Foreign Office at all may acquire a pivotal importance, so that it affects our interpretation of all the rest of the evidence. And that is one of the reasons why the technical historian can never be content with mere selections, and can never feel that his work is done.[15]

Butterfield never denied the great achievements of Namier and those who had worked closely with him. He praised the thoroughness of their researches, and referred to the emergent *History of Parliament* as 'a type of achievement hardly paralleled in the historiography of our time'. The dispute lay at another level: at the level of interpretation, of deciding what the limits of structural analysis were. Butterfield believed that Namier had done invaluable work in exposing the naivety of one approach to the eighteenth century, but that he suffered from a similar limitation of understanding. It was a mistake 'to drain the intellectual content out of the things that politicians do'. Butterfield was not suggesting that men always act from the highest motives. But ideas and modes of thought were themselves part of the texture of history, and this was true for the first twenty years of George III's reign. An aversion from Burke was not a sufficient ground for ignoring the impact of his ideas. Butterfield believed that Namier's distrust of any tendency to exaggerate the conscious will and purpose of individuals had produced an inclination to underrate the role of individuals in history. If Namier's attitude were to be carried to its logical conclusion, it would be difficult to see why the study of history should be thought to have any importance for anybody. It was possible to become doctrinaire, too ideological in one's opposition to ideology, too wilful in one's emphasis on the wilfulness of history.

Critics were able to show that some of Butterfield's charges were wild and inaccurate. Jacob M. Price pointed out that the Butterfield who was so unrelenting with Whig historians had a warm place in his heart for the Whigs themselves. He claimed that Butterfield was indifferent to the 'rival claims of research methodology, the true glory of the Namierites'. The Namierites saw interpretation as a function of research; for Butterfield interpretation seemed to have a life of its own. 'Thus, while they demand the utmost verbal attention from their readers, he seems no more interested in semantic rigour than in any of the other niceties of methodology'. Price complained that Butterfield shifted his ground throughout the book, and he could not resist asking whether all the contradictions added up to Butterfield 'the Whig historian', a Butterfield 'for whom Rockingham and Fox still sit on Olympus'.[16] Nevertheless, what one historian has called Butterfield's long rearguard action against the Namierite interpretation has to some extent been justified by events. A number of younger historians now see Namier's own psychological presuppositions and methodology as too limited. Although this is not to say that Butterfield's attack was either fully justified or satisfactorily sustained in every detail, it suggests that he was doing more than tilt at windmills.

Butterfield was always aware of the limits within which the academic historian worked and the restricted significance of his work. In the preface to *Man on his Past* he summed up with some poignancy the transient fame associated with historical scholarship:

The death which the outmoded historian has to suffer is more complete and pitiful than ordinary death. A man who has written a single lyric may outlast the centuries, living on in perpetual youth; but the author of a hundredweight of heavy historical tomes has them piled upon his grave, to hold him securely down. A mere literary dressing would seem to be insufficient to defend such an author from the ravages of time. The historian who survives seems to be the one who in some way or other has managed to break through into the realm of enduring ideas or gives hints of a deeper tide in the affairs of men.[17]

Butterfield was uneasy about the growing tendency for research students to work on what he called vague and indefinite subjects. He remained convinced that a piece of diplomatic history was as good a training as any for the young historian. He was dubious about the benefits of intellectual and social history for the inexperienced research student. Here he was setting his face against a tendency which gathered pace in the 1960s: the suggestion that only social or economic history or history viewed chiefly as a form of sociology had any relevance for those whose primary concern was less the understanding of the past than the transformation of society. Experience has proved that Butterfield's misgivings were sound. Despite gloomy predictions history has made a considerable recovery in the face of challenges posed by social science, sociology and the cult of the history of ideas.

This is not to deny the value of social history or of any other kind of history, but to reaffirm the value of traditional types of historical study. Butterfield was never concerned with the construction of abstract schemes of speculative history. He had no interest in philosophies of history or the discernment of cosmic patterns in the unfolding of events. Rather he was committed to the study of history as a craft shaped by the cultural experience of the eighteenth and nineteenth centuries. He saw the historian as a fallible mortal but without him there could be no history. He was always sceptical and sometimes scathing about those who thought that some technical innovation would solve the problems of historical understanding. It was wholly typical that he should end his lecture on the origins of the Seven Years' War with a tribute to Ranke: 'In the last resort, sheer insight is the greatest asset of all.'[18]

In the Michaelmas Term 1948 Butterfield delivered a course of lectures on Christianity and history in the University of Cambridge. These were so successful that they were delivered in a revised form in a series of broadcasts in April and May 1949 and later the same year published in book form. They met with wide acclaim. Butterfield had achieved what many academic historians dream about but few accomplish: he had communicated with a wider public without compromising his professional status. His lectures gave meaning to the study of the past in a way which transcended the technicalities of research or the pressures of routine learning. Among undergraduates his influence was immense: his work added another dimension to historical study. His lectures were read by clergymen of all denominations, and many a sermon, whether delivered in a parish church, a college chapel or a nonconformist Bethel, ended with the closing words of *Christianity and History:* 'Hold to Christ, and for the rest be totally uncommitted.'

Much of what Butterfield said was particularly appropriate to the climate of opinion immediately after the Second World War, when hopes for international understanding and world peace were being eroded by the beginnings of the Cold War. Men sought meaning in history, but their mood was one of sober realism, and the sense of catching a deeper tide in the affairs of men than any form of shallow optimism could provide was one of the main reasons for the success of *Christianity and History.* One reviewer, Sir Maurice Powicke, was distressed by Butterfield's emphasis on human sinfulness: 'He hammers away on the importance of his message so incessantly that it loses something of its persuasiveness, and becomes rather a prophetic message for the present than a lesson drawn from a spacious survey of the past.'[19] But there is a depth to prophecy which academic caution cannot match, and Butterfield would probably not have resented being likened to an Old Testament prophet: he was known to incorporate into a lecture on the origins of diplomacy a discussion of the Assyrian embassy to Jerusalem as it is recorded in the eighteenth chapter of the Second Book of Kings, and much of what he said in *Christianity and History* showed a keen appreciation of biblical prophecy. His main theme was that the God of the Bible was pre-eminently the God of history, and that this was fundamental to an understanding of both Judaism and Christianity. Butterfield contrasted the religion of the God of history with nature and fertility cults. A profounder insight into the problems of good and evil was closely linked with the contemplation of history, which was not only the story of mankind but the record of God's dealings with men.

For the Christian, religious thought was inextricably bound up with historical thought. Christianity, rooted as it was in the life of Christ, was an historical religion in an unique sense. But precisely because this was so, Butterfield argued that superficial or defective history could be a more serious obstacle to Christian faith than natural science. It was also significant that Marxism, which Butterfield described as the most formidable contemporary challenge to Christianity, was itself an ideology equipped with a particular version of history. Those who sought God only in nature were liable, in Butterfield's view, to debase religion; those who were concerned only with man-in-nature were likely to 'degrade history into a wilderness of atrocity and crime'.

A sense of history was the greatest security against facile optimism and superficial pessimism. But this meant more than romantic day-dreaming or a mere nostalgia for the past. Butterfield argued that Christians ought to be committed to demanding the most exact type of history, since only the accurate rediscovery of the past as it really was could be adequate for the demands which the Christian made upon the past. Whenever historical writing claimed the status of finality it was to be searchingly examined, and the analogy between the historian and a detective was used to emphasise the constant re-examination of the evidence which was so much a part of the historian's task.

History, Butterfield argued, was a peculiar science 'in that it depends so much on things which can only be discovered and verified by insight, sympathy and imagination'. Historians sought to discover the past in a sense which would be free from party bias, but many disliked this matter-of-fact approach. 'And so it is that the liberal and the Jesuit, the Marxist and the Fascist, the Protestant and the Catholic, the rebel and the patriot – all cry out against our modern forms of exposition, saying what a bloodless pedestrian thing academic history is.' Even the student could feel that history was lacking at the most demanding level of all: 'Above all, the young student who does not know where he stands amongst all these partisans but goes round with a hungry look seeking for something like an interpretation of life – even the student who comes to history itself for his education, on the assumption that life will somehow explain itself if you study a greater length of it – he tells us that whereas he asked for bread, he is in reality only being given a stone.'[20]

Butterfield claimed that if men had found no philosophy or religion in their own experience of life it was unrealistic to expect academic history to provide them with one. To complain that history did not provide a meaning to life was to fall into two grievous errors: first, by asking of an academic subject more than it could give, and secondly, by tempting the historian into yielding to a particularly dangerous form of self-aggrandisement. Butterfield suggested that this error was a heresy learned from secular liberals, who had deposed religion in order to exalt scholarship in its place. But for the Christian the appeal of technical history was understandable: his religious faith had already given him a clue to his conception of the human drama. His faith might be challenged by what he found in history or it might be confirmed by it, but in both cases the tension would be of a creative kind. History deepened our understanding of human relations, within the restraints of its modest attempt to provide 'a limited knowledge of the demonstrable connections between events'.[21]

Butterfield maintained that the study of history made men more aware of the fragile foundations on which civilisation rested. He stressed the frailty and fallibility of men, especially when they were at their most pretentious, and he depicted men caught up in the tragic predicaments of a sinful world. History uncovered man's universal sin and a study of history would lead to the questioning of facile optimism. Indeed, Butterfield believed that such optimism was itself likely to contribute to new catastrophes:

> It is like the Bishop who said that if we totally disarmed he had too high an opinion of human nature to think that anybody would attack us. There might be great virtue in disarming and consenting to be made martyrs for the sake of the good cause; but to promise that we should not have to endure martyrdom in that situation, or to rely on such a supposition, is against both theology and history. It is essential not to have faith in human nature. Such faith is a recent heresy and a very disastrous one.[22]

For some this Augustinian emphasis was disturbing, but for others it struck a note of welcome realism.

Butterfield went on to reflect on the tragic element in human conflict. He based much of what he said on the Old Testament prophets, drawing attention to the distinctive contribution of the Jews to the understanding of catastrophe and to the way that men could come to a more profound grasp of the meaning of life through suffering. The insight of the Old Testament prophets, and the Christian understanding of redemptive suffering, were alike grounded in history and in the distinctive reflection of a particular people on the meaning of their history. The imagery of the Suffering Servant was particularly important here: 'And though it might be a remarkable thing to find an example of the Suffering Servant existing in its absolute purity – though there may have been only one perfect fulfilment of it in history – it is impossible to deny this picture its place as the pattern, the working-model, of ideas which do in fact operate throughout the ages, helping to reconcile man with his destiny.'[23]

It was with this in mind that Butterfield discussed the tragic element in history and the way in which the historian could look back and see in particular historical crises factors which had eluded the notice of contemporaries. In the sixteenth century Protestants and Catholics had seen each other as foes, but the historian could see just how much both sides had in common, that they were allies who had fallen out, and that this had given an added poignancy to the conflict. History meant that tragedy replaced melodrama. The human achievement could be seen by the historian as a great co-operative endeavour. Christianity sought to bind men together in love, and Butterfield went on to suggest that the historian was the reconciler who sought through his work to comprehend and explain, revealing to men what the conflicts of the past had been about and what had caused them, and showing that however divided men were they shared in a common predicament.

This acute sense of human suffering gave greater weight to Butterfield's discussion of providence, where he sought to grapple with the way in which good may be brought out of evil. He used a musical analogy. The sequence of historical events was like the performance of a piece of music by an orchestra, where the composer was also the conductor and where, if the players played a wrong note, he could incorporate this discord into the overall shape of the piece. Butterfield repeated his warnings against self-righteousness. He was especially scathing about wars of righteousness and he praised the virtues of traditional eighteenth-century diplomacy, the idea that the preservation of an international order transcended temporary national advantage, and the notion of limited wars for limited ends, fought in the sober recognition that today's foes may be tomorrow's allies. It was this type of thinking – which Butterfield took somewhat further in *Christianity, Diplomacy and War* – which led Mr A. J. P. Taylor to describe him as 'that Christian defender of the balance of power'.

Non-Christians were and are quick to point out that most of Butterfield's ideas were drawn from Christian theology, the Bible, the experience of faith, rather than from the findings of scholarship. But Butterfield never pretended otherwise. He had written as a Christian, and he always claimed that personal experience was the clue to the deeper meanings men found in history. History alone could not solve life's problems. He stated his position in language that was unambiguous and moving:

> I do not think that any man can ever arrive at his interpretation of the human drama by merely casting his eye over the course of the centuries in the way that a student of history might do. I am unable to see how a man can find the hand of God in secular history, unless he has first found that he has assurance of it in his personal experience. If it is objected that God is revealed in history through Christ, I cannot think that this can be true for the mere external observer, who puts on the thinking-cap of the ordinary historical student. It only becomes effective for those who have carried the narrative to intimate regions inside themselves, where certain of the issues are brought home to human beings.[24]

Butterfield consistently pleaded for humility among scholars. He pointed out that humble and unlettered folk could have visions of truth and goodness, could experience love and devotion, could manifest fidelity and courage, in ways often denied to those who prided themselves on their learning. Like C. S. Lewis, Butterfield regarded spiritual pride as the besetting sin of intellectuals and a particularly obnoxious one when associated with the writing of history. It was so easy for history to degenerate into polemical tracts written for sectarian or political purposes. Yet the Christian faith was embedded in history, as the church had appreciated when insisting on the full humanity as well as the divinity of Christ. Christianity would be unable to maintain the characteristics of an historical religion if the Christ of the theologians became divorced from the Jesus of history. It was necessary to combine belief in God with elasticity of mind. Christianity was less imprisoned within contemporary patterns of thought than many realised. It was this which explained the famous close to the book: 'We can do worse than remember a principle which both gives us a firm Rock and leaves us the maximum elasticity for our minds: the principle: Hold to Christ, and for the rest be totally uncommitted.'[25]

Butterfield's writing was remarkable in its variety and scope, but it held closely together. Even a survey as brief as this will have shown how certain themes recurred throughout his career. Few did more to enlarge the understanding of history in his time. Because he related the study of history to those ultimate questions which everyone has to face for himself he communicated something of the excitement and thrill of personal discovery to his audiences. His critics have argued that his reputation was built on a slight, early essay. Others have claimed that he did not chart out new developments in historical methodology (which usually means that he was not in agreement with those developments they personally favoured). Those who see history as essentially devoted to some utilitarian or political purpose have branded him as a reactionary. His work, like that of all historians, is vulnerable to the advances of research and to the changing emphases which each generation brings to the study of the past, but it remains a significant achievement, civilising in its implications, humane in its import. It is of abiding interest to those who bring to their historical studies more than the arid functioning of intellect divorced from experience, and who seek to understand the past with nothing less than the whole personality, a condition which, while not one of absolute simplicity, still costs not less than everything.

NOTES: CHAPTER 11

1 *The Peace Tactics of Napoleon* (1929), p. 3.
2 ibid., p. 168.
3 *The Whig Interpretation of History* (1931), p. 11.
4 ibid., pp. 31–2.
5 ibid., p. 47.
6 ibid., p. 68.
7 ibid., p. 92.
8 ibid., p. 96.
9 ibid., p. 132.
10 *History*, April 1932, p. 86.
11 B. L. Manning, *Essays in Orthodox Dissent* (1953), p. 29.
12 *The Englishman and his History* (1944), p. vii.
13 ibid., p. 6.
14 *English Historical Review*, vol. LXV (1950), p. 529.
15 *George III and the Historians* (1957), pp. 30–1.
16 *Journal of British Studies*, vol. I, no. 1 (November 1961), p. 92.
17 *Man on his Past* (1955), pp. xii—xiii.
18 ibid., p. 170.
19 *History*, October 1950, p. 196.
20 *Christianity and History* (1950), p. 20.
21 ibid., p. 24.
22 ibid., p. 47.
23 ibid., p. 87.
24 ibid., p. 107.
25 ibid., p. 146.

NOTE ON FURTHER READING

This chapter is best followed up by reading Butterfield's own works. In some ways his *Napoleon* (1939) makes a good start, before tackling more substantial works such as *The Peace Tactics of Napoleon* (1929) and *George III, Lord North and the People* (1949). *The Whig Interpretation of History* (1931) is essential, but it should be supplemented by *The Englishman and his History* (1944) and by several of the essays printed in *History and Human Relations* (1951), particularly those entitled 'Moral judgement in history' and 'History as a branch of literature'. *Man on his Past* (1955) is for the specialist. A reading of *George III and the Historians* (1957) should be accompanied by looking at some of Namier's writings: Sir Lewis's *Crossroads of Power* (1962) contains several important essays, and see also the note on further reading to Chapter 9. *Christianity and History* (1949) is fundamental to any appreciation of Butterfield's work, but two pieces by other Christians are helpful by way of comparison: the first is C. H. Dodd, *History and the Gospel* (rev. edn 1964), especially the chapter 'Christianity as an historical religion'; the second is B. L. Manning's lecture 'The witness of history to the power of Christ', printed in *Essays in Orthodox Dissent* (1953). In addition to the reviews referred to earlier, Carl Becker's review of *The Whig Interpretation of History* is worth reading: it is printed in *The Journal of Modern History* (1932), vol. 4, pp. 278-9. E. H. Carr makes several criticisms of Butterfield in *What Is History?* (1961), at times with more wit than accuracy. A useful collection of Sir Herbert's occasional papers and essays has recently been published: H. Butterfield, *Writings on Christianity and History*, ed. C. T. McIntire (1979). It contains an interesting introduction.

12 *Fernand Braudel*

Fernand Braudel was born 1902, in Lorraine, studied history at the Sorbonne and taught in schools in Algeria (1923–32) and Paris (1932–5), and at the University of Saõ Paulo, Brazil (1935–8). Spent the war years in a German prison camp writing *La Méditerranée et le monde méditerranéen à l'époque de Philippe II,* which he defended as a thesis in 1947 and published in 1949. He instantly took his place at the top of the French historical profession, being made professor at the Collège de France (1949) and president of the VIth Section of the Ecole Pratique des Hautes Etudes (1956–72). From 1956 to 1968 he edited *Annales d'histoire économique et sociale.* He has published *Le Monde actuel* (1963); an enlarged edition of his *Mediterranean* (1966); a study of *Civilisation matérielle et capitalisme* (Part I, 1967; by 1978 the remainder of this work had not appeared); and *L'Italia fuori d'Italia,* a long essay on the achievements of Italians outside Italy which forms part of a multi-volume collective history of Italy published by Einaudi of Turin. Selected essays were published as *Ecrits sur l'histoire* (1969). He is now at work on a history of France.

In 1949 there appeared in Paris a book which is commonly regarded as the most remarkable historical work to have been written this century. Its title was *The Mediterranean and the Mediterranean World in the Age of Philip II.* Its author, then 47 years old, was Fernand Braudel. Despite the many important contributions to history which Braudel has made since, it is with this book, his masterpiece, that I shall be mainly concerned in the pages which follow.

The Mediterranean is a massive book. In its first edition, before it was enlarged, it already contained some 600,000 words, making it the size of six ordinary volumes and a hundred times as long as this essay. It is divided into three parts, each of which exemplifies a different approach to the past. It may be useful to discuss these three parts in reverse order, in other words in order of increasing originality. The last part, which one suspects was written first, and is in any case the least unconventional of the three, is concerned with 'Events, politics and people' in the Mediterranean area in the second half of the sixteenth century. It deals with such well-known events in European history as the abdication of the Emperor Charles V (1555), the peace between France and Spain signed at Cateau-Cambrésis (1559), the Turkish siege of Malta (1565), the defeat of the Turkish fleet at Lepanto (1571), the Spanish intervention in the French Religious Wars, and the peace between France and Spain signed at Vervins (1598).

This third part of *The Mediterranean* is a substantial work on its own account. It is a fine piece of relatively traditional political, diplomatic and military history, solidly based on documents from the archives of Rome, Genoa, Florence, Paris and above all from Simancas, where the Spanish state papers are kept. Braudel provides brief but incisive character-sketches of the leading actors on the political stage. We meet Don García de Toledo, a man of 'strategic vision', 'capable of sharp observation', with a taste for operations on a grand scale; the 'narrow-minded and politically short-sighted' Duke of Alba; 'the astonishing and overpowering personality of Pius V', an apparently fragile old man who was at once dynamic and decisive, visionary and intransigent; and Philip II himself, slow, hard-working, cautious, secretive, a mystery even to his own courtiers.[1] Battles and sieges and tortuous negotiations are described in considerable detail.

However, this narrative of political and military events is more remote from traditional 'drum and trumpet' history than may appear at first sight. Time after time Braudel goes out of his way to emphasise the limitations on the freedom of action of individuals and the relative unimportance of events. In 1565, for example, Don García de Toledo, at that time the Spanish General de la Mar, the naval commander in the Mediterranean, was slow to relieve Malta, then hotly besieged by the Turks. 'Historians have blamed Don García for his delay', comments Braudel. 'But have they always examined thoroughly the conditions under which he had to operate? . . . A commander seeking to concentrate his fleet in a hurry had to contend not only with distance but also with all the many patrol, transport and supply duties the navy was called upon to perform in a sea where corsairs threatened every shore.'[2] He makes similar points about Philip II, whose well-known and oft-condemned slowness to react is not to be explained entirely in personal terms, but also as a result of communications difficulties over his vast empire, financial exhaustion and the existence of a 'double burden', of simultaneous problems in two areas, the Netherlands and the Mediterranean.[3] Like the failures of Don García and Philip II, the success of Don John of Austria at Lepanto must not be seen simply in personal terms. Don John was 'the instrument of destiny' in the sense that his victory depended on factors which he did not know about.[4] Even the battle itself, which the Christians of the time greeted as a glorious victory, is for Braudel interesting above all as an example of the limitations of 'the history of events' (*l'histoire événementielle* – a technical term in his vocabulary). Lepanto ended the Christian 'inferiority complex' relative to the Turks, but it did not have, and could not have had, serious military results. 'All one can say is that after all Lepanto was only a naval victory and that in this maritime world surrounded and barred by land-masses, such an encounter could not destroy Turkey's roots, which went deep into the continental interior.'[5]

In one of his first publications, a long article on 'the Spaniards and North Africa' (1928), the young Braudel had set himself the task of relating the African campaigns of the sixteenth century to the Spanish and indeed to the European history of the time. In a similar manner, and on a far grander scale, *The Mediterranean* is concerned to show the impossibility of understanding what is happening in one area if one does not know what is happening elsewhere at the same time. The Turks, for example, were inactive in the Mediterranean in the late 1560s because they were preoccupied with a revolt in the Yemen, and they may have attacked Cyprus in 1570 because they knew that the Spaniards were preoccupied with the revolt of Granada. 'History can do more than study walled gardens.'[6] The historian has to break through these walls, to study his subject 'globally' (*histoire globale*, in this sense, is another of Braudel's technical terms).

In short, Braudel is concerned to place individuals and events in a wider context, to make them more intelligible at the price of revealing their fundamental lack of importance. The history of events, he suggests, although 'the richest in human interest', is also the most superficial, dealing with what, in a typically poetic image, he calls 'surface disturbances, crests of foam that the tides of history carry on their strong backs'.[7] To understand what happened it is necessary to go deeper.

The stiller waters which run deeper are the subject of Part Two of *The Mediterranean,* entitled 'Collective destinies and general trends' (*Destins collectifs et mouvements d'ensemble*), and concerned with the history of structures – economic systems, states, societies, civilisations and the changing forms of war. While the history of events flashes past, the history of structures moves at a slower pace, in generations or even in centuries, scarcely noticed by contemporaries yet carrying them along with it just the same. For example, changes in Spanish policy will not make sense to anyone who does not know about changes in the government's financial resources, so Braudel discusses loans from Genoese bankers and imports of silver from the mines of Peru. Philip II's notorious slowness of reaction needs to be related to the structure of communications in the later sixteenth century. 'Historians have paid too little attention to the gigantic tasks demanded of the Spanish administrative machine', which had to govern an exceptionally far-flung empire in an age when transport was difficult, expensive and slow, so much so that 'the Mediterranean crossing from north to south could be expected to take one or two weeks', while the crossing from east to west took 'two or three months'.[8]

Yet the sixteenth century was favourable to large states, states like the opposing Spanish and Turkish Empires which dominated the Mediterranean. 'The course of history', writes Braudel, 'is by turns favourable or unfavourable to vast political hegemonies', and 'the period of economic growth during the fifteenth and sixteenth centuries created a situation consistently favourable to the large and very large state'.[9] Like their political structures, the social structures of the two great empires resembled one another. The main social trends in Anatolia and the Balkans in the sixteenth and seventeenth centuries parallel the trends in Spain and Italy (much of which was under Spanish rule). The basic trend in both areas was one of economic and social polarisation. The nobility prospered and migrated to the towns, the poor grew poorer and were increasingly driven to piracy and banditry, while the middle class disappeared or 'defected' to the nobility.

And yet the historian has still not reached the bottom. Beneath the social trends there lies yet another history, 'a history whose passage is almost imperceptible, that of man in his relationship to the environment, a history in which all change is slow, a history of constant repetition, ever-recurring cycles'.[10] This is a kind of historical geography or, as Braudel calls it, 'geo-history', and it is the subject of Part One of his *Mediterranean*, which is devoted to mountains and plains, coastlines and islands, climate, land-routes and sea-routes. The aim is to show that all these geographical features have their history, or rather, are part of history, and that neither the history of events nor the general trends can be understood without them. The section on mountains, for example, discusses the culture and the society of the mountain regions: the cultural conservatism of the mountaineers, the social and cultural barriers between mountaineers and plainsmen, and the need for many of the young highlanders to emigrate, to become mercenary soldiers, for example, as the Corsicans and Albanians so often did.

Turning to the sea itself, Braudel contrasts the western Mediterranean, which was under Spanish domination in this period, with the eastern Mediterranean, which was subject to the Turks. 'Politics merely followed the outline of an underlying reality. These two Mediterraneans, commanded by warring rulers, were physically, economically and culturally different from each other.'[11] Yet the Mediterranean remained a unity, more of a unity (according to Braudel) than Europe was or is, thanks to the climate and to the vines and olives which flourish in it, not to mention the sea itself.

Braudel's achievement in this remarkable book is to change our notions of both space and time. He makes his readers conscious of the importance of space as few (if any) historians before him have done. He achieves this end by making the sea itself the hero of his epic, rather than choosing a political unit like the Spanish Empire or an individual like Philip II; and also by his repeated reminders of the importance of distance, of communications, in an age when many goods travelled at the pace of mules and it often took two weeks to sail from Marseilles to Algiers. Most spectacularly of all, Braudel helps his readers to see the Mediterranean as a whole by moving outside it, in a section which clearly reveals his conception of 'global history', his 'desire and need to see on a grand scale'. This section describes what he calls the 'Greater Mediterranean', from the Atlantic to the Sahara, on the grounds that 'If we did not consider this extended zone of influence . . . it would often be difficult to grasp the history of the sea.'[12]

Still more important, for Braudel and for us, is his original treatment of time. In 1976, looking back on his achievement, he emphasised that *The Mediterranean* was above all a demonstration that 'le temps n'est pas unique', in other words, that time does not move at a uniform speed. It is convenient to divide it into the long-term, the medium-term, and the short-term: 'geographical time, social time, and individual time'. It is the consciousness of the long-term in particular (*la longue durée*), the consciousness that all 'structures' are in fact changing, however slowly, that is, according to Braudel, the historian's special contribution to the social sciences, disciplines from which (he has often said) the historian has much to learn. Braudel has little patience with frontiers, whether they separate regions or disciplines. He wants to see things whole, to integrate the economic, the social, the political, the cultural into a 'total history'. 'Total', like 'global', is one of his favourite words.

The global approach is again apparent in his second major work, of which only the first volume has been published so far: *Capitalism and Material Life*. It is something like an extension of Part Two of *The Mediterranean* to the whole world in the last four centuries before the industrial revolution, dealing with population, food, houses, clothes, technology, money and towns. The first chapter, for example, points out that the rise in the population of Europe between 1400 and 1800 was simply part of a larger trend, the rise in world population, a point which calls into question the conventional Europe-centred explanations for this phenomenon. Later chapters discuss the relation between maize-growing and despotism; the social history of the chair; the differences between camels, oxen and horses as sources of power;

and other fascinating topics rarely treated in this comparative way. The discussion of the rise of capitalism is still to come, although it is common knowledge that Braudel will follow the American historical sociologist Immanuel Wallerstein in his emphasis on a 'world-economy' divided into centre, periphery and 'semi-periphery', and his stress on the mutual dependence of commercial capitalism in Western Europe, serfdom in Eastern Europe and slavery in the New World.

Published at a time when most historians, in France and elsewhere, were still practising the history of the short-term, and normally within national frontiers at that, *The Mediterranean* came as something of a shock. In 1923 the 21-year-old Braudel had begun work on a relatively conventional piece of diplomatic history, a study of the Mediterranean policy of Philip II. In the thesis Braudel defended twenty-four years later, Philip had virtually disappeared from a stage which now stretched from the Atlantic to the Sahara.

All the same, *The Mediterranean* is no isolated phenomenon. The book has its place in a tradition. 'What I owe to the *Annales*, to their teaching and inspiration, constitutes the greatest of my debts.'[13] *Annales* is the title of a journal founded in 1929 by Marc Bloch (who is discussed in Chapter 8 of this volume) and Lucien Febvre, two French historians who were profoundly dissatisfied with the inward-looking, narrative political history which was dominant at that time. They wanted, and they practised, a history which was open to the social sciences, problem-oriented and analytic rather than a mere story of events, and concerned with economic, social and cultural life as well as with politics.

The senior partner in this alliance, Lucien Febvre, had published a book about *Philip II and Franche-Comté* (1911), a book which might have been more accurately called 'Franche-Comté and Philip II', because of its emphasis on the economic and social history of the region at the expense of its political history. He had gone on to write *The Earth and Human Evolution* (1922), a study of historical geography which rejected determinism but recognised the importance in history of geographical factors, whether opportunities or constraints. Febvre was a tireless missionary for his new kind of history. He encouraged Braudel to turn his 'Philip II and the Mediterranean' into *The Mediterranean and Philip II*. It was to Febvre that Braudel sent instalments of his thesis, written in exercise-books, from his prisoner-of-war camp near Lübeck. It was to Febvre that he dedicated the book with 'the affection of a son'. It was to Febvre's positions at the Collège de France and the Ecole des Hautes Etudes and to his editorship of *Annales* that Braudel succeeded. His *Mediterranean* owes much to *The Earth and Human Evolution* and is organised in much the same way as *Philip II and Franche-Comté*; both books start from the physical environment, move on to economic and social structures and end with a narrative of events. It was Febvre, too, who asked him to write on material culture and capitalism between 1400 and 1800.

As for Marc Bloch, Braudel met him only once but took his work very seriously: 'I think I can honestly say that no aspect of his thought is foreign to me.'[14] Already in the 1920s Bloch was concerned with long-term historical trends; his *The Royal Touch,* for example, discusses the belief in the healing power of kings from the Middle Ages to the eighteenth century. Bloch both preached and practised comparative history, and the systematic comparison of the Spanish and Ottoman Empires, the western and eastern Mediterranean, is one of the great strengths of Braudel's masterpiece.

Behind Febvre and Bloch stand other influential figures. There is François Simiand, for example, an historically minded economist who was fascinated by long-term economic trends, and who put into circulation the pejorative phrase *l'histoire événementielle* to refer to the history of 'mere' events. There is Paul Vidal de la Blache, a pioneer of social and historical geography (*la géographie humaine*); it was his kind of geography which Febvre and Bloch and Braudel all practised. There is the great sociologist Emil Durkheim, who was criticising the history of events as 'superficial' in the 1890s. There is Karl Marx, about whom he is somewhat ambivalent. Braudel admires Marx, finds him stimulating, agrees with him on some issues, but finds it necessary to keep a certain intellectual distance from him, to avoid being trapped inside a framework he regards as too rigid. Still further back, there is Jules Michelet, the revolutionary-Romantic historian from whom Braudel learned to indulge his gift for poetic images and to write of regions as if they were almost persons. The oft-quoted first sentence of Braudel's book – 'I have loved the Mediterranean with passion' – is pure Michelet.

Braudel also learned from his contemporaries while he was writing his *Mediterranean.* Among the colleagues who impressed him most were the Brazilian Gilberto Freyre, sociologist and social historian of the family, the housing, the cooking, the sexual and the race relations of his native north-east; and the economic historian Ernest Labrousse, whose great work on wages and prices in eighteenth-century France, published in 1933, is constructed round the contrast and the interaction between short-term trends and trends *de longue durée.*

In its turn *The Mediterranean* has made a powerful contribution to the formation of a historical tradition, to the rise of the new kind of history associated with the journal *Annales.* From the 1950s onwards, an increasing number of French historians turned from political to social history and from a preoccupation with events to a concern for structures. One of the first and one of the most remarkable was Pierre Chaunu, who tried to imitate (if not surpass) Braudel by taking the

Atlantic as his subject. Between 1955 and 1960, with the help of his wife, Chaunu published a twelve-volume study which centres on the rise and fall of the trade between Seville and the New World from 1501 to 1650. In places, this work reads like a caricature of Braudel, but Chaunu is one of the few living historians capable of taking a similar global view of a subject, and his study is another important and in many ways successful attempt to integrate space into history, to deal with changing problems of communications.

Although most of them lack these territorial ambitions, other French historians, especially those concerned with Spain and Italy, have been writing works which bear the mark of Braudel in other ways. These works include Henri Lapeyre's study of the Ruiz, a sixteenth-century Spanish merchant family (1955); Jean Delumeau's study of Rome in the second half of the sixteenth century (1957–9); Jacques Heers's book on fifteenth-century Genoa (1961); Bartolomé Bennassar's book on sixteenth-century Valladolid (1967); and many more. It has, in fact, become standard practice for French historians to write books which begin with the geographical setting, pass on to economic and social structures and end with a study of 'conjoncture', that is, of trends over time, usually a hundred years or more.

Historians outside France have also interested themselves in Braudel's methods, notably in Italy, Spain, Poland and, more recently, in the United States and in Britain. The Spanish and Italian translations of *The Mediterranean* go back to 1966, while the English version was published in 1972–3. A book on this scale is little more likely to provoke imitation than Gibbon's *Decline and Fall;* but there is little doubt that Braudel has led many of his readers to look at the past in a different way.

Now (in 1979) over thirty years old, *The Mediterranean* has never, so far as I know, been the object of an explicit critique by French historians of the younger generation, although a critique may be implied by what they are currently doing. The most brilliant of Braudel's pupils is, by common consent, Emmanuel Le Roy Ladurie, who succeeded him at the Collège de France as Braudel succeeded Febvre. Le Roy Ladurie owes much to Braudel and resembles him in a number of respects – imaginative power, wide-ranging curiosity, the multi-disciplinary approach, ambivalence to Marxism. However, he has found it necessary to keep his intellectual distance from Braudel just as Braudel did from Marx. His thesis, published in 1966, is, like *The Mediterranean,* a brilliant piece of 'total history', and it is of much the same length, but it is constructed on a very different geographical scale. It is concerned with the peasants of Languedoc from the fifteenth century to the eighteenth. It begins, as one has come to expect, with the geography of the region, but it is not organised into long-, middle-

and short-term. Instead it is divided into periods. Within each period the analysis of demographic and economic trends is followed by an account of 'prises de conscience', the conscious responses of the peasants to the changing situation in which they found themselves, with particular emphasis on movements of protest and revolt, from the Carnival of Romans in 1580, a festival which turned into a battle between the haves and the have-nots, to the guerrilla war conducted by the Camisards, the Calvinist peasants of the Cévennes, against the royal troops sent to stamp them out in the early eighteenth century.

The Peasants of Languedoc may be said to imply a criticism of Braudel by its divergence from his model. It may also be useful to discuss some of the explicit criticisms which have been levelled at The Mediterranean in the course of the last thirty years, and also to discuss the question which the appearance of a masterpiece inevitably raises – should we all be trying to approach history in this way or not?

Of the various criticisms made of Braudel's work, a number are worth taking seriously. Two of these points may be called 'local' criticisms in the sense that they focus on specific sections and concern sins of omission. The first of these concerns Part One of The Mediterranean, in which, as an anonymous reviewer in The Times Literary Supplement once put it, 'insufficient attention is paid to animals and plants and their effects on the human and natural environment'.[15] Despite his admiration for Maximilien Sorre, a French geographer who was already concerned with what he called 'human ecology' in the early 1940s, Braudel has given us a relatively static geo-history rather than a more dynamic eco-history. To turn from The Mediterranean to W. G. Hoskins's The Making of the English Landscape (published six years later, in 1955) is not only to recognise similar interests, whether in trade routes or drainage schemes, but also to see something of what Braudel missed. 'The Making of the Mediterranean Landscape': what a marvellous book that would be! Emilio Sereni has given us part of the story in his History of the Italian Agrarian Landscape (1961), but much work remains to be done.

A second 'local' criticism concerns Part Two, and the relatively small role in it played by attitudes, values or, to use the favourite Annales term, 'mentalities' (mentalités collectives). A brilliant historian of material culture, Braudel, despite his aspirations towards a 'total history', has much less to say about immaterial culture, even in the chapter entitled 'Civilisations'. In this respect he differs from both Febvre and Bloch. Beliefs obviously mattered in the Mediterranean world in the age of Philip II: religious beliefs, for example, whether Catholic or Muslim. Did they interact, or was the intellectual frontier between Christendom and the world of Islam a firm one? Some historians have, in fact, addressed themselves to this question. In his Structure of Spanish History, Amérigo Castro discussed the interpenetration of Christian and Muslim culture in the Spanish peninsula. As for Eastern Europe, already in the 1920s F. W. Hasluck had studied the interaction between Christianity and Islam at a popular level: the Christian shrines which were frequented by Muslims and the other way round, and the Albanian Muslim mothers who baptised their children as a charm against werewolves or leprosy.

Another part of the history of mentalities which lends itself to study at the Mediterranean level, as some social anthropologists have discovered, is the concept of honour, a dominant part of the value-system in Algeria as in Spain, in Sicilian villages as in Turkish ones.

The two criticisms discussed so far have the disadvantage that they fault Braudel's 600,000-word book for what it leaves out. Could he reasonably have been expected to put anything more in? Surely not. Does this mean that 'total history' is impossible? In the literal sense, yes; the historian must always select. Braudel would not deny this. It must be understood that he talks of 'total' or 'global' history as a shorthand for a history less limited by geographical or disciplinary frontiers than history used to be.

A third criticism, and the one most frequently made of Braudel by historians of a traditional stamp, is that his history is history with the politics left out. At the 'local' level, this is not true. Part Three of *The Mediterranean* deals, as we have seen, with political events, while Part Two contains chapters on 'Empires' (including a discussion of the resources and weaknesses of the state), and 'The forms of war' (which is, after all, a continuation of politics by other means . . .). It would be more accurate to say that Braudel, like Febvre and to a lesser extent Bloch, has broken with the traditional dominance of political history; that he has deliberately chosen not to write his history within a political framework. It may also be true that some historians associated with *Annales* have not taken political history seriously enough, in reaction against an earlier generation of historians for whom politics was virtually everything that mattered. It may be revealing that the subtitle of *Annales* is 'Economies. Societies. Civilisations.', with no mention of states. British historians have been particularly unhappy with this rejection or at least demotion of politics, a reaction which may have something to do with British parliamentary traditions. However, the question of the relative importance of politics within a history which aspires to 'totality' is still very much an open one. It is Braudel's achievement to have presented us with an alternative framework to the political one, whether we all feel at ease inside it or not.

Allied to the question of the importance of politics is that of the importance of individuals (especially political and military leaders) and their decisions. Some historians are highly suspicious of Braudel's concern with 'collective destinies and general trends', which they see as impersonal forces producing an almost inhuman history. As John

Elliott once put it, 'Braudel's Mediterranean is a world unresponsive to human control'.[16] Just how important are individual decisions or events? This of course is one of the oldest debates in the history of history, the debate between those who believe that men make their own history and those who think that fortune, or providence, or climate or economic trends play a greater role. Did Philip II's character and abilities (or lack of them) really make so little difference to the history of the later sixteenth century? If so, was this because Spaniards and Turks were evenly matched and fought to a stalemate, or is it the case that the leaders never matter? Could Braudel have adopted the same approach if he had been writing about the age of Alexander the Great or Napoleon? Can individuals or events never break the structures which constrain them? How else can the structures change? Did events break through in 1789 (for example) or 1917, even if they did not do so between 1555 and 1598? Anyone with a taste for irony will relish the fact that it was an eruption of the despised *histoire événementielle*, the events of May 1968 in Paris (*les événements par excellence*) which brought Braudel flying back from Chicago and led him to put *Annales* under new management, resigning the editorship to a group of younger men. Events seemed to take their revenge on the historian who had scorned them. But one still has to ask what difference these events really made to French intellectual life, to French society. Ten years later it is still too soon to judge. In the long term Braudel may yet have the last word.

The traditional historians' critique of Braudel's determinism would of course apply equally well to most Marxist history. However, the Marxists are as ambivalent about him as he is about them. He finds them too dogmatic; they find him too much of an eclectic, and insufficiently rigorous, in his economic analysis in particular. Would it be possible to show more rigour without also showing more dogmatism? Like Febvre and Bloch, Braudel has always been unwilling to assert the predominance of the economic factor even in the long term. Like them he stresses the interaction of economic and social, political and cultural. His *Capitalism and Material Life* concludes by saying that one should not talk about 'economies' or 'societies' but about 'socio-economies', and even then one has to bring in the state and culture as well. However, the *Annales* group has much in common with Marxists, especially the more 'open' Marxists, notably the interest in structures and the desire to penetrate the 'surface' of events in search of an 'underlying' historical reality. It is no surprise to find Braudel expressing admiration for Marxists such as Eric Hobsbawm, Immanuel Wallerstein or the Polish economic historian Witold Kula, an admiration which is certainly reciprocated.

Another charge against *The Mediterranean*, most sharply formulated by the Harvard historian Bernard Bailyn, in a review of the first edition, is that of incoherence. 'Braudel', he wrote, 'has mistaken a poetic response to the past for an historical problem'.[17] The book disintegrates, so Bailyn suggests, because Braudel was not prepared to set limits to his subject and also because he isolates the geography, the sociology and the politics of the Mediterranean world from one another in different parts, thus giving himself no opportunity to discuss their interaction.

That the historian should study problems not periods was a proposition as dear to Lucien Febvre as to the British scholar Lord Acton. Braudel himself once wrote that 'The region is not the framework of research. The framework of research is the problem.' Could he really have neglected his own advice? I put the question to Braudel in an interview with him in 1976, and there was no hesitation in his answer. His book did focus on a problem: 'my great problem, the only problem I had to resolve, was to show that time moves at different speeds', that events move fast while society changes more slowly and the environment scarcely budges at all.

The question of the links between geo-history, social history and the history of events is a more difficult one. Braudel does believe that they are all part of a total history, that the three levels are 'transparent', as he puts it, that at a given moment we should be able to see them operating simultaneously. But how does one make this possible? In Part Three of *The Mediterranean* there are references to the constraints under which individuals like Don García de Toledo operated,[18] but perhaps not frequently enough to get his message across. One can see why Le Roy Ladurie, in his *Peasants of Languedoc,* chose to emphasise their *prises de conscience,* the way in which they became conscious of the constraints and (usually without success) rebelled against them. Such a link between structures and events can be found for the history of one social group in one region; it may be asking too much to expect anything comparable in a history of the whole Mediterranean world.

Should one even try to write history on such a grand scale? Traditional historians have often expressed suspicion of Braudel's generalisations. They think it the historian's business to deal with the particular, not the general, and they wonder how these general statements could ever be documented. A careful reader of footnotes will notice that whereas Part Three, the most conventional part of *The Mediterranean,* is firmly based on archive sources, Part Two is simply illustrated from archive material, while Part One refers very little to documents at all – though it should be added that the main source for the geo-history of the Mediterranean is the landscape itself.

It remains true that a large part of the work of the greatest historian of our time is based on secondary sources. It is not in finding evidence but in using evidence that Braudel excels. It is not the use of new documents but the choice of subject, the selection of material, the illuminating comparisons, and above all the quality of the analysis which make *The Mediterranean* into a masterpiece. In an age of over-specialisation and of the proliferation of monographs on small subjects, Braudel's most outstanding characteristic is his desire (and of course ability) to see things whole. He chose an enormous subject, the history of the Mediterranean world, and then tackled it by going beyond it; beyond the Mediterranean to the Atlantic and the Sahara, and beyond history to geography and sociology. Few people will want to imitate this book, and fewer still will be capable of imitating it, but one may still say of it, as of *War and Peace* (which it resembles not only in length but also in its poetry, its awareness of space, and its sense of the futility of individual actions), that it has permanently enlarged the possibilities of the genre in which it is written.

NOTES: CHAPTER 12

All references to *La Méditerranée et le monde méditerranéen à l'époque de Philippe II* are to the translation from the second edition, published in 1972–3, and referred to as *Mediterranean*.

 1 *Mediterranean*, pp. 1012, 1056, 1027 ff., 1082 ff., 1053, 1137, 1236.
 2 ibid., pp. 1017–18.
 3 ibid., p. 1042; cf. pp. 966, 372.
 4 ibid., p. 1101.
 5 ibid., p. 1104.
 6 ibid., p. 22.
 7 ibid., p. 21.
 8 ibid., pp. 372, 363.
 9 ibid., pp. 660–1.
10 ibid., p. 20.
11 ibid., p. 137.
12 ibid., p. 170.
13 ibid., p. 22.
14 loc. cit.
15 *Times Literary Supplement*, 10 February 1968, p. 156.
16 *New York Review of Books*, 3 May 1973.
17 *Journal of Economic History*, 1951, pp. 377–82.
18 See p. 189 above.

NOTE ON FURTHER READING

Braudel's *Mediterranean* has been published in English (1972–3, translated from the second edition). So has the first volume of his *Material Civilisation and Capitalism* (1973), and *Afterthoughts on Material Civilisation and Capitalism* (1977), which offers a foretaste of the unpublished volumes. Also available in English is his most famous essay 'History and the social sciences' (in *Economy and Society in Early Modern Europe*, ed. P. Burke, 1972), and an article he wrote together with F. Spooner, 'Prices in Europe from 1450 to 1750', in *The Cambridge Economic History of Europe*, Vol. IV, ed. E. E. Rich and C. H. Wilson (1967).

There has as yet been little serious criticism or evaluation of Braudel's work. Among the essays on him in English, see B. Bailyn's review of the first edition of the *Mediterranean* (*Journal of Economic History*, vol. 11, 1951), J. H. Elliott's review of the second edition (*New York Review of Books*, 3 May 1973) and the special issues devoted to Braudel of the *Journal of Modern History*, vol. 44, 1972 (especially J. H. Hexter's description – and affectionate parody – of the 'Monde Braudelien') and of *Review*, vol. 3, 1978.

Index

Luther, Martin, Butterfield's concern with 174–5
Lydney, excavations 159, 168
Lyte, Henry Maxwell, collaboration with Maitland 110

Mabillon, Bloch's comment 133
Macaulay, Thomas Babinton: on writing history 1; motives 55–7; on progress 58–62, 67–8; Whig sympathies 60–1, 64–5; accused of caricature 65–7; on the Rockinghams 138; 8, 13, 14, 41, 173, 176, 177
Machiavelli 38, 58, 171
McFarland, Sir Basil, at Salerno 161
Mackintosh, Sir James 56, 58–9, 64
Madras Museum 163
Magna Carta 64, 108, 177
Maiden Castle, excavation, 160, 166 168–9
Maitland, Frederic: on past and present 13–14; as lawyer 108; importance of legal history 105–6, 110, 114, 116; on the County Court 107–10; on Parliament 110–14; *History of English Law* 114–17; reputation 117–18, 124, 127
Malesherbes, Chrétien de 70
Manning, B. L.; critical of Butterfield 176–7
Marcus Aurelius 24, 26
Maria Theresa 42
Marie-Louise 146
Marlborough, 1st Duke of 65–6, 67
Marston Moor, battle 5
Martin, Henri; French historian 51
Marwick, Professor A. on Namier 136
Marx, Karl, historical materialism 87–8, 92, collaboration with Engels 88–9; methods of work 90–1, 93; influence of Hegel 91–6, *Communist Manifesto* 96–8; settles in London 99–101; 13, 182, 194, 195, 198
Maximilian I, Ranke on 39
Mayer, J. P., on Tocqueville 72, 83–4
Mazarin, Cardinal 43
Medici, Catherine de 37, 48
Michelet, Jules 73, 194
Middleton, Conyers, Gibbon rejects 20
Mignet, François 51, 73
Mill, John Stuart 72, 88
Mohammed, Gibbon on 30
Momigliano, Arnaldo 33

Montaigne; Ranke on 51
Montesquieu; influences Gibbon 21–2, 27, 29; Tocqueville 73
Montfort, Simon de 112
Mosheim, used by Gibbon 24, 29
Munich settlement 10, 149
Murat, Joachim 172
Muratori, used by Gibbon 23

Nain de Tillemont, Le, consulted by Gibbon 23
Namier, Lewis Bernstein: History an art 15; family origins 137; on George III 137–9; structural analysis 139–41, 147–8; influenced by Freud 141–4, 146; on Revolutions of 1848 144–5; work for Zionism 13, 145, 149; change of name 146; demanding scholarship 149–50; criticised by Butterfield 178–81; 1, 8, 90
Napoleon Bonaparte 9, 70, 73, 77, 83, 146, 156, 171, 172, 174, 198
National Museum of Wales, Wheeler's work at 157
Neale, Professor J. E. 140
Necker, Jacques 21, 79
Nero; Gibbon on 26
Newcastle, Duke of; Namier on 140, 150
Newton, Sir Isaac 57, 88
Nodens, worship of 168
North, Lord 12, 21–2

Oakeshott, Michael; on historical causation 3
Oates, Titus 10, 65
Objectivity in history 7–8, 74
Ordeal at law, Maitland on 109–10
Ottoman Empire 24, 31, 42
Oxford Honours School 36

Pakistan, archaeology in 164
Palmer, R. R. on Atlantic Revolution 77
Papacy, Ranke on 40–1, 129, 174–5
Pares, Richard, on Butterfield 178
Paris, Peace of 139–40
Parliament, Maitland on 110–14
Parsons, Robert, influence on Gibbon 20
Party, Namier on 138–9
Pascal, Blaise; influences Gibbon 21
Past and present; relationship 11–14; Tocqueville 70, 83–84; Maitland 104,